Advance Praise for *The One-Week Job Project*

"*The One-Week Job Project* is a remarkably original idea that will inspire a new generation of young people to stay true to themselves, shed the noise around them, and set out to define their own roads in life. **This book will help you to take a critical look at your own future, and all the possibilities that lie waiting.**"

—Mike Marriner, co-founder of Roadtrip Nation and author of *Roadtrip Nation: A Guide to Discovering Your Path in Life*

"With 52 jobs, 52 experiences and 52 lessons learned, Sean Aiken has done all the dirty work for young individuals who are looking to embark on their own career journey. *The One-Week Job Project* is **eye-opening, entertaining and will help answer the question on any young individual's mind: what do I do when I graduate?** Sean has done it all in less time than it takes to graduate from college and has pulled all of his knowledge into **one book that can and will change your life for the better.**"

—Dan Schawbel, author of *Me 2.0: Build a Powerful Brand to Achieve Career Success*

"At a time when the traditional path to success is fading from view, Sean Aiken has emerged as a role model for making the best of the inherently unstable life of today's workforce. Most people will likely work a number of different jobs in a variety of different fields over the course of their lifetimes, and most people will feel uneasy during transition. Aiken's book shows 52 transitions, and they add up to **a vital message that job hopping is productive and can help you find a better career, and build a better life.**"

—Penelope Trunk, nationally syndicated career columnist and author of *Brazen Careerist: The New Rules for Success*

"Who says job hopping is a bad thing? Sean Aiken worked 52 jobs in one very busy year and documented the life-changing experience in his wonderful new book, *The One-Week Job Project*. Sean takes you on a rollicking journey across the U.S. and Canada to gigs as an astronomer, brewmaster, cowboy, and deejay (among many others). He shares hilarious stories and valuable advice from mentors in pubs and tattoo parlors, on dairy farms and movie sets, and in kitchens and cubicles. I loved the opportunity to tag along on Sean's year of career enlightenment without having to sleep on 55 couches and trek more than 46,000 miles. I think you will too. *The One-Week Job Project* is **a great read and a terrific resource for anyone looking for inspiration on the job**."

—Pamela Skillings, career coach and author of *Escape from Corporate America: A Practical Guide to Creating the Career of Your Dreams*

"It started as a simple idea: work a different job every week for a year. But as Sean put his plan into action, it quickly became **a life-changing, cross-continental, action-packed adventure. After reading *The One-Week Job Project,* you'll know how to bring the most extraordinary things out of life, and how to score some choice jobs along the way!**"

—Kyle MacDonald, author of *One Red Paperclip*

"**A fresh approach** to the long-held idea of 'trying on' jobs before you 'buy' them."

—Richard N. Bolles, author of *What Color Is Your Parachute?*

"*The One-Week Job Project* is **a terrific read for young people wondering what to do with their lives, and for anyone looking to change his or her life for the better.** Sean Aiken's audacious, inspiring book packs a good dose of humor and reminds us that the only thing standing between you and your dreams is yourself!"

—Keith Ferrazzi, #1 *New York Times* bestselling author of *Never Eat Alone* and *Who's Got Your Back*

PENGUIN CANADA

THE ONE-WEEK JOB PROJECT

SEAN AIKEN graduated from Capilano University in North Vancouver, British Columbia, with a degree in business administration in 2005. At the top of his class, with a 4.0 cumulative GPA, he was voted class valedictorian. He started the One-Week Job project in February 2007, at age twenty-five, and finished his 52 weeks in March 2008.

Connect with Sean
Website: www.oneweekjob.com
Email: sean@oneweekjob.com
Facebook: www.facebook.com/oneweekjob
Twitter: www.twitter.com/seanaiken

APPLICATION FOR EMPLOYMENT

THE

☒ ONE- ☐ TWO- ☐ THREE- ☐ OTHER-

WEEK JOB PROJECT

This section to be completed by applicant. Please print clearly

NAME OF APPLICANT:

APPLICANT PHOTO:

Sean Aiken

ONE: ☒ **MAN,** ☐ WOMAN,

1 YEAR, 52 JOBS

Office use only:

IMPRINT: **PENGUIN CANADA**

CITY: **TORONTO**

LOGO: PENGUIN CANADA

PENGUIN CANADA

Published by the Penguin Group

Penguin Group (Canada), 90 Eglinton Avenue East, Suite 700,
Toronto, Ontario, Canada M4P 2Y3 (a division of Pearson Canada Inc.)

Penguin Group (USA) Inc., 375 Hudson Street, New York, New York 10014, U.S.A.
Penguin Books Ltd, 80 Strand, London WC2R 0RL, England
Penguin Ireland, 25 St Stephen's Green, Dublin 2, Ireland (a division of Penguin Books Ltd)
Penguin Group (Australia), 250 Camberwell Road, Camberwell, Victoria 3124, Australia
(a division of Pearson Australia Group Pty Ltd)
Penguin Books India Pvt Ltd, 11 Community Centre, Panchsheel Park,
New Delhi – 110 017, India
Penguin Group (NZ), 67 Apollo Drive, Rosedale, North Shore 0745,
Auckland, New Zealand (a division of Pearson New Zealand Ltd)
Penguin Books (South Africa) (Pty) Ltd, 24 Sturdee Avenue, Rosebank, Johannesburg 2196,
South Africa

Penguin Books Ltd, Registered Offices: 80 Strand, London WC2R 0RL, England

Published in Canada by Penguin Group (Canada), a division of Pearson Canada Inc., 2010
Published simultaneously in the United States by Villard Books, an imprint of The Random House Publishing Group, a division of Random House, Inc., New York

Book design by Simon M. Sullivan

3 4 5 6 7 8 9 10 (WEB)

Manufactured in Canada.

LIBRARY AND ARCHIVES CANADA CATALOGUING IN PUBLICATION

Aiken, Sean
The one-week job project : 1 man, 1 year, 52 jobs / Sean Aiken.

ISBN 978-0-14-317051-8

1. Aiken, Sean. 2. Vocational guidance. 3. Occupations. 4. College graduates—Canada—Biography. I. Title.

HF5381.A415 2010 331.702 C2009-907526-1

American Library of Congress Cataloging in Publication data available

Visit the Penguin Group (Canada) website at **www.penguin.ca**

Special and corporate bulk purchase rates available; please see
www.penguin.ca/corporatesales or call 1-800-810-3104, ext. 2477 or 2474

To Mom and Dad—
I'm here because of you.

Twenty years from now you will be more disappointed by the things you didn't do than by the ones you did do. So throw off the bowlines. Sail away from the safe harbor. Catch the trade winds in your sails. Explore. Dream. Discover.

—Mark Twain

PREFACE

"FIVE!"

A crowd gathers behind me and cries out in unison. My fingers clutch the railing of the metal bridge. The platform on which I stand leads to empty space. On either side of the 160-foot river canyon, peaceful snow-capped trees taunt me with their calm. I turn to the crowd and craft an exaggerated fearful expression, then force a smile.

"FOUR!"

Once they get to one, I need to jump. I *have* to jump. It'll be so anticlimactic if I don't. Everyone knows you can't back out of a countdown. Even if I jump five seconds after the fact, it won't matter—a countdown is a countdown.

"THREE!"

My toes creep over the edge of the bridge to which I'm attached by only a thick bungee cord. I glance toward the picturesque mountain backdrop, and for a moment I forget my current reality, lost in appreciation of the beauty that surrounds me.

"TWO!"

The cheer from the crowd jolts me back to the task at hand. I peer past my toes. One hundred sixty feet below, the river eagerly awaits my descent.

"ONE!"

I tell the muscles in my legs to contract. They don't want to. My precious seconds of leeway are about to run out. If I don't jump, I'll hear the sighs of a disappointed crowd. The people who are rooting for me now will suddenly lose interest. Little do they know, this is the most important jump of my life.

I have no idea what the next year will hold, where my different jobs will lead, what I'll end up doing, or who I'll meet. I wonder if I'll get enough job offers, where I'm going to sleep while on the road, how I'm going to travel from city to city, and how I'll support myself for an entire year without pay. Most important, I question if I'll be able to heed the insights I gain when my journey is over. The uncertainty is loud, my self-doubts determined, fear pervasive. But I'm excited. I've made excuses for too long. Ready or not, it's time to take the leap.

"BUNGEE!"

I take a deep breath, check my harness one last time, and step off the bridge.

THE ONE-WEEK JOB PROJECT

IN MY PARENTS' BASEMENT, I woke up ready to start my morning routine—hop in the shower, brush my teeth, put on some clothes, grab something to eat, then run out the door. A moment before I tossed my covers aside, I realized that I didn't have to go to school. And it wasn't just that day. For the first time in my life, I didn't have to go to school again, ever.

I'd felt ready to graduate for some time. I wanted to do my own thing, to start working toward something. The only problem was that I had no idea what this something was.

For as long as I could remember, my life had been organized for me. The most major decision making I did came every four months when I'd spend an hour looking at a course calendar and chart my life for the next semester. Advisors told me how many credits I needed, the courses required to earn my degree. A schedule told me when to be at school. Teachers told me when assignments were due. If I paid attention in class, they'd even tell me how to get a good grade. I was so focused on receiving the best grades I could that I didn't care whether I was actually learning something. I was taught to focus on grades, and I gave my teachers what they wanted. After all, good grades are what got me into a decent university and what would land me a decent job. Good grades are what would give me "value."

When summer came, I enjoyed my freedom, never feeling any guilt over not doing something else, something more. There was no need to worry about the long term. I had a simple plan—finish my degree. I'd be back at school in the fall and so could spend the next four months making money, partying with friends, taking weekend road trips—whatever, it didn't matter. There was no need to stress about anything, least of all the job I got. It was just a summer job. And I, after all, was just a student.

When I graduated, it all changed. No longer a student, I was suddenly expected to provide a legitimate answer to the question "What do you do for a living?"

I wanted to accomplish great things, help others, make a difference. I wanted to do everything and be everywhere. I had big ambitions, but I was totally directionless. I'd been thrown ill-prepared into a wide open landscape in which I could create anything. I thought this freedom was what I'd longed for—a chance to achieve my goals, to live up to this alleged potential many saw in me. But with no course schedules or professors to guide me, I experienced this freedom as a daunting reality rife with expectations. Now it was up to me to determine my path.

In the back of my mind I knew that I was lucky to have options at all—since so many people, especially at a time of economic downturn, don't—yet I found myself overwhelmed by the expectations of others and my own self-doubts.

A few months removed from my student status, I became depressed. I lay awake at night asking myself life's big questions, and I wasn't finding any answers. In July, I and a group of close friends went a few hours up the west coast of British Columbia to my friend's cabin on Savary Island, as we did every year. I wasn't much fun to be around. Admittedly it would have taken some extra energy given the best of circumstances—I was the fifth wheel in a weekend getaway with my two best friends, their girlfriends, and their dogs. I'd go for walks on the beach by myself and think about the routineness of everything. I could see my entire life laid out:

I'd come home from my unfulfilling nine-to-five job and cook dinner. Then, by the time I'd cleaned up, I'd finally have a moment to relax. Exhausted from the day, I'd flop on the couch, flick on the TV for a couple of hours, then go to bed and wake up and do it all over again the next day. My friends and I would keep our annual tradition and go up to the cabin. But now we'd sit in lawn chairs, watch our kids run around, our dogs dig in the sand, and reminisce about the past.

It wasn't just the thought of routine that scared me but the idea of not having passion in my life. Life without passion meant finding trivial ways to pass the time. Nobody could convince me otherwise.

In search of answers, I decided to travel. I spent the next year and a half alternating between stints on the road and back home in Port Moody, BC (20 kilometres east of Vancouver). I backpacked throughout Europe and Southeast Asia, taught English in Thailand, and moved to Quebec to learn French. I never stayed in one place long enough to feel that I needed to plan more than a day ahead.

Avoidance became my self-prescribed coping mechanism. If I was always in transition, there would never be enough time to build up the expectation that I should be doing something more with my life. As soon as questions about my future began to surface, I could move on, hoping an answer would appear in the process.

Travelling taught me a lot about myself. I experienced new cultures, met all sorts of people, and was forced outside of my comfort zone on a daily basis. I learned to appreciate the small moments where life becomes simple and the beauty in all that surrounds us is crystal clear. On the road, people I met accepted who I was that day, in that moment. A certain anxiety always accompanied me when it was time to go home, where friends and family had preconceptions about me and what I should be doing. At home, it was all too easy to slip back into comfortable routines and conform to the established expectations of familiar faces.

Around Christmas, a year and a half after I graduated, I moved home, knowing that travel wasn't providing the answers I wanted. The holiday season made for an easier transition. Friends were between semesters or on vacation from work, and there was always something to do.

But when the new year came, my friends went back to their normal lives. And there I was, twenty-five years old, living in my parents' basement, and still without a clue about what I wanted to do with my life. I didn't even know where to start. I knew that unless I still wanted to be living in my parents' basement at age thirty, I had to do something.

I thought back to a dinner conversation with my parents and older sister in my senior year of university. My sister, Natalie, decided she'd put me on the spot. "So, Sean, what are you going to do after graduation?"

Silence followed as everyone awaited my answer, or rather, the chance to voice an opinion. My hesitation granted my family permission to bombard me with ideas on the direction I should take. My mom suggested teaching. My sister suggested that I use my business degree and look for an entry-level corporate job. My dad was the only one who didn't have a specific path in mind. He is a man of few words, and the table went silent when he began to speak.

"Sean, it doesn't matter what you do; just make sure it's something you're passionate about." He paused thoughtfully. "I've been alive for nearly sixty years and have yet to find something I'm passionate about besides your mother."

My dad never had the luxury of making job satisfaction a top priority. In 1976, recently married, he and Mom left their home country of Jamaica, which was beset by political strife and crime, in search of a safer environment in which to raise a family. They followed some friends to Canada. They'd never been to Canada, nor did they know many people here. It was a new culture. They had five thousand dollars to their name and a baby, my older sister, on the way. As a new immigrant, my father simply wanted a decent job so he could put a roof over his family's heads and food on the table. He endured long hours at his tedious accounting job, deriving his happiness from the pride in knowing that my sister and I would always have something to eat, a safe place to call home, and the opportunity to one day go to university.

Reminded of my dad's sacrifices, I renewed the promise I'd made to myself that night after dinner: I'd find a career that I would be passionate about, something that I'd love doing. And if there ever came a time when that career was no longer fulfilling, I'd have the courage to change it.

I'm going to spend the majority of my life working, I thought. *I don't want to spend that time always wishing it was the weekend, counting down the minutes to 5 P.M. I want to be as happy in my work as possible. I want to be one of those annoying people who say, "I'd do this job even if I didn't get paid."*

With some new-found inspiration, I scoured various job boards and flipped through newspaper classifieds. All the important and ambiguous job titles sounded enticing, but I had no clue what the jobs would actually be like.

And that's when I had an idea.

What if I was able to try out these different jobs? I thought. *Then I could see what I like, what I don't like, and find out what I need in a career to be happy.*

The more the idea sank in, the more I liked it. At the end of January, I went to my best friend, Ian, with the idea. "So, you know how I'm trying to figure out what I want to do?" I said.

"Yeah. Have you decided?"

"Well, I think I'm going to do a different job each week for a whole year."

He laughed. "You're going to do *what*?"

"I'm going to accept job offers from different companies or individuals, for one week at a time, for a whole year."

"You're serious?"

"Yeah, fifty-two jobs in fifty-two weeks. I'm thinking that I could start a website where anybody can offer me a job for one week. Then I'll travel anywhere somebody is willing to hire me and try out a different job each week to see what I like and don't like." I thought the idea was brilliant and waited for his response.

He stared at me blankly. "So . . . wait a second here," he said. "And who is going to hire you for only one week?"

"Umm, I don't know—anybody. I haven't thought that far yet," I said. "But I'm sure people will be open to the idea."

"I don't know, man, seems pretty . . ." He paused, then smiled. "But hey, why not, right? Go for it."

For years I'd gone to Ian with my ideas for various adventures, yet I'd never had the courage to pursue any of them. I had always wanted Ian to say, "Great idea, Sean. Let's do it together." I was on my own with this one, but just knowing that I had Ian's support was enough to help me move forward.

Over the next couple of weeks I went to the local library with my laptop every day to prepare content for the website. I composed my resumé and background information, including my motivation behind the project and how employers could offer me a job.

I wasn't doing the project for money, but for the experience. I wondered how I could use my journey to help others at the same time.

I decided that I'd ask my employers to make a donation to Make Poverty History, a campaign I support that fights extreme poverty by advocating policy reform. It just felt right. I'd help raise money and awareness for a great campaign, the company that employed me would get a tax receipt for their donation, and I'd embark on a year-long internship in which I could *try out* fifty-two different professions with no commitment to stay at the job.

I didn't know how I could finance the whole thing, but I wanted to take the first step. I had a few hundred dollars in my savings to get me started. However, if I wanted to keep it up for the year, I'd need to somehow find a way to support myself.

Part of me questioned whether the project made sense—wasn't it just another prescription for avoidance (albeit a more creative one)? After all I'd eventually have to get a real job once I quit my daydream. Still, I was happy to stay busy planning.

The following weekend I went to Ian's apartment in Vancouver.

"So, what are you going to call this project?" he asked.

"I don't know. Maybe . . . Job-a-Week?"

"Hmm. How about . . . One-Week Job?"

"Yeah. I like that," I said. "One-Week Job it is."

Ian's fiancée, Karen, purchased the domain name www.OneWeekJob.com, and Ian and I began to design the website. I felt a little guilty taking up Ian's time to design a website that I wasn't convinced I'd use. But I kept moving forward, step by step, refusing to acknowledge my doubting inner voice.

By late February, my website was complete. I'd reached the final step—I needed to tell people about One-Week Job in order to get job offers. I composed an email to friends and family explaining the project:

Hey Everyone! I wanted to let you know about a project that I'm starting. Basically, any individual or company can offer me a job for one week. The job can be absolutely anything, anywhere. I will then travel to the city, work the job offered for the week, blog about my experience, and any proceeds that my employer is willing to pay me, they donate to the Make Poverty History Campaign.

I don't know what I want to do for a career, so this is my way of figuring it out. I would really appreciate your support to get the project off the ground. If you have a blog, personal website, or use MySpace or Facebook, it would be great if you could post a link to: www.OneWeekJob.com. Thanks! —Sean

Stalling, I reread the email several times. Then I stared at the screen a while longer with my mouse hovering over the Send button. Once I sent this email, there would be no turning back.

One tap of the index finger and it was off. Now I needed to find myself a job. Monday was a workday.

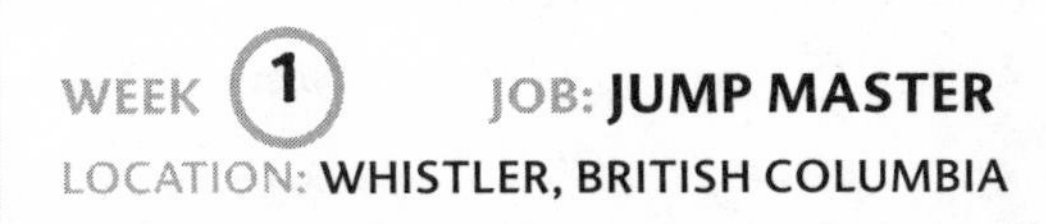

EMPLOYER: **WHISTLER BUNGEE**
WAGE: **$10–$15 HOUR***

INDUSTRY IQ:

- In Vanuatu, a boy's acceptance into manhood involves jumping off a wood platform over two storeys high with only vines attached to his feet (his head must touch the ground).
- The world's highest recorded jump is 232 metres, with 4–5 seconds of free fall, reaching speeds up to 200 kilometres an hour.
- Each bungee cord lasts about 600–800 jumps and costs approximately $800–$1,300.

APPLICATION PROCESS: My soccer coach is part owner of the company.

WHAT I LEARNED: Jumping off a bridge attached to an elastic cord is surprisingly safe.

Many jump masters say it's safer than driving your car to work. That comparison has never offered me much comfort, but I'm told that one bungee jump is as dangerous as driving a car 160 kilometres. Since most people don't drive 160 kilometres to get to work, I guess I'll buy it.

*Source: employer. Most of the wage information I've included has come from my employers. I will specify when I've used other sources. The notation "BLS" is used for information from the U.S. Bureau of Labor Statistics' *Occupational Outlook Handbook,* 2008 (www.bls.gov/oco/).

You can't overthink it. You just gotta jump.

—MATT, jump master, Whistler Bungee

THE CHEERS FROM the crowd quickly faded as I plummeted 160 feet toward the river below. My eyes struggled to stay open as wind crashed against my face, then resonated loudly in my ears. Ten feet short of the river, I felt a sharp tug on my harness and my view quickly shifted to the metal bridge above. Moments later, I was suspended in the river canyon while Matt lowered a rope to me.

It was only when I was back with both feet on the bridge that I realized how much fun I'd just had. Now I was one of the crowd. I could add to the peer pressure of the countdown that faced the next jumper—jump or face the disapproving sighs of the peanut gallery.

It was my first day on the job, though I didn't dare tell that to the jumpers who desperately sought some form of reassurance as I tightened their harnesses. "No worries," I'd say. "You'll love it." Then I'd politely ask that they sign the waiver that would absolve the company of any responsibility if something happened to go wrong.

It was a week of firsts for me; I also got my first cellphone. Even though Zack Morris had introduced me to cellphones at a young age, I'd never had one. I still didn't wear a watch, but now that I had a cellphone with official satellite time, I was confident that I'd be able to cure my habit of being five minutes late to everything—never ten or fifteen, always just under five. I've always suspected that this has something to do with what I call microwave time.

Almost every day after middle school I'd come home and put last night's leftovers in the microwave for a minute and a half. Then I'd grab a glass from the cupboard, take some juice out of the fridge, pour some into the glass, put the juice back into the fridge, take a long, dramatic drawn-out drink, stare out into the backyard to watch the birds take turns at the feeder, and ponder my homework. Then I'd walk to the living room, flip on the TV, tune in to a brilliant lineup of late-afternoon programming: *Saved by the Bell*, *Full House*, and *The Fresh Prince of Bel-Air*. Then, stalling for time, I'd slowly meander back to the kitchen and glance at the microwave, and there'd *still* be at least twenty-five seconds to go. Microwave time takes forever. Sometimes I'd rush around to see how much I could do before the microwave beeped. To this day, it never fails to surprise me. And so, I blame microwave time for my false sense that I can fit more tasks into a fifteen-minute period than is humanly possible.

But back to my week of firsts. That week, I also had my first-ever radio interview. I sat in the interview chair across from Bill, a well-known Vancouver radio host. Somewhere in his sixties, Bill spoke with his deep radio voice and a "Can you believe this guy" attitude: "This morning we have a young man who thinks he's a jack-of-all-trades. Sean Aiken graduated from college top of his class, a 4.0 GPA, he was even voted class valedictorian—one would think that he could find himself at least one decent job. But Sean says he wants fifty-two! Welcome to the show, Sean."

"Thanks for having me," I replied.

"So, tell us a bit about this idea of yours," he said, a hint of mockery in his voice.

I felt like I was being set up. "Well, I don't know what I want to do for a career, but I made a promise to myself that whatever it is, it's going to be something I'm passionate about," I cautiously replied. "So I came up with this idea to try out different jobs, to see what I like and don't like, and learn from others about how they decided on a career."

It was like he hadn't even heard me. "This is just so wacky," he said with a smirk. "So, you want employers to hire you with no prior experience, spend the time to train you, and then at the end of the week, you say Goodbye, then go elsewhere?"

"Yeah, that's right," I said.

He couldn't get past the concept and didn't even try to grasp my reasons. I admit, my idea was a little wacky, especially when compared with the traditional route: Go to school, get a job, buy stuff, start a family, buy more stuff, retire, die. But far more wacky is the number of people who get out of bed in the morning and absolutely dread going to work because they hate their jobs. I was trying to avoid that fate. I wanted to find something that I'd love. Something that I'd gladly spend forty hours of my life doing each week and that would allow me to pay the bills. Whether this was possible or simply the unrealistic hope of an inexperienced, idealistic twenty-something, I wasn't sure. But I worried this same hope could easily become regret if I didn't find out for myself.

Back on the bungee bridge Friday afternoon. A teenage girl looked up at me skeptically while I tightened her harness. "So, is this thing, like . . . safe?"

"Yeah, *totally* safe."

She didn't seem convinced. "Seriously," I assured her. "One might even say . . ." I paused for effect, then compellingly added, ". . . safer than driving your car to work."

WEEK 2 JOB: **TV TALK SHOW INTERN**
LOCATION: **VANCOUVER, BRITISH COLUMBIA**

EMPLOYER: ***URBAN RUSH***
WAGE: **NONE—TYPICALLY VOLUNTEER**

JOB DESCRIPTION: Greeted guests in the green room, helped out around the studio, learned how to work the camera, brainstormed ideas for future shows, and shot a couple of short segments.

APPLICATION PROCESS: Jay, a producer at the show, heard my previous week's radio interview and contacted me through the One-Week Job website.

WHAT I LEARNED: Passion increases productivity.

All the staff at *Urban Rush* love their jobs, and so they happily work hard to ensure the show's success. They're often laughing, generally in a good mood, and always eager to contribute their ideas for the show at the daily meeting.

During my week, the hosts of the show, Mike and Fiona, would mention on air how they were doing their best to make my experience at the studio worthwhile, then they'd cut to a shot of me organizing their wardrobe, washing windows, being loaded up with a ridiculous number of tapes to sort through, or walking one of their dogs. This fun attitude created a positive work environment, but more important, it added to the creativity of the production. Simply put, people who love their job do it better.

WEEK 3 JOB: **SNOWSHOE GUIDE**

LOCATION: **NORTH VANCOUVER, BRITISH COLUMBIA**

EMPLOYER: **MOUNT SEYMOUR**

WAGE: **$10–$15 HOUR**

INDUSTRY IQ:

- Traditional snowshoes were made with wood frames and rawhide lacings. Today, most use light metal or plastic.
- We burn 45 percent more calories snowshoeing than walking or running at the same speed.
- Snowshoeing originated in present-day central Asia between four thousand and six thousand years ago.
- The lowest recorded temperature on earth is –128.6 degrees F. (–89.2C), in Antarctica (not ideal snowshoeing conditions).

APPLICATION PROCESS: My friend Erin replied to my initial email about the project. She said that I could work with her as a snowshoe guide giving daily tours to high school students. I didn't want to take many jobs from people I knew, but with only a couple of days to line up my next position, I accepted the offer. As I drove up the mountain with the sun shining, eighteen centimetres of fresh snow on the ground, and the promise of unlimited hot chocolate, I was glad I did.

WHAT I LEARNED: I really enjoy working outdoors.

I never thought I'd be someone to work outdoors. But now that I've experienced it, I can understand why many who do never go back to an office environment.

WHEN I ARRIVED at the lodge, I was introduced to a man in his forties named Garry. Garry had recently moved to Canada from England, where he was a software developer for a successful IT firm. Now, halfway across the globe, Garry was a snowshoe guide for high school students. Most of the other guides were in their twenties; needless to say, Garry, with his thinning grey hair and English accent, stood out. "All right, Sean, looks like you're with me this morning on trail maintenance. Let's get going," he said, then handed me a pair of snowshoes.

It was late in the season. Temperatures were rising, and the snow had begun to melt. Each morning the trails had to be walked to ensure that routes were still safe to pass and to fix signs that had been knocked down.

Snowshoes and backpack in hand, Garry eagerly made his way for the door. We strapped on our snowshoes and set out into the crisp morning sunlight. The mountain hadn't opened to the public yet, and so only employees were visible—several prepared the main lifts, while others shovelled the walkway into the base lodge. There was a heightened awareness to the calm; we knew that with the fresh snow, the crowds would soon arrive.

We passed the final chairlift and entered the first trail. With no tracks to follow, we were guided by large fir trees on either side. It was quiet, except for the clicking of our metal snowshoes as they cut through the light powder. The striking scenery removed any obligation to make idle conversation and at the same time added a sense of purpose to each exchange.

"Erin mentioned that you were a software developer back in England," I said. "That's quite the career change."

Garry's stride and facial expression were unchanged, and I wondered whether he had heard me. I decided to probe further. "How did that lead to the snowshoe guide job in Canada?" I asked.

"Well, I've always loved the outdoors," he said after a long pause. "So, when my wife got a job that would bring us to Canada, she said, 'Well, if you love the outdoors so much, why don't you try for a job in the outdoors?' "

Following his passion came with a huge pay cut, Garry said. But he assured me he'd made the right decision. "My friends back in England can't believe the change that I've made. They can't imagine making that leap themselves," he said. "But, I'm finally doing a job that I'm passionate about. I really love this job. It's fantastic—the best job ever."

We continued to tread through the dense forest, following the trails, picking up toppled signs and wedging them into firmer snow.

In taking a much lower-paying job in a new field, Garry could be accused of suffering a midlife crisis. His father thought he was crazy. But after I'd spent a few hours with Garry, it was obvious to me that he knew exactly who he was and why he'd made the choices he had.

"Why was it so important for you to make such a drastic change and pursue something you loved?" I asked.

"Life's about chances. It's too short not to take those chances. The way I always look at it is, I don't want to be sixty-five thinking, Ah, I wish I'd done that. If I do it and it doesn't work out, then fine, it didn't work, try something different. But I don't want to be sitting there for the rest of my life regretting the things that I didn't do, because I think that's a sad waste of your life."

I was glad I'd asked. Not only did Garry seem to share my perspective, but things tend to sound more profound in an English accent.

"Have a play around in the job market, do jobs that you think you're going to enjoy, and if you don't enjoy them, get out and go try something else," he continued. "It's a lot easier to do when you're young than it is when you're my age."

Shortly after our talk, we emerged from the trail and spotted the base up ahead. Several large noisy groups of school kids were running around, throwing snowballs at one another, as a couple of other snowshoe guides attempted to calm them down.

Garry laughed. "You sure you're ready for this, mate?"

"Yeah," I said, smiling. "I'm ready."

JOB: **COACH: VOLLEYBALL CAMP**

LOCATION: **BURNABY, BRITISH COLUMBIA**

EMPLOYER: **VOLLEYBALL BC**
WAGE: **$15 HOUR**

JOB DESCRIPTION: Along with two other coaches, I organized the camp schedule, led skill demonstrations, training drills, and various games.

INDUSTRY IQ:

- Approximately 10 million children attend camp annually in the United States.
- The average salary for a NCAA Division I-A college football coach is over $1 million.

APPLICATION PROCESS: I played on the men's varsity volleyball team at university, so I had many friends involved in the volleyball community.

WHAT I LEARNED: Sometimes you can never be well enough prepared.

I only had one day to organize the schedule with the other two coaches before the camp started, but even if we'd had the entire previous week, I doubt it would have mattered. After my first day I realized that it would be an astounding feat to successfully hold the attention of fifty kids, age ten to fifteen, for eight hours a day. Especially when those kids were spending their spring break indoors at a volleyball camp. I had no chance—even school doesn't last eight hours.

WEEK 5 **JOB: REPORTER**
LOCATION: VANCOUVER, BRITISH COLUMBIA

EMPLOYER: *VANCOUVER 24 HOURS*
WAGE: $31,690 YEAR [Source: BLS]

INDUSTRY IQ:

- A columnist is often not an employee of the newspaper. The columns are purchased with a first publishing right, after which the columnist can sell the same piece to other publications.
- Columnists are paid per word or a flat rate for each piece.

APPLICATION PROCESS: A reporter from *Vancouver 24 Hours* had interviewed me two weeks earlier. I brought up the possibility of writing a column as a One-Week Job. She went to the editor with the idea, and when I didn't hear back, I called the following week and spoke to the editor directly. I said things like, "extremely excited" and "opportune opportunity" and "pretty please." And he said, "Sure, Sean."

WHAT I LEARNED: You're not official until you get a key.

On my first day I entered the building through the public entrance. But on my second day I spotted a door marked EMPLOYEE ENTRANCE. Now that I was an official employee, a reporter with *Vancouver 24 Hours,* I confidently stepped up to the door, smugly glanced at the lettering on the window, and even paused to take a few photos in front of it for my website. Then I pulled at the handle. Locked. Not as official as I'd thought. I had to walk around the building to the front door with the other visitors and have reception buzz me in.

THAT FIRST DAY, I sat in the lobby and waited for the editor in chief, Dean, to escort me into the newsroom. On the coffee table I spotted the current issue and flipped through it. Typically when I'd pick up a newspaper, I'd skim headlines and read the articles. But not today. Without realizing it, I denied this tendency and instead analyzed the layout, the type of stories covered, the names of reporters, the colour scheme, the advertisements. I was no longer a typical reader—now I was a reporter.

Dean arrived. He wore dark, rectangular glasses, and his hair was short and messy (yet inadvertently stylish). I guessed him to be in his late thirties. He seemed tired and busy; I got the impression he had a lot on his mind.

"Welcome, Sean. Come with me," he said, extending his hand. Then he led me through the office to the newsroom.

The newsroom was a stark contrast to the stillness of the lobby with its soft elevator music and comfy leather chairs. A sense of urgency filled the air as people buzzed around, phones rang, keyboards tapped, and colleagues discussed the day's hot news items. I took a seat in Dean's office and we went over my ideas for potential articles: redefining the word *career,* the trade-off between money and happiness, my generation's outlook on the workplace. He was quick to give me the go-ahead. I wondered if he was convinced of my ideas or simply had more important things to take care of. Either way, I was off to my desk to conduct interviews, gather information, and write my pieces.

To research, I visited a couple of campuses around Vancouver and interviewed students about what they wanted to do after university, why they thought so many members of our generation have difficulty deciding on a career, and what they're specifically looking for in a career.

I was quick to play the part—notebook and pen in hand, I'd approach a group of students and immediately assert my credibility. "Hi, I'm a reporter with *Vancouver 24 Hours.*" I'd ask my question, put on my best Anderson Cooper face (an inquisitive, unchanging stare), then listen intently while jotting notes in my reporter's notebook. With several usable quotes, I hurried back to the office to write up the story before my deadline at the end of the day.

I began:

> My generation, those born after 1980, has been described as a "Peter Pan generation," "adultescents," "kidults," and a host of others to describe how we are putting off the transition into adulthood later than previous generations; generally taking longer to finish college, get married, move out, start a family and enter the workforce. If you asked me when I was ten, I probably would have told you that I would be well into my professional career and expecting my second child by now. But at the age of 25, I have no idea what I want to do as a career, I still live at home, and could not conceive of getting married at this point in my life. Guess what? I am not alone.

After only one day, I could understand why Dean seemed so preoccupied all the time. It must be stressful being responsible for putting together a new paper each day. He had to manage a team, edit several pieces, decide what stories to cover, and attempt to make each paper better than the last. I imagined there's a point every day when the pressure mounts and the staff doubts whether they'll be able to pull it all off.

Dean left the office late, clearly exhausted but, I'd guess, satisfied, with a sense of completion—another paper was ready to go to press and hit the newsstand. The next morning, while sipping a cup of coffee, he'd see the result of everyone's hard work. But he'd dare not linger too long in admiration—there was always another paper to produce, more decisions to be made, and the next deadline quickly approaching.

The credibility I sought in announcing my new "reporter" title was short-lived when I returned to the office the next morning and was denied by the employee entrance.

But then I got my next assignment. Dean sent me out with another reporter to research a homicide that had occurred the night before at a high school party. I felt like a police investigator. The few details we had about the incident were vague. We had to visit the crime scene and interview neighbours, friends, and police, and visit the high school the victim had attended.

It was a sad story, and I didn't feel right being among every major media station in Vancouver trying to capture a few good quotes and names to construct a complete story. A reporter's job is to ask the tough questions and uncover the facts. As a neighbour explained how he awoke to yelling outside early that morning, reporters pushed him to describe in detail what he saw when he rushed from his house and found the victim lying wounded in the driveway. Perhaps some of my discomfort was a result of my inexperience, but I felt like I was prying into the lives of others and getting involved in something that was none of my business.

After we finished at the crime scene, we made our way with the rest of the media caravan to the victim's high school. It was close to noon, and the students would soon be on their lunch break. With no reporters allowed on school property, we all waited at the curb to pounce on students as they stepped off school grounds. The goal was to find a friend of the victim to speak with.

"Hey, look, there's a couple kids with flowers. They seem sad. Quick, over there." When one reporter found a student willing to talk, others would rush over, tape recorders and cameras in hand. "When you heard the news this morning, how did it make you feel?"

"Tell us about your friend, what was he like?"

"What's it like to know that you will never see him again?"

After a visit to the police station to solidify details of the incident, the story was complete. We drove back to the city and typed out the article; I made it home in time for dinner. Tomorrow would be a new day, a new story. In a profession that deals with such tough circumstances daily, being a bit detached may be the only way to cope with the job. I wonder. For me, it was all too real.

A testament to the stark contrasts in the world of daily reporting, my next assignment was to help cover a wine-tasting festival in downtown Vancouver. After visiting a few booths, I met Bill Hardy of Hardys wine. An older man, probably in his sixties, he picked up a bottle and in his Australian accent said, "This one's named after my grandfather. And this one over here after my grandmother." He wasn't keen on my suggestion that he name one after me.

He explained how the festival worked and the etiquette of wine tasting. I was lucky that I ran into him when I did. I was going on my fifth tasting and was astounded by the countless rows of booths representing different wineries. I couldn't understand how people could withstand this for an entire day. After I'd tasted a couple of varieties of the Hardys label, Bill said, "You know, Sean, you don't have to drink all of each sample. That's why they have spit buckets next to each booth." You really do learn something every day.

I like the immediacy that comes with reporting. I found it easy to stay engaged and motivated knowing that there was a deadline at the end of the day. For me, if a project is too long-term, it can be easy to lose interest. It needs to be broken down into short-term, achievable goals to keep me motivated. In the news world, each day you leave the office never certain what tomorrow will bring. For me, tomorrow brought good news in an email from a man named Manuel:

> Hello Sean, Just saw an article about your project while I was in Edmonton this week. It reminds me of when I had no idea of what I wanted to do for a living at age 25. I'm now 40 and I don't think it's a generational

issue. Some people know what they want to do, some don't. Some think they know (often under parental influence) and realize their mistake later on.

There is a good fit between your initiative and our job search engine, NiceJob.ca, and I would like to help you.

The next week we met for coffee, and it was settled. In exchange for a banner on my website and mention in media interviews, NiceJob.ca would give me $1,000 per month to put toward travel expenses. The One-Week Job project officially had a sponsor.

It was time to hit the road.

EMPLOYER: **BEST BUDS FLOWER COMPANY**
WAGE: **$23,950 YEAR** [Source: BLS]

INDUSTRY IQ:

- In Canada, approximately 156 million fresh-cut flowers are sold for Valentine's Day.
- In North America, women account for 65 percent of fresh-flower purchases; 33 percent of these purchases are for themselves.
- In medieval and Victorian times flowers were used to convey messages depending on the composition and type of flowers—it was known as the "flower language."

APPLICATION PROCESS: Robert Manolson, a career-development professional, called me. He was excited about the project and wanted to help by giving me some contacts in the Edmonton area. I sent emails to several of the businesses and heard back from Kim, the owner of Best Buds, who said she'd be happy to get involved.

WHAT I LEARNED: How to prepare a simple bouquet.

1. Sparsely position some of the small pieces (foliage, twigs), which will act as a foundation.
2. Then place the largest flowers; these will dominate the arrangement.
3. Place slightly smaller flowers to fill out the bouquet.
4. Last, use small foliage as accents.

I love being the person behind the scenes, being able to design and create something that will bring a smile to someone's face.

—KIM, florist, Best Buds Flower Company

EVEN THOUGH I now had a sponsor, I still had to make sure I stayed on budget. To keep costs down, I decided to post a note on my website and on Craigslist to try to find a ride with someone headed to Edmonton. Later that same afternoon, Olivia, an animated Italian in her early twenties, sent me an email.

> Hey Sean, I saw an article about you when you were on Urban Rush. I can totally relate. I recently graduated and have spent the past 6 months probably thinking about a lot of the same things you are. Anyway, I can give you a ride, though I'm planning on leaving tomorrow.

Road trips are fun. Even last-minute road trips with strangers to unfamiliar cities, with no idea of where you'll sleep upon arriving. We were five hours into the thirteen-hour drive from Vancouver to Edmonton, where I'd be a florist with Best Buds Flower Company. Olivia spent the first hour trying to decide if I was a serial killer, though after a few corny jokes, she'd concluded I was harmless.

Hitting the road felt like the true start to the project. I'd left the simple comforts of home, and from now on, I'd have to live out of a suitcase and find a new place to crash each week. But I was excited about the challenge. For some reason I felt like the project needed to be a bit difficult to be worthwhile.

I'd left my hometown of Port Moody many times before, but this time was different. I felt like I was really setting out on a journey. I think it was the whole searching thing that brought it out. We're told that if we want to find something, we must search for it. To search for it, we must go on a *journey.*

So, a journey it was.

I turned to Olivia and asked, "Have the past six months given you any clearer direction about what you want to do?"

"Yes and no." She adjusted the volume on the stereo. "I ended up returning to what I wanted to be when I grew up as a kid—which is a journalist—preferably an international reporter. But it takes a long time to get there. I'm doing an internship right now and have applied to some grad schools." She paused a moment. "I don't know, I sometimes wonder how spoiled I am to be able to think about this kind of stuff, because most of my family never had the opportunity—they just had to make money somehow."

"I know what you mean." I gazed out the window and watched the landscape speed by. I felt a bit spoiled myself. After all, I was on my way to try out life as a florist. In Edmonton.

Before Olivia picked me up that morning, I'd posted my cellphone number on the website in hopes of finding a place to stay before I arrived in Edmonton. Three hours outside of the city, my cellphone rang. It was my friend Mike. "Hey, Sean, I checked with my girlfriend, and she said that it's cool if you crash at her place while you're in town."

I'd met Mike a year earlier in a language program in Quebec. I knew he'd gone to school in Edmonton, but I didn't know he still had a girlfriend there. I was glad to find out he did. "That's huge, Mike. Thanks so much!" I said.

I'd never been one to make plans far in advance, but I could tell that this year would put my easygoing, things-will-work-out-even-if-I-leave-it-to-the-last-minute mentality to the test.

I hung up and looked down at my first-ever cellphone in awe—so *that's* what cellphones are for, I thought. I couldn't understand how I'd managed to live without one for so long.

I only hoped that my new-found mastery of cellphones could also translate into helping with my inexperience in the floral industry.

• • •

When I pushed open the front door of the shop on Monday morning, a bell attached to its metal frame announced my presence. It was bright. Each wall was painted in a solid colour—three different earthy greens and one maroon. Arrangements of flowers sat on tiered displays lining the shop floor, and a walk-in glass cooler housed more flowers. A couple of workers busily cut and arranged flowers on the two tables in the back as I approached the front counter. Kim, the owner, was one of them. She appeared to be in her mid-twenties and had curly dark hair and big blue eyes. She walked over with a pleasant smile on her face and handed me a piece of paper. "You're a popular guy, Sean. First day on the job and people are already asking for you," she said.

I glanced down at the paper. It was a list of names and numbers of various TV and radio producers who had called the shop looking to interview me. It turned out that word about my project had begun to spread over the internet, and the media was picking up the story.

"I'm sorry, Kim. I don't know why they'd call here—my email and cell number are on the website."

"No trouble at all," she assured me, and introduced me to the other staff members.

That afternoon I arranged more interviews than bouquets. All of a sudden, it was assumed that I possessed sweeping insight into the psyche of an entire generation. They asked why I started the project, about my promise for passion, my generation, and my previous five one-week jobs. I had to retell the story of my dad's advice at the dinner table over and over as if it were the first time. It felt weird. A bit like a show. I'd wrap a bouquet, cut stems, or man the register with a camera crew filming. We'd step aside to do an interview, then they'd leave and I'd go back to work. I did about fifteen interviews in the first two days. After a while, it seemed as if my answers to their identical questions had become rehearsed.

I wasn't sure if Kim was happy about the publicity or if it was a nuisance, but it definitely created a new dynamic. When I was working on set at the television talk show during Week 2, the cameras were part of the job. In the floral industry—not so much. On one hand I was happy for the exposure. Kim's business got some publicity after she had been kind enough to take the time to teach me her profession. For those who saw or heard the segment, it would open up a dialogue about finding passion at work. Finally, it would help me land some more one-week job offers. But on the other hand, I questioned how it would impact my experience.

All the interest from the media suggested to me that I wasn't the only twenty-five-year-old who didn't know what he wanted to be when he grew up (though I might have been the only one who still employed the expression "when I grow up" as if it was in some distant future).

Whether we're coming out of school and entering the work world, thinking about a career change after twenty years in the same position, or victim of a layoff due to the changing economy, most of us at some point will look deep inside ourselves for an answer to the question "What should I do with my life?" Ultimately I think we all want to be happy. But what that really means—and how to get there—remains uncertain. I suppose my journey—my pursuit of happiness—represented that search for many people.

By Wednesday, I'd learned a lot about the flower industry. I could arrange and wrap a bouquet and even tell the difference between a Fuji mum, an Asiatic lily, and a Gerber daisy. Most occasions that warrant flowers are happy. The customers are generally happy too, as they know the flowers they purchase will put a smile on someone's face. This aspect of the job contributed to the positive work environment I experienced—something I'd certainly look for in my career. I imagine it'd be difficult to find a similarly upbeat environment at a call centre that deals with customer complaints (even if they too had a cookie jar filled with homemade cookies on the counter).

I had also learned to appreciate the creative aspect of arranging flowers.

Kim handed me a green block of foam and laid an assortment of flowers on the table to choose from. My task was to stick flowers into the foam, piece by piece, until I created a full arrangement. I'd pick up a flower, then turn to Kim. "What if I put this one here? Will that look good?" Kim, working on constructing her arrangement, would casually reply, "Whatever you think, Sean." Of course this only filled me with anxiety. I always want to make the right choice. There were so many ways these flowers could be arranged, and I took my flower arranging very seriously.

It's the simple decisions I've always had difficulty with. A spontaneous road trip? Why not? Show up in a city with no place to stay? No problem. Backpack through a foreign country where I don't speak the language? Sure. But, hand me a four-page dinner menu? I hope no one's in a hurry to eat.

In school, my teachers always claimed they were teaching me skills that would prepare me for the "real world." That they made a point of distinguishing it from whatever world I was in at the time made this so-called real world a bit intimidating to me. I could never quite make the connection between learning the number of electrons in a sigma bond (that's two) and preparing for this real world.

As I stared at the sparse block of foam surrounded by an assortment of flowers and foliage, I questioned where those real-world skills were when I needed them.

I organized the various pieces on the table in front of me and plotted out my next steps. I was careful to keep in mind the techniques and patterns that Kim had taught me earlier—"Keep it simple, start with the small things like the foliage and twigs, then the biggest flowers that will dominate the arrangement, then the slightly smaller flowers, and lastly back to the foliage to fill it out." Easy enough.

Then something hit me.

My teachers *had* taught me real-world skills, and I was currently using them—just indirectly. In school, what I was learning wasn't nearly as important as the fact that I was being taught *how* to learn, and therefore how to make better decisions. A lame comparison, yes, but it made me recognize that the skills that had enabled me to be successful in certain areas of my life—namely, school and sports—were in fact the same skills that would provide the framework for success in this real world filled with green foam blocks and a ridiculous number of flower varieties.

After all these years, I finally understood what the after-school specials tried so hard to get through to me: School, in fact, *is* cool.

When I returned from lunch that afternoon, I noticed that my arrangement had sold. The "Well, how do ya like that?" expression that I immediately shot toward Kim soon morphed into one of puzzlement as I thought, Really? Someone actually bought that?

WEEK  JOB: **YOGA INSTRUCTOR**

LOCATION: **EDMONTON, ALBERTA**

EMPLOYER: **LOTUS SOUL GYM**

WAGE: **$34,310 YEAR** **[Source: BLS]**

JOB DESCRIPTION: Tidied mats, swept the studio floor, welcomed members. Attended approximately six hours of yoga classes a day, sometimes participating, other times absorbing teaching techniques by watching Henri, Lotus Soul Gym's owner.

On Friday, it was my turn to teach. I forgot a couple of postures and had to sneak a few glances at my notes while the students' eyes were closed, but overall it went well—even though apparently (as the students told me afterward) I'm a hard teacher.

INDUSTRY IQ:

- Over 1.5 million Canadians practise yoga.
- Approximately 75 percent of yoga practitioners are female.
- There are two levels of Yoga Alliance certificates—200-hour and 500-hour. Most yoga studios require that only the 200-hour certification be completed to obtain employment.
- There are many types of yoga. Hatha yoga is the most popular type in Canada, as it's great for beginners. It focuses on balancing mind and body through dozens of postures performed slowly and smoothly.

At a social gathering it's common that the second or third question is "What do you do for a living?" And it's almost like what you do defines who you are as a person. But I think that many young people are saying that's not who I am, I'm a lot more than whatever it is that I do for a living.

—Henri, yoga instructor, Lotus Soul Gym

LATE MONDAY MORNING I hesitantly stood at the door of Lotus Soul Gym on Whyte Avenue in Edmonton. I wondered how many people show up to their first day of work with everything they own—fully equipped to move in permanently if the job demanded it. Short of bringing a blanket and pillow, that was me. I had to bring all of my stuff to work since I wouldn't be introduced to my next couch until that evening. And so under the weight of my suitcase, computer bag, and backpack, I climbed the stairs to the second-storey gym.

Double French doors separated the studio from the waiting room. Suddenly the doors swung open. A class had just finished. Natural light streamed through the windows on the far side of the room and reflected off the polished hardwood floor. Feeling slightly out of place, I took a little more time and care than necessary to remove my shoes as the students gathered their belongings and headed for the exit. I glanced across the studio and spotted a tall, pleasant-looking grey-haired man whom I estimated to be somewhere in his late fifties. Henri, I thought to myself.

Our eyes met. With a warm touch on a student's shoulder, he finished his conversation and made his way toward me. Long grey locks flowing behind him, he moved with the deliberateness of a Buddhist monk, and his smile was warm and comforting.

"Hi, Henri. I'm Sean, your newest instructor."

"Welcome, Sean. We're happy you're here," he said.

No classes were scheduled for the afternoon. As the studio

emptied we began exchanging stories and perspectives on life. He shared his philosophy of yoga: "Yoga is so much more than learning how to do a posture," he said. "While we're doing a posture, we're learning to connect with the limitations in our body, but we're also beginning to understand how we operate under those conditions—what do we do with those challenges? Do we become critical? Do we become judgmental? Do we want to give up? Let's face it, everybody in this world deals with challenges—it's how we respond to those challenges that determines where we go from there."

The journey that led Henri to open a yoga studio at the age of fifty-six is a unique one. One of his career decisions stood out to me. In his forties, he and his partner started a successful catering company. After seven years, it was doing $1 million worth of business annually. Things looked great financially, and Henri and his partner found they could afford the finer things in life. There was only one problem. Years of working so many hours each week had left them totally burnt out. They realized that growing the business and their material wealth had come at a great cost—their happiness. So they sold the business.

"The catering business was not feeding my soul," he said. "It was just paying the bills. And the thing about being in your own business and making good money is that it's always hard to leave that money. It takes a little bit of soul searching to say, 'Okay, so I can make this much money, but this is what I have to give up to do it.' Some people can never make that choice. It's not something that everybody would be comfortable in doing and not have regrets."

After selling his business, Henri decided to move to the Cayman Islands and take up something he always wanted to do—become a scuba diving instructor. Even though his salary was a fraction of what he had made with his catering business, he was much happier. "Sean, I was so happy to have that first cheque in my hand. I wanted so bad to frame the thing," he said. "And I would have, but I *really* needed the money."

I could see Henri standing there, a warm breeze blowing off the Caribbean Sea, holding his check with both hands, beaming with pride as tourists prepared their scuba equipment in the background. "I believe the biggest travesty of many people's lives is that they never take the time to put themselves under scrutiny. Well, how can we ever grow if we don't do that? For as long as I live I'm going to have that memory—that I chose to follow my heart. It is what I really wanted to do, and I followed it, and there are no regrets. None. And that's a very liberating feeling."

Henri's calming presence made him very easy to connect with; I caught a glimpse of the clock and saw that two and half hours had passed. If I was to make it back in time for my first lesson that evening, I had to grab a bite to eat.

I left the serenity of the studio and walked into the chaos of rush hour, but it didn't faze me. I felt energized and alive but somehow calm at the same time. When I remembered that I had to teach yoga classes in four days—and my first-ever visit to a yoga studio had occurred just moments ago—my nervousness quickly returned.

When my big day finally arrived, I felt as if I'd been studying for a final exam all week. Now it was my turn to teach a class.

The students were seated facing me, eyes closed, in the meditative position that begins each practice. Soft music bathed the room. Henri sat on a mat beside me.

My mind drifted to the conversation we'd had on Monday. I remembered the genuine admiration in his gaze when Henri said, "Sean, you inspire me. I can't wait to see what you're doing in twenty years, because you are going to do some amazing things in your life."

It felt good that others had confidence in my future, but I didn't always share it. Sure, I wanted to do "amazing things" with my life. But what did that even mean? In the past, there had always been an equation. Take notes in class, do your homework, study for exams, and it will help you get a decent grade. Train hard, improve coordination, work out regularly, and you're on your way to becoming a decent athlete. But now, how was I to satisfy this ambiguous "amazing thing" scenario?

How does anyone define the moment at which they become successful or fulfill their true potential? For some, maybe it's an echelon achieved through the acquisition of wealth and status. For others, maybe it comes from experiencing a certain level of happiness or enlightenment. Or maybe it comes after an explicit number of people have been positively affected through our actions. Whatever method we choose to keep score, how do we decide when it's enough? When do we stop aspiring for more? And, most important, when does it become "amazing"?

The students looked so peaceful seated before us, cross-legged, deep in their own thoughts. I hesitated to begin the class, worried that a tremble in my voice would give away my nervousness. The silence grew louder. A bead of sweat slid down my temple. I glanced in Henri's direction. He nodded, then gave me a reassuring smile. And I began.

WEEK 8 JOB: **DAIRY FARMER**

LOCATION: **RIMBEY, ALBERTA**

EMPLOYER: **THE SLOMP FAMILY**

WAGE: **$49,140 YEAR [Source: BLS]**

INDUSTRY IQ:

- A cow's gestation period is about nine months.
- Dairy farmers typically purchase bull semen by mail order for artificial insemination. The catalogue features a picture of the bull and lists its statistics: breed, stature, strength, daughters' udder quality (a solid addition to any coffee table's reading material).

WHAT I LEARNED: To deal with dung.

After trying to avoid it for the first fifteen minutes, I finally gave up and realized there was no way around it—having cow feces all over my hands and occasionally splashed in my face is simply part of the job. It's like walking in the rain. We may initially struggle to avoid it, but no matter how fast we walk, or how many puddles we manage to jump over, we're inevitably going to get wet. But if we can accept that getting soaked is unavoidable, then we allow ourselves to stop worrying and actually enjoy the experience.

GEORGE, THE HEAD of his family's 120-hectare organic dairy farm, and his wife, Solene, converted their computer room into my bedroom for the week. I was fast asleep when George provided my wake-up call with a knock on the door. I crawled out of bed and slowly made my way into the living room. It was still pitch-black outside, and for a second I questioned if George was just messing with me. There were no lights turned on in the house, but with the help of the moonlight that crept in through the kitchen window I managed to discern George's outline across the room.

"Morning, Sean," he whispered. "Big day ahead of us."

We quietly made our way to the back door while his wife and newborn slept peacefully in the other room. George handed me a blue full jumpsuit that reminded me of something a mechanic might wear and a large pair of thick rubber boots. I slowly stepped into the jumpsuit and pulled it up over my legs. I was half-asleep though alert enough not to allow its well-worn brown-crusted exterior to touch my comparably clean shorts and T-shirt. With my boots on and jumpsuit zipped up, I followed George out into the moonlight and we headed toward the barn.

An intelligent twenty-seven-year-old with blond hair, blue eyes, and wire-rimmed glasses, George grew up working on the family farm until he went away to university. After he finished his degree, he'd returned to the farm to settle with his new young family.

George opened up the barn door and the cows stirred accordingly—they knew the routine. We walked through the barn to wake up the approximately eighty cows and direct them toward the milking area. We clapped our hands, made grunting sounds, and smacked the few cows who decided they wanted to sleep in.

The milking area was the size of an auto mechanic's garage. It was connected to the barn and had white walls, fluorescent lighting, a distinct odour, and the hum of machines at work. The cows entered the milking area through two sliding wood doors, which funnelled them into a single lane on either side of the farmer. As we herded the cows, George explained the milking process.

"In the past, they'd milk each cow by hand—a long and labour-intensive process. Now there are milking machines that do the work. It's faster, more sterile, and easier on the cow."

We stepped down to a lower-level dugout, which put the cows on either side of us around waist height. George said that this gives the farmer easier access to the cow's udder. I've since determined that these are the most precarious moments. While my hands flirted in dangerous territory and the cow shot me an unwavering docile stare, I could never be certain when one was going to force me to embrace yet another "walk in the rain" experience.

George continued: "Each milking machine has four suction tubes that attach to each individual teat. Once all four suctions are attached, press the Start button, and move on to the next cow." George pointed to a tube that pumped the milk.

"The milk is then sent through this tube into a filtering process, and then into one large storage vat in the next room, where the milk truck will come and pick it up."

"How often does the milk truck come?" I asked.

"Every other day, rain, shine, even Christmas—nothing stops the milk truck. Well, once rain and flooding did postpone it for a day, but one day in twenty years is not bad."

"Do you ever drink the raw milk?" I asked.

"Raw unpasteurized milk is illegal to sell. But I can drink the milk from my own cows," he said. "The health authorities think it's foolish, but I swear by raw milk, since its enzymes are not destroyed, making it more digestible. This means that your body gets more nutrients out of the milk and the milk sits well in your stomach. But I cannot stress how illegal raw milk is—we don't sell it."

After all the cows on one side had been milked, George opened the metal gate in front of the first cow and they walked forward back into the barn. "Once the lane is clear, we close this metal gate at the front," he explained. "Then we open the sliding wood door at the back, and the next six are allowed to enter."

With six milking machines per side, twelve cows could be milked at one time. The whole process took around two hours. Then it was time to sweep and hose down the milking area, feed the calves, and work around the barn until it was milking time again in the afternoon. On average, each cow produced about thirty litres of milk per day.

George told me that dairy farming works on a quota system. "All farmers buy the right to produce *x* gallons of milk per year. This is their quota. Once they buy it, they own it until they sell it. There's no yearly renegotiation or fee—it's a commodity. A farmer must ship within one percent of *x* gallons or else be penalized. If he ships too much, he'll be fined—he's better off dumping it down the drain—and if he doesn't ship enough, quota will be taken away. On our farm we produce around 132,000 gallons [almost 500,000 litres] per year, and we have quota to match that."

The life of a dairy farmer is forever tied to the cows. The workday doesn't end with the late-afternoon milking session. There's always barn work to complete, and George will often check on the cows again before he goes to bed. If George ever wants to take a day off, the cows still need to be milked because full udders can be painful.

Although I'd never say that I enjoy having cow excrement all over me, once I managed to convince myself that it was somehow comparable to walking in the rain, it didn't bother me as much. It was just part of the job. Then I could focus on more important things—like learning to swiftly sidestep an onslaught of cow piss (surprisingly warm) or avoid getting kicked in the face by the rear hoof of a cow not in the mood to be milked. Both, I'd learn, are important skills for a dairy farmer to master.

WEEK 9 JOB: SKI-RESORT STAFF

LOCATION: LAKE LOUISE, ALBERTA

IT WAS A "work hard, play hard, party even harder" mentality at the resort. I did my best to keep up, though, as it was the end of April, the season was complete, so most employees boasted six months of practice.

Throughout the week I worked in different departments: trail crew, lift attendants, snow-school instructors, and with the events team to help run the spring wrap-up event for the season. The event featured a full lineup of free concerts, demos, bike-trial riders, and a bunch of other activities. There was even a hot-dog–eating contest. I considered signing up but in the end decided that stuffing my face with whole hot dogs, drool pouring out of my mouth, forcing back the gag reflex, and then secretly vomiting under the table out of the view of the audience wasn't something I felt inclined to experience. It was fun to watch though.

It was the first one-week job where I tried out different departments within the same company. It gave me a unique perspective. There are more than six hundred employees at Lake Louise, and I got to see how much work and organizing goes into effectively operating such a large company.

I never thought I'd enjoy working for a large company. I assumed that it would be difficult to develop a sense of teamwork and to see how I was contributing to the company's overall success. But each department I worked with was made up of smaller teams, and each team had its own unique culture within the context of the larger company. This seemed to help things run smoothly and made all employees feel like they play an important role.

• • •

On Wednesday I was in the cafeteria at the base of the mountain when I overheard a conversation between a visitor and an employee. The employee, in her early twenties, was justifying her minimum-wage seasonal job. The visitor didn't appear to be passing judgment, but the employee still played down her current situation, as if to convey her awareness that she should be doing something more significant. She seemed to want him to know not to judge her based on her current job, because she had a plan.

I heard several similar conversations throughout the week. The majority of the employees loved their jobs. They worked at one of the most spectacular mountain resorts in Canada, where they got a free season pass and could hit the mountain at every opportunity. To sweeten the deal, there were always festivals and events coming through town. Yet still many seemed to feel guilty for putting off the "real job" route (or to at least feel enough external pressure to give this façade to an outside observer).

For as long as I could remember, I'd always entered social gatherings ready to report on "my plan"—ensuring that I'd communicate a desire to get ahead and an awareness that I could do better. For some reason it never seemed acceptable to be content with my current situation. I'd always assumed that other young people knew how they were supposed to spend their time after university—that I was the only one struggling to figure it out. They'd state their plans with conviction and confidence almost as if rehearsed. When I was among them, I did it too. We'd validate one another's plans and then carry on with another day. When I was busy, I didn't question this. I was in it and it felt good. But when things were quiet, part of me wondered if it was all a show—were we trying to convince others as much as ourselves? Lately, I'd begun to suspect that the majority of young people were just like me—simply making it up as they went along.

WEEK 10 JOB: COMPUTER-SOFTWARE SALES

LOCATION: VANCOUVER, BRITISH COLUMBIA

ANOTHER MONDAY MORNING. Sitting in rush-hour traffic in Vancouver en route to yet another first day on the job, I was exhausted. It's hard to change jobs every week. As soon as I got settled in a position, Friday came. I said my goodbyes, and it was time to start all over again—new location, new dress code, new co-workers, new boss. Most people dread their first day of work. I'd already had ten, and if I could keep this going, I'd have many more.

I came back to Vancouver because my best friend, Ian, was getting married the following weekend, and I was going to be his best man. I took my first office job, at a Vancouver company called SustaiNet Software Solutions that sells computer software.

I wasn't looking forward to it. I got into town on Friday, packed up a small backpack of clothes, then immediately headed out for Ian's bachelor party weekend, which didn't end until after one o'clock Monday morning. I woke up five hours later (thankfully in my own bed) and then left for work.

It felt weird that my friends were starting to get married. That we were approaching *that* stage in life. It's funny to think that there's an age at which we start to feel we should get married. Before long, friends would discuss having babies at the same time so that they could go for walks in the park together, chat on wooden benches while watching their kids play on the jungle gym, and not be the only ones at the party who had to leave before 8 P.M. Me, I was just trying to get through my first day at the office.

I thought of offices as the places where "real jobs" happen. Here is my desk. Here is my computer. I come *here* to work. On the wall there is a clock. When the clock says 5 P.M., I stop work and go home. No more work. When I work outside of that nine-to-five box, I somehow feel rebellious.

I liked the idea of offices. It seems to attach a legitimacy to the job. I'd definitely enjoy saying things like "Just send it on over to my office" or "I'll call you when I get into the office." And having meetings in boardrooms with big comfy leather chairs, congregating around the water cooler, discussing who got kicked off *Survivor* the night before. In theory, I thought offices were great—they bring people together and facilitate communication so that more can be accomplished. I just didn't think I could do it every day. Then again, I'd never tried it.

I arrived at the ninth-floor downtown office and met my boss for the week, Howard. He appeared to be somewhere in his fifties. Balding and bearded, he had a great smile and a lot of energy.

"Hey, Sean, welcome!" he said in a South African accent.

The office was unsurprisingly office-like. There were desks, chairs, computers, stationery, a coffee machine, and a couch for visitors with scheduled appointments. Howard led me into his office, and I took a seat across from him at his desk. His office seemed pretty standard, with a few personal touches: pictures of Howard skydiving and riding horses; a family portrait on his desk. The choice of floor lamp instead of typical overhead fluorescent lights added a human element. Hip but office-like, I decided.

We discussed the history of the company, and I sat in on the weekly Monday-morning meeting. Then Howard showed me to my workspace. I took a seat, and he handed me an informational booklet about the company. "Here, Sean, have a read. This will give you a better idea of what we do here," he said, then returned to his office.

I glanced down at the pamphlet, "SustaiNet Software Solutions."

"Okay, here we go," I said, attempting to pump myself up. I looked to my left and saw the water cooler across the hall. I got up, grabbed one of the paper cups next to it, filled it up, then returned to my desk and tried again. "Okay, *now* here we go." I took a sip of my water and began reading. "SustaiNet Software Solutions is a distributor and implementer of web-based information management systems that are designed to assist organizations to efficiently manage the wide range of information gathered to achieve their environmental and social sustainability goals." Yeah, I'm still not sure what that means.

After a few hours of reading through information on the software and on the protocol for the trade show we'd be exhibiting at on Thursday, I glanced up at the wall clock—11:30 A.M. My mind drifted. Could I be sitting at that same desk performing similar tasks at 11:30 A.M. one year later? I wasn't sure that I could. Then again, maybe it'd just need to be the right task. Howard appeared to love his job. He owned the company and so was more invested in its growth. He was very motivated, and he got excited when he talked about the company. He knew where he wanted to take it.

It must be nice to have a routine, I thought. But I wasn't quite ready for it. I found that a routine took away much of my preoccupation with day-to-day decision making, thus granting me far too much time to question myself and my lack of direction. At that point in my life it was much easier to just keep moving, exploring, trying new things.

By Friday, things hadn't gotten much more exciting than they were the first day.

My co-workers were great. They were very generous with their time and fun to be around. It was my cubicle that I disliked. But the reality was, I couldn't possibly learn the skills of the other employees and implement them in only one week, so I didn't get to do any of the interesting things that probably make their jobs worthwhile.

I spent the majority of my last day at my desk, inputting contact information from business cards we picked up at the trade show the day before. Leads, as the industry calls them. Howard said he'd come and grab me at the end of the day, but it felt like I'd been trapped in a business-card abyss for hours. I was beginning to think that when I finally emerged from my dwelling all the lights in the building would be off, chairs would be neatly tucked in, and everyone would have gone home for the day. I'd have to manoeuvre through a maze of red laser beams to avoid setting off the alarm.

It had been a quiet day. The confines of my cubicle and the dull, calming hum of the overhead fluorescent light fixtures got me thinking. Did I genuinely believe this next year would help me figure out what I wanted to do with my life, or had I just figured out a creative way to trick myself into believing it would? Was this all just an elaborate form of procrastination in which I could continue to hide from myself, escape my fears, silence the external pressure of others, and avoid getting a real job?

Those who know me well say I live in a dream world. My friends call it Sean's World. A place where anything is possible and "happy thoughts" decide whether things go right. In other words, Neverland.

I questioned whether I should give up on my fairy-tale adventure and stop trying to convince myself that I'd actually be better for this experience. I wasn't the first to have doubts about my direction in life or to question the status quo. Surely most people went down this same path at some point, struggled with the same decisions, asked themselves the same questions. And, judging solely by the number of times I'd hear others complaining about their jobs, perhaps most had come to the same conclusion: That is just the way it is. Accept it. Get a real job.

I've yet to figure out what makes one job any less "real" than another, but I have a strong suspicion that to be accepted as a real job, it has to be something you don't enjoy. Furthermore, that it requires formal attire and time spent sitting in traffic. To have a job that I love and at the same time make enough money to live the lifestyle I want would almost make me feel guilty—as if I'd somehow be cheating the system.

Guilty or not, that was the goal I'd set out to achieve. But what if I didn't find it? I'd taken that first step, put myself out there, opened myself up for criticism and adventure, but what if I tried my hardest and still failed? Then what? Would I have to accept a more mundane means of existence?

A year earlier in Thailand, I'd met a man who said he was a lot like me when he was my age—idealistic, set on finding a passion rather than a career. Then he went to business school, got the large salary, the Porsche, the big house, and the girl, and left behind his ideals.

"What changed?" I asked. "Why did you have to give up on your ideals?"

Although he was only twenty-nine, he sat back in his chair like a wise old man. "You will find out yourself one day," he said.

I smiled, then politely replied, "I hope not."

But that was just it. I *hoped* not. Sometimes I felt naïve to want these things, to believe that it was possible. Perhaps one day I too would learn to compromise my ideals and accept a job that I wasn't passionate about.

But this belief, this hope, that there was something more—was the one thing that kept me going. And, for the time being, allowed me to silence any doubts about the project.

The sound of approaching footsteps broke the incessant hum of the overhead fluorescent lights and brought me back to reality. Howard popped his head into my workspace. "Hey, Sean, that's all for today. Time to go home."

I packed up my things and headed for the elevator. The window at the end of the hall granted my first glimpse of the outside world since lunch. And what do you know, it was still light outside after all.

WEEK 11 JOB: ELDER CARE WORKER
LOCATION: TROIS-PISTOLES, QUEBEC

A COUPLE OF DAYS after Ian's wedding in Vancouver, I hopped on a plane and made the trip out east to my next one-week job in the small town of Trois-Pistoles, Quebec.

In my last year of university, I heard about a government-sponsored program that encourages Canadians to learn French. I figured if the government was going to pay for me to live somewhere else in the country for five weeks, thereby allowing me to further put off any major decision making after graduation, I was in.

I got accepted into the program in Trois-Pistoles and was placed with a host family along with eight of the three hundred anglophone students enrolled in the session. It only took a couple of days to realize that it would be a special experience.

The population of Trois-Pistoles is about four thousand. Very few speak English, which forces the students to learn the language quickly in order to communicate. The school organizes cultural activities—movies, field trips, concerts—every week, which allow the students to learn about Quebec culture and interact with one another. When I first arrived in town with the other students on the train, only a few previously knew one another and everyone was very quiet and kept to themselves. Five weeks later, when it was time to go home, we were all in tears, sad to leave the friends we'd become so close to.

After my first five weeks in the spring of 2005, I returned for the summer session and again the following year. I loved it. I was hidden in my own world with no expectation to have a detailed map of my future. Life was simple. It was as if we'd all gone back to elementary school. Class started and finished at the same time each day. The schedule of after-school activities was posted on the fridge with a magnet. Our only responsibility was to soak up the experience, learn the language, and show up at mealtime.

I stayed with the same host family each time, and as a result we'd become very close. They call me their adopted son, and I consider them my French family. Robin, Caroline, and their two daughters, Kim and Kristina, had been hosting students in their home for sixteen years, but I don't think they'd ever hosted one like me—I refused to leave.

Robin, known as Tiggy to his friends (I call him Tigs), set me up with a one-week job at the local home for the elderly. Tigs owns a window-and-door-installation company in town and suggested that I work with him the following week. I never pass up an opportunity to visit Trois-Pistoles (especially when the language school is in session).

It felt good to be back there. There's always an added energy that comes in situations restricted to a limited amount of time—everyone's game for anything as they try to take away as much as possible from the experience. It was mid-May, and there were three weeks left in the spring session, so I decided that I'd stay and work three different jobs in town.

I'd always wanted to spend time at a home for the elderly. But it was in the same way that I'd always wanted to read Tolstoy's *War and Peace*—I liked the idea but had never bothered to actually do it.

Now I had to.

Late Thursday afternoon I sat next to Gretchen in a room with about forty other elderly bingo enthusiasts. Several rounds of single lines, four corners, and postage stamps later, we were working on the full card. Things were looking good for me and Gretchen—just one more number to go: G48.

Bingo had been the highlight of the week. I was excited to hear the different perspectives from the elderly residents on what I was doing and tap into their wealth of life stories. But now that I was there, finally taking time out of my busy life, ready to listen, learn, and heed their profound wisdom, it seemed that no matter the topic of conversation, it always found a way back to my hair.

Elder folks were more overt in their curiosity about my dreadlocks than other people were. I'd be saying something about the weather, careers, politics, my excitement about bingo after lunch, anything really. Then someone would interrupt as though to add an opinion to the discussion, but instead it'd be something like, "So, is that your real hair?"

Others simply sat in silence and stared at me as if in a trance, their eyes following me around the room, perplexed expressions unwavering.

People have always had questions about my dreads, but they hold off asking until the right moment. I'll be at a party, a few small groups engaged in separate conversations. Then the person I'm speaking to will ask, "How long have you had dreadlocks for?" All of a sudden there's only one conversation in the room.

I'd had dreads for almost five years. Growing up, I always had a short clean cut. I'd wanted to have long hair at least once in my life. I figured that university would be the best time to grow it out before I'd be expected to clean myself up and get a real job. I also had the security that came from being in a long-term relationship. Dreadlocks were the last step. I planned to cut them for my final year of business school, but then I never did. And so the valedictorian of the business department had long blond dreadlocks. I found the juxtaposition funny, though I don't think the dean was too happy with the image it portrayed.

Inevitably, the next question is "How do you get them like that?"

Traditionally dreadlocks are formed over time when hair is not washed or combed—not the most hygienic technique. In straight hair, a combination of back combing and palm rolling a section of hair makes a dread. As hair grows, it grows into the already formed dread.

Now that the near-strangers are feeling comfortable in the conversation and I appear to be cool with answering their probing questions, we get into what everyone really wants to know. Working at maintaining a fine neutral-reporter face, one of both intrigue and nonjudgmentalness (the elderly tend not to be so great with this subtle display), someone will finally ask, "And so, do you wash them?"

Yes. I'm able to wash my hair because it's so knotted that it won't come undone with shampoo, but I still have to avoid conditioner.

Since the start of the One-Week Job project, I'd had this exact same conversation at least once a week. This week it was about several times a day, as new people entered the room with a bewildered look on their face. Others would simply forget that they'd already asked me a half-hour earlier.

"G forty-eight," the young female caregiver at the front of the room called out.

"All right!" I said, then passed the final chip to Gretchen, who hadn't yet realized this would complete her card. She took the chip and looked down. "Oh, would ya look at that," she said, as she covered G48 with the chip and slowly stood up. "BINGO!" she cried out, waking up those who had drifted off to sleep.

With a proud smile on my face I watched her walk to the front and claim her, or rather, *our* winnings—as I knew that this win would not have been possible had I not pointed out earlier that N34 and I29 had already been called.

With a grin on her face and the crisp $10 bill in her hand, she looked toward me and waved it like a winning lottery ticket. I smiled back at her and gave a spirited thumbs-up. People clapped, then stood up and began to pack up their chips and cards and head for the exit. I gathered up the rest of our chips and cards and debated whether I'd give Gretchen a high five or a hug when she returned.

I decided on a high five transitioned into a hug.

But when I looked up, cards and chips in hand, she was walking out the door arm in arm with an elderly man. Our shopping spree at Dollarama would have to wait.

That weekend the language school had a trip planned to Quebec City. I decided to tag along, as I'd made some new friends over the week (excluding Greedy Gretchen of course). But there was one in particular who motivated me to hop on the yellow school bus and make the three-hour trip with the rest of the students. Her name was Danna (pronounced "*Dan*-nah").

I saw her everywhere I went that week—at the concert at school, outside the post office, riding my bike through the park. In a town with only one traffic light, I probably passed most people a few times each day. But Danna was different.

When I saw her at the corner store (the third time that day) I debated employing the "Are you following me?" line—where of course we'd both laugh at the coincidence, then I'd continue to visibly mull over my chocolate-bar selection to convey that I was actually there with purpose, that I wasn't a stalker, that in fact I was actually a funny guy—maybe even someone she should ask out for a cup of coffee. The groundwork would be in place for a more meaningful conversation the next time we saw each other, and she'd be left thinking, Hmm, he seemed nice.

Yeah, that would have been good—smooth even.

But instead I managed an awkward half smile that could only suggest a creepy fetish with choosing chocolate bars.

The next day I saw her again outside of the school. This time she was talking to Matt, one of the students who lived at my house. I quickly made my way over to get in on the conversation before they went their separate ways.

"Hey, Matt, how's it going, buddy?" I said, perhaps a bit too eager.

"Good, man." He turned to his right. "Sean, this is Danna. She's in my class."

I turned and faced her.

Wow, she is beautiful, I thought. Not a magazine, done-up, Photoshopped kind of beautiful, but a natural beautiful. I was positive she could wake up in the morning after only a few hours sleep, no makeup, hair everywhere, and she would only be more beautiful.

Oh, what a coincidence. Coincidences are fun, I thought, hoping that my facial expression would reflect the thought.

I debated explaining the whole awkward chocolate-bar-fetish thing or trying the following-me line, but before I could say anything, she beat me to it. With a wry smile, she said, "You're the one that was following me around yesterday, right?" She laughed.

Oh, she's good, I thought. Definitely someone I should ask out for a cup of coffee.

"Well, I should get going," she said. "Matt, see you in class?"

"You bet," Matt said.

She turned to me (one might say, "with purpose"). "Nice to meet you, Sean."

"Nice to meet you too, Danna."

She headed for the front doors. "And I'll be sure to stop following you around," I called out. Immediately, I wanted to take it back.

I hadn't had a meaningful conversation with Danna yet, but I couldn't help but be intrigued. With her green eyes, shoulder-length blond hair, genuine smile, slim build, and unassuming demeanour, she possessed a down-to-earth allure draped in coolness that immediately drew me in.

I turned to Matt. "Hmm, she seemed nice."

"Yes, Sean." He laughed, sensing that I'd taken to her. "Yes, she is."

In Quebec, we stayed in the dorms at the university campus just outside of the city. After a night out on the town with a group of the students, several of us, including Danna, were back at the dormitory, sitting on the patio. We talked until early morning. The sun would be rising soon and the conversation dwindled.

I saw Danna slip back inside.

I searched for a way out of the conversation. I yawned and stretched, giving the "time for bed" routine, then went inside. Danna had just turned into a stairwell down the hall. In my desperate attempt not to lose her, I called up ahead, "Hey, Danna, where are you going?" I hurried to catch up.

She'd already started up the stairs. "I'm going to try and get onto the roof to watch the sunrise," she called back.

She ran up the stairs, and I ran up after her. I only hoped that she wanted to be followed—that it was her plan for us to watch the sunrise together and she had very tactfully led me there. That's the scene I'd created in my mind, anyway. And at the time it gave me enough courage to continue my pursuit.

But it turned out I wasn't the innocent victim of a premeditated romantic setup. The truth is she wasn't ready to go to bed and wanted to watch the sun come up over the city. The rooftop of the dormitory was the obvious choice.

We grabbed two chairs from the top floor, crawled out a window onto the gravel rooftop, and placed them beside each other. The sky was cobalt blue with pink brushstrokes that traced a silhouette of the city's skyline. In such a setting, it was easy to fall into a conversation about life.

"We are *so* lucky," Danna said, admiring our surreal view. "It really puts things in perspective and reminds me to appreciate the small things, and to just be grateful for this opportunity at life." She paused, then continued, "I don't know, I just find it incredibly humbling."

If there was a book titled *Sean's Life Philosophies,* incorporating all my beliefs and passionate views on life, Danna had studied it. During our conversation she naturally recited passages I'd subconsciously collected over the years. It was as if someone had prepped her beforehand and put her up to it, kind of like the time when Ian put a personal ad in the university newspaper. To mess with him, I created a fake email account and sent him admiring letters. Because I know Ian so well, it took only a couple of emails before he thought he'd found his perfect match. He was thrilled, until he found out it was me. I only hoped this wouldn't end with the similar joke-taken-too-far, bitter result.

With Danna, I was speechless. I felt I couldn't contribute anything meaningful to the conversation—especially since she shared so many of my opinions. All I could do was nod and say "Yeah." And then change it up every once in a while with a "Yeah, I *totally* know what you mean," in an attempt to communicate my sincerity and deflect any suspicion that I merely wanted to woo her (yes, *woo* her).

There's something about staying awake until the sun comes up that feels epic. At least when you've decided to do so. When you end up walking home, still sobering up, wearing the clothes from the night before, while coping with the judging eyes of those on their way to work and the sun's piercing rays that have never been so bright, that is somehow not so epic.

Tonight was the epic sort.

We finally said good night. We stood up and paused to take one last look at the peaceful city with the sunlight beginning to creep into its shadows. I turned toward Danna, summoned all the authenticity I could, and tried to pack my words with as much meaning as possible. "Danna, I *really* enjoyed talking to you tonight"—my weak attempt to create a moment.

I wanted to express how much I'd enjoyed our conversation. That I looked forward to seeing her again. That I felt something special between us. That quite simply, she amazed me. But I wanted her to feel it too, without it having to be said.

Still staring at the view, looking lost in appreciation, she smiled and casually replied, "Yeah, it was fun." Then she headed toward the stairs.

I guessed she hadn't had the same wow moment that I did. Ouch.

WEEK 12 JOB: FRAMER

LOCATION: TROIS-PISTOLES, QUEBEC

GROWING UP I wasn't a skilled handyman, but I liked to construct things. Whether it was a precarious rope swing in the backyard or an elaborate Kinder Surprise egg, at the end of the day it felt like I'd accomplished something. I could say, "I did that."

Back in Trois-Pistoles working with Tigs at his installation company (Portes et Fenêtres Bernier), I realized how many jobs involve constructing the ordinary items that we use every day. I attached a mesh screen to a window frame and thought, There's a company that simply makes mesh screens. That's probably all they do, mesh screens. Where someone finds the inspiration to start a business that specializes in mesh screening, I'm not sure. Perhaps the same place one finds the inspiration to produce a monthly catalogue that sells bull semen.

It had been a quiet week at the shop. Tigs took it easy on me, which meant that I got to spend more time with Danna. Over the past week when I wasn't at work and she wasn't at school, we were together.

"I love how positive you are, and just your whole view of the world," I said as we walked through town one evening.

"Thanks!" she said, smiling. "I say that I'm in my oyster phase."

"Oyster phase?"

"Yeah. The world's my oyster."

She explained that a few years earlier her parents had divorced and how the event impacted her. All of a sudden, everything that she was brought up to know—her family, her home—all seemed false.

"I didn't understand how my entire world could crumble so quickly," she said. "I became very resentful, and kinda started spiralling downhill. Until, after a couple of years, I hit rock bottom."

"What turned it around?" I asked.

She reflected on the thought, then answered. "I just remember looking at myself in the mirror one morning, and I was like, 'Oh my God, is this who you want to be?' It was weird. I had this, like, eureka moment and suddenly realized that the world didn't revolve around me. That I needed to stop blaming everyone else for my problems and take responsibility for my own life."

She smiled. "And so now, oyster phase it is."

By the end of the week, I was confident that Danna had had her wow moment too.

How could she not? We jumped in puddles, shared ice cream cones and sunsets and life stories, and stargazed while the entire town slept silently.

A pebble tossed at the window signalled the commencement of our late-night rendezvous, while the birds, our voice of reason, chirped every morning to inform us that it was time to say good night. The beautiful church in the centre of town, the calm streets, old buildings, and other students were merely the backdrop to our young romantic cliché.

It was incredible how fast things moved. We were both hesitant to embrace our feelings. One moment we expressed how much we liked each other, so grateful to have met, excited about what the future held, and the next moment we'd doubt everything. "We don't even know each other." "It doesn't make sense." "We shouldn't be feeling this way."

Then we would fall even further.

JOB: **RESEARCHER ASSISTANT**

LOCATION: **TROIS-PISTOLES, QUEBEC**

WORKING AT THE language school this week, I realized that whatever I ended up doing long-term, I needed to be in a creative role.

On my first day, I sat down with Yves, president of the Center for Language Education and Development, in his office for a brainstorming session. The centre wanted to increase the number of language programs offered in town throughout the year—currently there were only the two 5-week sessions during spring and summer, when many university students are out of school. We discussed the French immersion programs they currently had, programs they were thinking about developing, and Yves's passion to share the French language and Quebec culture.

He looked tentatively at me across the table. "So, what do you think, Sean?"

"I think it would be great to start a third session in the winter," I said. "Either a short three-week intensive program over Christmas break, or perhaps a longer semester program to target students who want to do a semester on exchange."

He nodded, contemplating the possibility.

I continued, "Or what about targeting an older demographic—perhaps baby boomers who are retired, though still active, and looking for a unique cultural experience? They'd have the flexibility to come during the fall or winter semester when university students are still at school. It'd be like a cultural exchange, where we could help them organize housing, then they live in the town for a few months and take language classes with other couples from the same demographic."

He nodded again, his lips now puckered as he mulled the possibilities.

I kept going. "Or maybe part of the course could be online and part of it they could come here for. The program could start online to introduce them to the language with assignments and textbook stuff, then they'd come for a few weeks for the practical component, with organized activities for practising the language."

I was excited about my ideas and where they could lead. I owe many great memories to this program, and so finding ways to make the opportunity more accessible to others gave me a lot of energy. I continued to fire off suggestions. We discussed how they could work, problems that could arise, and what steps they would entail. I wanted to make them happen and get started on mapping out the process.

I'd previously grouped all office jobs together and didn't see them as particularly desirable. But in a way, this was an office job. It was just one that interested me.

"These are great ideas, Sean," Yves said. "Thanks for your help."

Then he assigned me to input unrelated statistical data collected by the language program over the years. I returned to my desk and watched from across the room while he put in place a strategic plan based on our discussion.

I wanted to get involved—to help take the ideas we had and put the foundation in place to make them happen. I wanted to help build something. I felt like a kid again when my big sister would hoard the Lego pieces, then hand me a deck of cards in consolation and say, "Here, go play solitaire."

To be fair, my sister had been around longer than me. I'd have to put in my time and grow several inches before I'd get to be in charge. Likewise, Yves was the director. If I wanted to be involved at a higher level, I'd have to clock my hours.

Back at my desk inputting the data, I found that the only thing that kept me energized was the hope that Danna would come by and visit. Thankfully, she did often.

I'd met this girl a little over two weeks earlier. I didn't understand how I'd fallen for her so quickly. We were at the same point in our lives—not looking for anybody and wanting to carve out our own paths.

There was only one week left in the program. One week before I left for my next job, in Montreal. One week to make a decision.

It had to be one way or the other—either I leave with no need to think about her ever again, or I decide she was worth the long-distance heartache and move wherever she was the moment I was able to.

I pictured myself many weeks down the road:

I'm a lobster fisherman sitting on a boat gazing out toward the ocean off the coast of Prince Edward Island. The weather is perfect, the landscape incredible, the people kind. But with each lobster catch I haul in, I grow more distracted by the enchanting siren songs of Danna beckoning to me on the wind.

Or: I'm a rancher in rural Saskatchewan, doing whatever it is that ranchers do. Most likely galloping on a horse into the sunset, throwing my cowboy hat into the wind, traversing beautiful streams, things like that. But it doesn't matter, I'm unable to enjoy it anyway. All I can think is, I wish Danna could be here to see this.

By the morning she left there wasn't a decision to be made.

Shortly after our final goodbye I called Ian back home, and the reality hit me—this girl was trouble.

"Hello?" he answered.

I couldn't speak.

If I opened my mouth, tears were sure to fall. My face grimaced with pain, I clenched my muscles, held my breath, and forced my emotions to stay put. The lack of sleep from staying up until sunrise every day had finally caught up with me. Danna had a theory: "If we don't go to sleep, perhaps time will stand still."

I was an easy sell.

What am I doing? I've known this girl three weeks, I thought. This is ridiculous. I'm committed to finishing the fifty-two weeks. I don't need another distraction. The rational excuses as to why I shouldn't have felt this way kept coming. It makes no sense to get involved with someone I wouldn't be able to be with for so long, I told myself. I don't have time to fall in love.

But Danna was different. And I knew it.

WEEK 14 JOB: **JOB RECRUITER/ HEADHUNTER**

LOCATION: **MONTREAL, QUEBEC**

EMPLOYER: **VENATUS CONSEIL LTD.**
WAGE: **$61,000 (BONUS TO $114,000) YEAR**

INDUSTRY IQ:

- There are more than 40,000 employment websites worldwide.
- There are two kinds of job recruiters/headhunters: internal recruiters (who work within an organization) and third-party recruiters (who work for many clients at a time).
- A recruiter's commission can be from 10 to 35 percent of the applicant's first-year salary.

WHAT I LEARNED: The interview goes both ways.

The interview process should be equally focused on the interviewee asking him- or herself, "Why do I want to work for this company?" as it is on the employer asking, "Why should I hire this person?"

The interview is an opportunity to discover what working for the company would be like and if it's something the applicant would want to do. The employer wants to find the right employee as much as the candidate wants to find the right job.

I never forget that I work with people, for people.

—NATHALIE, president, Venatus Conseil Ltd.

I PUT ON MY ONLY SUIT, took out a map, and hopped the metro headed to the offices of Venatus Conseil, an executive-recruiting firm in downtown Montreal.

Thirty minutes later I was sitting across the table from the president, an attractive middle-aged woman named Nathalie. Nathalie had started the company ten years earlier.

Ironically, in trying to find the kind of job that would be a good fit for me, I'd landed a one-week job at a headhunter—a firm that tries to fit a candidate to a specific job. Now I'd get to see the career search from a different perspective. I'd search the firm's database for qualified candidates, review job descriptions, observe initial telephone interactions, and sit in on face-to-face interviews.

"Why did you choose to start a headhunting firm?" I asked Nathalie.

She offered what had become a familiar response: "I'm not sure that I chose my career. In a way, I'd say it chose me. At the time, I'd recently had a child and was working part-time from home on a contractual basis, mainly in recruitment and human-resources consulting for companies. I enjoyed it, but I didn't want to be a stay-at-home mom. I wanted to work in a professional business environment.

"After I spent some time searching for a new career, it became clear that I was already making a living doing what I loved. So the decision to start a headhunting firm was an easy one—it would allow me to continue in recruitment and consulting but also be in a professional business environment."

Once Nathalie identified the characteristics that she needed in a career, the choice became obvious. I wondered if the same would be true for me once I finished my fifty-two weeks.

Nathalie's attention turned to a piece of paper on her desk. "So, Sean, you're in luck," she said, picking up the paper. "Today we received a new contract. You'll be able to see the recruiting process from the beginning."

"Great," I said, and she escorted me to the office of Derek, the associate responsible for finding a qualified candidate to fulfill the new contract.

I quickly found out that the job demands a lot of cold calling and researching corporate websites to find appropriate candidates. It was kind of like detective work—generating leads on potential candidates, qualifying those candidates to ensure that their skills fit the position, then narrowing down the field until we find the right one. The majority of time was spent on the phone calling people who often were not grateful for the unique opportunity to meet a stranger over the telephone. It's tough to make friends on unsolicited phone calls—especially because the people answering the calls were all well aware that it's their right to be rude or immediately hang up on any stranger who calls out of the blue.

In order to find candidates who possess the required qualifications, the headhunting firm will often call executives at other companies who have a similar job description. Once on the phone with a potential candidate, Derek would gauge their tone and answers in order to qualify them. Did they immediately hang up, or did they colourfully describe their disgust at being cold-called, and then hang up? Were they genuinely happy in their position, or did they hesitate to respond about their current job satisfaction? Were they open to hearing about other possibilities?

Many didn't want to give the impression that they were interested. Some would play the aloof, half-paying-attention-but-if-you're-going-to-tell-me-I-will-listen routine. "No thanks, I'm not interested," they'd say, then casually add, "Though, just out of curiosity, what's the job description and salary like?"

I concluded that as long as the caller "volunteers" the information, the person called can have a clear conscience.

Derek told me that he can sense if he's called a candidate when a co-worker is in the room or happens to enter during the conversation. "Their tone might suddenly change, or they will ask that I call back another time. People don't want their co-workers or boss to know they're considering moving jobs. It would feel disloyal."

If he gets the answering machine, he leaves only his name and phone number. "I won't mention the company or reason I'm calling. It increases the chances that they will return the call—even if just out of curiosity," he said. "Also, you never know who will pick up the messages. It might put the employee in an awkward situation if their co-workers suspect they're actively seeking a new job."

After each call, Derek would add notes to the client database about the conversation—date of the call, reaction of the candidate, her attitude toward changing jobs, when to call back, her interest in hearing about future opportunities. Depending on the response, he can then bring the candidate in for an initial interview.

It's not until several steps later in the process that the hiring organization—the company looking for a new employee—is brought in. By contracting a recruiting firm to fill a position, the hiring organization can continue to focus on its day-to-day business activities and be confident that it will meet only the most qualified candidates.

"It's not about finding just anyone to fill the position," Derek said. "We need to find the *right* candidate so that both the company and the new employee are happy. If we don't, the employee might not make it through the probationary period, and then I'll be stuck trying to fill the position again."

This happened with a candidate Derek had placed only a couple of months earlier. At first it had seemed to be a good fit—the candidate had the required experience, her personality seemed to complement the company's corporate culture, and both the candidate and the company reported that they were happy. But then an issue cropped up. It seemed there was a conflict over the interpretation of what was meant by "some" travel required in the job. The candidate had a family and was not willing to travel often. But this had not been clearly expressed in the interview stages, and the job wasn't a perfect fit.

As Derek said, "If you're not upfront about your needs and don't spend the time to uncover what a company is all about, you may find yourself dissatisfied a couple of months later, and once again flipping through the classified section."

My week in Montreal at the headhunting firm was my first week away from Danna. During the week, I sent her picture to family, friends, even ex-girlfriends. I'd talk to complete strangers and bring her up within the first couple of minutes of the conversation. I wanted to share my excitement with everyone.

I spoke with Danna on the phone a few times during the week. We'd never spoken on the phone before, and at first it was a bit weird. It was hard to get past talking about how much we missed each other and reminiscing about our time in Trois-Pistoles. Now, with both of us back to our respective realities, it seemed as if it had never even happened at all.

I needed to see her again.

My next job was in Ottawa, only an hour and a half drive west of Montreal. Perfect, I thought. I'll hitchhike south for six hours to Toronto (Danna's hometown), then two days later hitchhike six hours north again to Ottawa.

My last ride dropped me off just outside the city at a gas station parking lot. Danna wasn't there when I arrived, so I sat on my suitcase on the sidewalk. I was nervous about seeing her. Part of me questioned whether our fairy-tale romance could exist outside the Trois-Pistoles bubble.

She pulled into the parking lot and jumped out of the car.

"Whassup?" she said, smiling.

"Hey, babe."

I gave her a hug, then we hopped into the car and headed back to her house. My feelings were reaffirmed. She had me at "Sup."

When we arrived at the house, Danna ran upstairs to get changed into her work uniform. (She was a server at a local pub.) I sat down on the bench at the front door and slowly took off my shoes. Danna hurried back down the stairs. "Sorry, babe, I couldn't get my shift covered." She grabbed her keys and gave me a hug. "But you can hang out with my mom," she said, then quickly headed out the door.

I was thrown right into it. When it comes to girlfriends' parents, I find mothers to be more welcoming than fathers. Or perhaps they're just better at extracting the same information without the intimidation factor. Either way, I wanted to make a good impression.

"Come in, come in, Sean. Make yourself at home," Mrs. MacLeod said, waving me into the house. As we walked toward the kitchen, I nervously wondered how I'd explain One-Week Job without appearing totally directionless. I'd tell her that it's completely practical for new grads to take a different job each week for a year—all the kids are doing it.

She put the kettle on and we sat down at the kitchen table.

"So, what is this thing that you're doing, a job a week?" she asked.

"Umm, yeah. Well, I couldn't decide on a career, so I decided to try different jobs," I said, not selling it very well.

"Where are you working next week?" she asked.

"Next week I'm an innkeeper in Ottawa," I said, happy to have a response.

"Great. And what about the week after that?"

"Umm, after that, I don't know yet."

"You don't know yet?"

"No, not yet. Usually I don't know until the week before."

"And so where do you stay?"

"Sometimes with my employer, sometimes people email me through the website and say I can stay with them."

"And you've never met them before?"

"Uh, no, not usually."

"And how do you travel from place to place?"

"Well, it changes. Sometimes I take the bus, sometimes I hitchhike, sometimes I—"

"Hitchhike? Is that safe?"

"Yeah, it's pretty safe," I said, fully aware that it's not likely as safe as driving her car to work.

"And do you get paid for these jobs?"

"Umm, no, not exactly."

At this point I imagined she was thinking that she'd brought her daughter up better than this. But what's great about mothers is that oftentimes they'll let you off the hook. She smiled, then in a very motherly, accepting tone, said, "Well, Sean, it all sounds quite interesting. Good luck."

After we'd shared several slow-sipping cups of tea and a long walk with their two dogs, Danna came home from work. I was relieved to see her. She changed out of her work clothes, and we went for a walk on the wooded trails behind her house.

"So, what did you think of my mom?" she asked.

"She seemed really nice," I said. "I could tell she was a little unsure about the whole one-week-job thing, and she probably thinks I'm a bit crazy. But it definitely could have gone worse."

"I'm sure she loved you," she said, then grabbed my hand as we wandered the trail. Before long, we were sharing the shortcomings of past relationships.

"I've been in some relationships that weren't all that trustworthy or honest," Danna said. "But when I started to focus on me and figuring out what I wanted, I just gave up on guys altogether. You can only get burned so many times before you start thinking, Well, what's the point?"

"How long ago was that?" I asked.

"That was about two years ago now," she said. "I haven't really dated anyone since."

We continued to walk, hand in hand, until we arrived at a wooden bridge over a small creek. Our meandering stroll came to a stop, and that's when Danna entered "big trouble" territory.

She turned to face me. Her hands buried in the sleeves of her sweatshirt, she anxiously fidgeted with the cuffs. "Sean, I don't know how you feel, but I know how I feel." Her gaze shifted to her toes. I knew where the conversation was going, and for a moment thought about cutting her off to beat her to it. But all I could do was smile.

She looked up into my eyes, "Sean, I love you."

Before I could say anything, she began to make excuses for me, giving a long-winded roundabout explanation that it was okay if I didn't feel the same way, but that it was important for her to tell me how she felt. I took her hand, gazed into her eyes, and silenced her insecurities: "I love you too, Danna."

It was going to be a long thirty-eight weeks.

WEEK 15 **JOB: INNKEEPER**

LOCATION: OTTAWA, ONTARIO

EMPLOYER: MCGEE'S INN

WAGE: $20,290 YEAR [Source: BLS]

McGee's Inn is family-owned, employing four members of the Armstrong family over two generations. Located in a beautiful heritage building, it offers Victorian decor, fourteen bedrooms, and gourmet breakfasts.

JOB DESCRIPTION: Cooked breakfast, served guests, cleaned rooms, made beds, worked in the yard, tidied common areas, visited with guests. By the end of the week, I could serve up a decent eggs Benedict, though my hospital corners still needed some work.

WHAT I LEARNED: Think "lifestyle."

The decision to operate a B & B is a major lifestyle choice—the ultimate convergence of social life and work. One reason the Armstrongs chose this profession was that it provides them with more time to spend with family and to raise their children. However, this benefit does bring challenges, such as needing to be careful not to allow any stress from work-related issues to impact the home environment.

This week I realized that when I choose a career, I won't just be choosing how I spend forty hours of my week. I'll also be choosing the lifestyle associated with that particular profession: salary, type of people, work environment, travel requirements, commute, vacation time, risk of transfer, and so on.

WEEK 16 JOB: RACE DIRECTOR
LOCATION: MARATHON, ONTARIO

I LIKE SMALL TOWNS. Small-town folks tend to be community-oriented and to welcome visitors warmly. I was invited into the small town of Marathon as the "celebrity" race director for the upcoming triathlon. Since my week as a florist when I'd received a lot of media coverage, the project had gained visibility each week as I entered a new city and websites would link to the site. I suppose the triathlon organizers figured I'd had enough coverage to warrant celebrity race director status. It was funny to be labelled a celebrity, but at the same time, I didn't want people to think that I thought of myself that way and then approach me with attitude. "So why does the brochure say that you're the 'celebrity' race director? I've never heard of you."

Thankfully, the town of Marathon doesn't have much attitude. What it does have is a population of 3,700 and a nice location three and a half hours east of Thunder Bay on the north shore of Lake Superior.

Most weeks I stayed with my employer or with one of my co-workers. It added so much to the experience because not only did I get a glimpse of their profession, but I also got to know my host outside of the work environment. They welcomed me into their family and I was able to experience each place as if I was living there—not simply as a tourist.

My boss this week was Pipin' Joe McGill, a high school teacher, triathlon enthusiast, and bagpipe player extraordinaire. Joe's friends Andy and Bev were kind enough to put me up for the week. Andy owns the pizza place in town, and each week during the summer he organizes a concert in the parking lot. While I was in town, he asked if I'd be the guest host and also invited me to perform. Although my musical ability is extremely limited, I couldn't pass up the opportunity to bang on a conga drum alongside Pipin' Joe on his trumpet and bagpipes.

It was the second annual Penn Lake Pursuit Triathlon—a sprint triathlon that involved a one-kilometre swim, a 20-kilometre bike ride, and a 5-kilometre run, to be undertaken over two days. On the second day, it was a staggered start based on the times from the first day. The competitor with the slowest time from the first day started the race on the second day. Then all the subsequent competitors started the race based on how much faster they finished on Day 1 compared with the slowest competitor. For example, the competitor who finished first on Day 1 had a start time on Day 2 close to forty-five minutes after the slowest competitor. Ideally, this makes for a great race as all the competitors should finish in close proximity.

The day before the start of the race, Joe picked me up at 9 A.M. to prepare the course. We set up fences and racks for the transition zone, placed wood barriers that would direct competitors, ensured that roadways were clear of debris, hopped in the lake to remove any large rocks near the shore, rounded up some last-minute volunteers and timekeepers, and discussed the protocol for race day. I didn't get back to Andy and Bev's place until 10:30 P.M. I had some candy and a beer, took a shower, and then was out the door again with some triathlon volunteers to go to the bar. It reminded me more of a bingo hall, the kind of place where you're just as likely to bump into your parents' friends as you are your own. Just one of the many reasons why I appreciate small towns.

On the morning of race day, we made final preparations on the course, positioned the volunteers along the route, assigned duties to the timers, and set up water stations. The competitors soon arrived and began warming up for the first leg of the race, the swim. I directed them to the transition zone, where they set up their bicycles and shoes for the second and third legs, then fifteen minutes before race time I brought all the competitors together and briefed them on the rules and course (information I'd only learned the night before).

With the volunteers in place and timers armed with their stopwatches, the gun was fired and the race began. Luckily there were two of us to help manage logistics as the race progressed, and everything worked out great. The second day would be much easier, as everyone knew the routine.

After the race on Day 2 was completed, I finally had a moment to relax. I walked away from the crowd of spectators and athletes to the small beach of the nearby lake. Shortly afterward, a girl in her late twenties cautiously approached me. She was shy, and I gathered she'd thought twice about coming to talk to me. Her name was Elana. We talked about One-Week Job for a bit, and she asked me if she could take a photo of me for a photo-essay project she was taking part in. I said sure, not thinking anything of it, then headed back into the crowd to toss some burgers onto the barbecue for the participants and spectators.

A month later, I heard from Elana again. She sent me the piece that she'd written for her photo-essay attached to a long email that explained how our interaction had affected her.

I was surprised. To be honest, I barely remembered our exchange. As I thought back on that day, I hoped that she didn't feel like I'd brushed her off. I was just so exhausted from the past few days of the triathlon.

About me she wrote:

> I am a skeptic, so part of me wondered if he was really as he seemed, or if all of the media and attention had gone to his head. From our first "Hello," I realized my fears were unfounded. He has a presence that is so infectious you cannot help but feel at ease. I got the sense that whether he knows it or not, the One-Week Job project is his "passion."
>
> While my vision of his future, and his vision of his future are more than likely on completely different scales, I can see him following in the foot-

steps of so many others who believed in something. No matter how unpopular or crazy it was.

My heroes are those who do not sit idly by and complain about what they see; they try to change it. Either through their own actions or words, they inspire others to do the same. They inspire people to take that first step, to turn something ordinary into something extraordinary, to make a change. What one single person does can make more of an impact than they might expect.

It is nothing I can fully articulate, but it is something that I feel deep in my core, that in these chance opportunities, something has changed . . . and that something . . . was me.

I remembered how Henri, the yoga instructor, was conscious of his impact on others and tried to make a positive difference through his classes. "When my students come into the class, it is my opportunity to impact the outer world through my inner studio," he said. "If I can change their mindsets, so that when they leave here, they are feeling calm and relaxed, that will alter how they experience the rest of their day and the other people they encounter. In doing so, I am creating a ripple effect with implications reaching far beyond what I could ever know."

But I'd never thought of myself that way. When I read Elana's photo-essay, I learned that we can never be fully aware of the impact our actions have on others. Sometimes I can be so wrapped up in my own world that it's easy to forget how I affect those around me. Every person who comes into our life, no matter how briefly, we have the ability to affect—through a kind word, a smile, a door held open. Each one of these simple interactions leaves us altered in some way—whether it's positive or negative change is up to us to decide.

That day I learned that the most important thing to remember in life is that whether we're aware of it or not, our ripples have an impact.

WEEK 17 JOB: STOREKEEPER
LOCATION: WILBERFORCE, ONTARIO

AFTER I READ the first few sentences of the email, I knew I had to go.

Hello Sean! Bring your hardworking self to Wilberforce to Agnew's General Store and experience the retail business in cottage country. A family owned and operated business since 1921, we're five generations deep. In fact, until Grama passed away just last month, you could have easily found four generations standing side by side on any given day!

And it only got better from there.

There's no end to the action around here. Just when you've finished helping Elsie find the butter and have Larry's plumbing needs all figured out, Eileen's Ice Cream shop needs an extra scooper. And when everyone is happily licking their cones, away you dash to load 30 bags of cow manure into someone's little Mazda.

Enjoy talking to the different groups that gather to chat, linger over the giftware or ponder whether they need one half or three quarter inch screws for that new deck. Some people rush in to get steak for the BBQ and others spend hours strolling through the outdoor Garden Shed, but each one has a story to tell.

In addition to above mentioned daily action, you may also have the pleasure of:

wrapping produce
running the cash register
finding someone a toilet plunger

filling the milk case
watering the flowers
sampling the fudge (yep!)
dusting the giftware
talking to some cottagers
cutting a key
mixing some paint
grinding some hamburger
filling the coffee pot
dead heading the petunias
putting together a wheelbarrow
or pricing the eggs
(but no grass cutting, that's Harley's job)

By Friday you'll know the difference between a Porterhouse and a T-Bone, you'll wow your friends with your knowledge of cottage plumbing solutions and in the future, you'll know exactly which flowers to put in that planter on the end of your dock!

I immediately wrote back and told them I'd love to come. It was only about 1050 kilometres from Marathon, and I could extend the small-town high I was already on. But getting to Wilberforce was a lot more difficult than I thought it'd be.

Wilberforce is too small to have a bus station. The bus only services a few neighbouring towns, but even these towns are too small to have a direct bus route. This turns a typically thirteen-hour direct car ride into a twenty-four-hour bus ride with a ridiculous number of transfers.

I hopped on an overnight bus that would take me four to five hours west of Wilberforce and decided that I'd hitchhike the rest of the way.

It was pitch-black, sometime after midnight, and most of the passengers were already asleep. I quietly made my way to the front of the bus. "Excuse me, sir," I said to the bus driver. "In the morning, I'm wondering if you could drop me off just outside of town alongside the highway? I'd like to hitchhike from there."

He turned to look at who would ask such a question. "Sure, I suppose so. That shouldn't be a problem," he said. "Do you have your bags on board with you?"

"Yeah, I do."

"Okay, well, just make sure you come up here when we're nearing town."

"Thanks, I will," I said, then headed back to my seat to try and get a couple hours of sleep. In the morning, adventure awaited me.

As we approached the town, I sat on the edge of my seat with my bags next to me, ready. The bus slowed down and pulled onto the gravel shoulder. I grabbed my things and headed for the front. Passengers slowly started to wake up and were no doubt wondering why we were stopped on the shoulder a few miles out of town.

"Thanks a lot!" I said, and waved at the bus driver.

I stepped off the bus into the early-morning sunlight. With my suitcase, computer bag, and backpack in hand, I watched the bus slowly pull off the gravel. The passengers sat snug in their seats with their faces pressed up to the window, looking confused.

I, on the other hand, was excited. I smiled and waved at the passengers. They stared back, their faces blank, as the bus pulled away.

That's not the life for me, I thought, trying to convince myself that I'd made the right decision. I'm different. I'm adventurous, out to take my chances on the open road, to stick my thumb out and see what happens. Onward I go, seeking fun, excitement, and random encounters. How many rides will it take? Who will I meet? Somewhere, someone is on a road trip heading in my direction. When they set out on the road that day, they didn't know that everything they did that morning—stop for gas, go for breakfast, take a photo at the tourist trap disguised as a giant wooden apple—would lead them to the perfect moment in which our paths would cross on this exact piece of pavement where they would see me standing, surmise my apparent harmlessness, and in a split second decide to hit the brakes, pull over, and pick me up. Now, *that's* adventure.

And this was how adventure started.

After a while, the muscles in my cheeks became sore from smiling at each car that passed, my right arm became tired from holding it outstretched toward the road, and I wanted to sit down but I wasn't sure how that would come across to prospective rides. I started to get a bit resentful as car after car passed with lots of room for extra passengers.

What was wrong with me? Didn't I look safe enough? *I'd* pick me up.

Then there were those drivers who gave false hope—they'd honk their car horn, smile, wave, force me to stretch my already aching smile a bit further to convey just how safe and fun I was, and even though I immediately pegged them as the false-hope type, I'd still indulge in the hope that they just might stop this time. No doubt they'd think they were doing me a favour, offering me some energy, as if to say, "Hey, that's fun, you're adventurous, you're hitchhiking, great!" Then they'd keep on driving, probably talking about me.

"Well, he looked nice. I hope someone picks him up."

"Yeah, me too. Not us though."

"At least we honked and waved at him. That must've heightened his spirits."

"Sure did, honey. Aren't we a fun couple?"

"Sure are. Road trip on!" Then they'd look at each other, smile, and high-five across the middle console.

And there'd be me, on the side of the road, standing next to my bags in the scorching midsummer sun wondering if I'd ever make it to my destination.

Then someone would stop. A new-found optimism and hope for humanity would fill me. I would grab my bags and jog toward the car. Can't casually walk, must be a subtle jog to express that I'm grateful and appreciate that the driver's time is valuable. I'd open the passenger door, say hello, and ask where I should put my bags to allow for a quick shallow judgment call, then hop in.

"Hey, thanks so much for stopping."

"No problem. Where ya headin'?"

"To a small town about five hours east of here. It's called Wilberforce."

"Oh. Well, we're actually on the west side of town right now. You're on the wrong side of town, partner."

After an adventurous walk past the bus depot to the other side of town, I stuck my thumb out once more. Again, nothing happened very fast. I couldn't believe my closed-lip smile accompanied with a head tilt and slight eyebrow raise wasn't working, not even with the added "Well, what can you do?" shrug. Nor was the shy "It's my first time hitchhiking, pick me up for my mother's sake" face proving all that effective. Maybe, I thought, I should let my hair down; a hippie driving an old VW van might drive by and feel obligated to stop. But I wasn't sure how that would fare with an older crowd. Maybe I should keep my hair tied back and put on a hat so people wouldn't see my hair at all.

Then, after a few more hours, someone stopped.

No jogging required this time—it was a police squad car. Great, exactly what I needed.

The cop stepped out of his car and walked toward me. He appeared stern, official, and purposeful, as police officers often do.

"Say, are you that guy doing a different job a week?" he asked.

"Yeah, actually, that's me."

"Thought I recognized the hair. Well, perhaps you'd have better luck if you made a large sign saying ONE-WEEK JOB GUY."

"Uh, yes, Officer, great idea," I said, unsure if I was in trouble or not.

"Well, I need to take your name down," he said. "You know, in case you go missing." He smiled to assure me he was kidding, though it came off more like foreshadowing in a murder mystery.

"Do people go missing around here often?" I asked, handing him my licence.

"Just a precaution," he said.

Luckily, on that highway hitchhiking was legal. He took down my information on his notepad, hopped into his patrol car, and pulled away.

Once I left the main highway, it was all small country roads. The scarcity of traffic made the last four hours into Wilberforce brutal. After six different rides, I was still over an hour away, it was getting late, and I'd been standing in the same spot for at least thirty minutes. I wasn't too worried. The elderly man in his truck who had dropped me off there had given me his phone number in case I got stuck. He lived twenty minutes away and said he'd come pick me up to stay at his place if I needed to.

Traffic thinned out and it started to get dark. The sky was still blue, but the sun had already dipped below the thickly forested road, making the trees appear like shadows.

An hour and a half later, in the pitch black, I started to feel a bit grim. I'd tried to call the old man's phone number along with several variations of it, but the operator repeatedly told me the number could not be completed as dialed. I had no idea where I was. The only sounds were mosquitoes and crickets. The only break in the complete darkness was the occasional set of headlights.

I didn't know what to do. I thought about trying to find some homes and knocking on doors, but I wasn't sure which direction to head. As each car passed, I made the expression on my face more and more desperate. Another one quickly passed and didn't look to be stopping. But as it crested a small hill a few hundred metres down the road, it stopped. All I could see were two red brake lights in the distance. The car paused, then suddenly went into reverse and sped backward down the country road. A change of heart. The car was loaded with stuff, but I didn't care. I was going to find a way to fit in that car. It was two guys in their early twenties, Tony and Sylvester, summer-camp leaders who were heading back to work after a long weekend. As fate had it, they were travelling right through Wilberforce. My cheek muscles were sore from a long day, but I couldn't wipe the smile off my face as I sat snug in the backseat, the car weaving through the darkness.

Fifteen minutes from town I called the owner of Agnew's General Store, Mary, to tell her I was going to make it that night.

"There's only one intersection in town," she said. "There's a bank, the old train station, and then our store with the ice cream shop across the street. I'll meet you guys out front of the ice cream shop."

"Ice cream?" I asked.

"I'll bring the key," she said.

Soon my fortunes had dramatically changed. An hour earlier, I'd been standing by myself at the side of the road in the middle of nowhere being eaten by mosquitoes in the pitch dark. Now, in the company of a few new friends, I grinned widely and clutched the biggest ice cream cone I'd ever seen. Adventure indeed.

True to the email, my week at Agnew's General Store consisted of many random tasks—packing meat, cutting keys, scooping ice cream, mixing paint, helping cottagers with their groceries. Agnew's slogan is perfect—"Everything from soup to nuts." I only wish I was able to cut the grass . . . but that's Harley's job.

WEEK 18 JOB: CATTAIL PICKER

LOCATION: MONTREAL, QUEBEC

I WAS KNEE-DEEP in sludge, the sun beating down, flies swarming and sweat dripping off my forehead. The muddy swamp water that slowly penetrated my supposedly waterproof coveralls made a memorable stench. The novelty of working in a swamp had quickly worn off, and the end of each workday couldn't come soon enough. At first I was intrigued to learn the practical use of cattails, but after spending the last few days slogging through mud, cutting the long stalks at the root and then peeling off the exterior layers to reach the soft centre, I decided that I couldn't care less.

It was weeks like these when I was thankful that each job lasted only five days. I was working with a distribution company that collects wild products (such as cattails, peppermint, and specialty tea leaves), then processes them and sells them to high-end restaurants and specialty boutiques in downtown Montreal.

At 5:30 A.M. I had crawled out of bed to start the workday. Now, twelve hours later, after another sweltering hot day in the bush, I was starving, exhausted, and ready to call it a day. Yet one delivery in town still remained.

My boss, Jean-Phillippe, was inside the restaurant talking with the owner. I was sitting in the car with my feet up on the dash, too tired to be impatient, when my phone rang. I flipped it open and was relieved to see that it was Ian.

Ian and I originally met in elementary school but didn't become friends until years later, in junior high. I invited him over for a game of Ping-Pong after he had so confidently boasted of his superiority during one of our classes together. I ended up winning every match, even neglecting to use a paddle in the last one. We started hanging out more often, until sometime in high school, after spending countless evenings in Ian's basement talking about girls, life, the future, and how we were going to climb the social ladder at school, we realized we'd become best friends.

For many years, people would say how similar we were from spending so much time together. We used the same phrases, had the same tendencies, even told the same jokes. We called it "Sean and Ian's grab bag"—either of us could pull a joke from it. We always laughed the hardest. Not so much at the joke but because we knew we'd used it so many times before.

One that we still inevitably use is the routine at a restaurant when the cheque arrives. It's almost become tradition. If I am the first to snatch it off the table, then Ian stays quiet with a smirk on his face and waits for the punchline. With the cheque in hand, I confidently lean back and review it, gesturing that I'm going to take care of it. Then in an overly noble tone I say, "Don't worry, guys, put your wallets away, it's no problem." Then I quickly toss the cheque toward Ian and add, "Ian's got it."

At which point Ian might choose to take out his wallet, purposefully flip through his cards, then swiftly pull out his library card, toss it onto the table, and say, "This should take care of it."

Throughout high school, for every project or presentation that was assigned, Ian and I would always ask to make a video. Ian was the camera guy. I and other friends would act out the scenes, then we'd edit the footage together. Ian had the idea that we should start our own production company when we got older. I had no idea what that meant. I remember he explained it to me one day. "They make movies," he said. Sounded cool to me. But I really just wanted to work with Ian.

"Hey, man, how's it going?" I said, slouching further in the car seat.

"Good. What are you up to?"

"Just sitting in a car, waiting for my boss, after spending the last twelve hours in a swamp picking cattails. You know, the usual."

"Ha. Nice."

"Yup."

"What are cattails anyway?" he asked.

"Ha, ahh, man . . . meh," I mumbled my disapproval.

"That good, huh?"

There is nobody who knows me better than Ian. A single remark, a vague observation, a certain smile, an incoherent thought, or a particular tone of mumble taps a catalogue of archived conversations and Ian knows exactly what I mean, the context, and the feeling behind it. We have so much material to reference that an outside observer can't possibly comprehend the layers beneath our words. At times this ease of interaction reduces our conversations to little more than one-word banter.

Ian has a Zen-like calm that is not easily shaken and an uncanny way of simplifying everything to where the correct choice becomes obvious—a helpful balance to my indecisiveness.

Sometimes we appear more like brothers, or like a bickering old married couple.

It's more than the typical "I can always count on him to be there," or "I could trust him with anything" stuff. It's deeper. Kind of like Frodo and Sam, without the awkward sexual overtones.

In short, I'm incredibly grateful to share a friendship like we do.

"So, I quit my job today," Ian said casually.

Immediately I thought, Great, now you can come out on the road with me.

I know he expected me to say it. I'm positive the same thought crossed his mind. We'd talked about it before and how cool it'd be if he came on the road to film the different jobs. But Ian had just gotten married two months earlier, and now he'd lost his only source of income; my idea represented a vague memory of when we both were unattached and free to take off on a moment's notice. But things had changed.

I knew his wife, Karen, wouldn't be thrilled with the idea, and so I fought the urge to bring it up. I simply listened to him explain why he'd quit and waited to see if he was thinking what I was thinking.

Ian had worked for an internet reservation-system company, and he'd felt there was no need to be at the office when he could do the same job, and do it better, from home. He asked if he could work at home one day each week. His boss wasn't willing to be flexible. So Ian quit. They lost a great employee, but it was the best thing for Ian. He could start freelancing, work from home, and if I could be tactful enough, he might even come on the road with me.

"So, what that *means* is . . . maybe I could come out on the road for a couple weeks," he said tentatively.

He'd opened the door.

"Dude, you've got to. It'd be so sweet," I said, energized by the possibility.

I'd been posting pictures and blogging on the website, but it had been difficult to accurately relate my experience and what I was learning. With Ian on the road, he'd be able to film the jobs, the interviews with my employers, and capture the overall experience. Not to mention I knew it would be great to have my best friend on the road. Our one last hurrah.

A couple of days later, and after what I'm sure was some entertaining early-married-life dialogue, Ian had convinced Karen that he'd be home in two weeks. And so it was decided. Ian would come out on the road with me to film two one-week jobs.

WEEK 19 JOB: BREWMASTER

LOCATION: **TORONTO, ONTARIO**

EMPLOYER: **STEAM WHISTLE BREWING**

WAGE: **$25,000 TO $100,000 YEAR***

INDUSTRY IQ:

- Beer is the third most popular beverage worldwide after tea and water.
- Approximately 7 million gallons of beer are consumed at Munich's Oktoberfest.
- Becoming a brewmaster requires no formal education, only a love of beer and years of industry experience (five to fifteen on average); however, there is a certificate course from the Institute of Brewing and Distilling in London that is internationally recognized.
- The Czech Republic consumes the most beer per capita worldwide, followed by Ireland and Germany.

WHAT I LEARNED: Making good beer demands true dedication.

Steam Whistle Brewing makes one type of beer, a pilsner. Marek, Steam Whistle's brewmaster, grew up in Pilsen, Czech Republic, where the first pilsner was brewed in 1842. In Pilsen they take their beer making very seriously. Marek went to a technical brewing high school for four years, graduating as a brewer. Then he went to university (Prague's Institute of Chemical Technology), where he completed his master's in brewing in five years. That's nine years of studying how to make good beer!

*Salary varies widely, depending on qualifications and size of the brewery.

STEAM WHISTLE

When you have a group of people in a work environment that are all happy, what that group can accomplish as a whole is pretty incredible.

—CAM, president, Steam Whistle Brewing

IT WAS MY first job in Toronto, Danna's hometown. I had been eager to take a few one-week jobs in her area, yet I hadn't had any offers. Well, I had received one offer, but even though my feelings for Danna were strong, I couldn't bring myself to accept it.

It was for the position of news anchor at *Naked News Daily Male. Naked News Daily Male* is like any major network's evening news program, but while the anchor is reporting, he takes off articles of clothing until he's naked. This tactic saves them from having to add the human-interest story to ensure that the broadcast finishes with a happy ending. I decided to save my family the embarrassment but agreed to the interview option in my underwear—a special half-naked news report. I've never been on the set of an adult film, but it felt a bit how I'd imagine that would be—an intimate living room scene, with plush couches, soft lights, cameras rolling in the background, half-naked people walking around—cue sultry music.

Luckily, it wasn't long after that that Steam Whistle Brewing contacted me.

It was 5:30 P.M. Van Halen's "Panama" was ripping on the newly installed stereo system of the Steam Whistle Brewing Party Bus, a refurbished, mint-condition 1965 Ford Blue Bird with multimedia centre, thirteen-inch LCD flat-screen, iPod plug, and DVD player.

Cam, Steam Whistle's president and co-founder, was at the wheel. In his early thirties, Cam resembled a surfer fresh from the beach. He wore his hair in a curly mop, laughed easily, and seemed more comfortable in shorts and sandals than business attire.

The twenty-seater bus was part of the brewery's fleet of vintage vehicles painted Steam Whistle green (somewhere between lime and forest). I sat next to Danna near the back. Ian was in the seat across from us with the video camera we'd purchased the week before. Along with about ten Steam Whistle employees scattered throughout the bus, we were headed toward the Toronto harbour, where Cam's boat was docked. We were going to surf off the back, then have a barbecue.

Only a half-hour earlier, the steam whistle had blown, signalling the end of the workday at the old roundhouse-turned-brewery in downtown Toronto. Cam had announced his spontaneous idea to a group of employees. I'd called Danna, who hurried down to join us. And after a hard day's work, our excitement followed us as we all filed into the bus.

Now the music rocked the bus's frame as we rolled through the streets of downtown. Everyone yelled the few words of the chorus we knew, substituting head banging and wailing on our air guitars for the words we didn't.

Near the front of the bus I spotted Greg, the other co-founder, with a huge childlike grin on his face. The day before, Greg had taught me a valuable lesson. Several years earlier, he was walking through a street festival in Ellicottville, New York, with a friend when they spotted a woman eating fresh-cut fries. Greg said, "Wow, check out those fries. I'd love to try one." His friend replied, "Let's ask," and then walked over to ask if he could try one.

To Greg's astonishment, she said yes.

Greg was left watching his friend chow down on a few fresh-cut fries. The lesson: "If you don't ask for the fries, you'll never get the prize."

Several years older than Cam, Greg was the father figure of

Steam Whistle (likely because he was a father himself). Greg shared many traits with Cam, including a love of doing things simply because they're fun—things like installing a gigantic stereo system in the Steam Whistle bus.

Testing the breaking point of the new speakers, Cam cranked the volume yet again and sent Van Halen echoing off the downtown skyscrapers. Greg was lovin' it. He stuck his head out the window and started hollering to passersby. We all immediately followed his lead and began cheering "Steam Whistle!" out the windows. Pedestrians couldn't help but smile and shout back.

Cam knew when to work and when to party. He blurred the line only when he knew he wouldn't lose the respect of his employees. He was the first person to tap the keg, the last person still knocking back brews when the party was winding down, and the first one back at the office the next morning. Cam was modest and didn't rely on others to validate his success—he exuded a relaxed self-confidence that only comes from someone with nothing to prove.

The bus pulled up to a red light. There were a few people standing at the curb, so Cam reached over and opened the door. "Hop in!" he yelled over the music, then beckoned them onto the bus for the ride.

I'd known Cam and Greg a very short time, but I couldn't help but love these guys.

At the harbour, we all jumped out of the bus, towels, sunblock, and cases of Steam Whistle in hand. Our energy was high as Van Halen still rang in our ears. The expression on my face must have been one of wonder. A fellow employee looked at me with a big smile and said, "Welcome to Steam Whistle, Sean."

From the beginning, I felt like a part of the team at Steam Whistle. On my first day, Cam offered Ian and me the use of his high-end, $4,000 video camera for the year after finding out that our camera didn't support wireless microphones. During our first conversation with Greg and his wife, Sybil, they invited me and Ian to stay at their house for the week. Shortly afterward, they extended the invitation to come up to their cottage for the weekend. This project continually reminded me of how many genuinely kind people there are out there. This week I was among some of the best.

Over the week I'd met the majority of the staff. All the way from the brewery floor to the office upstairs it was obvious—people liked to work for this company. After a few interactions with the co-founders, it was easy to see why. Cam and Greg understood that the best way to run a company is to earn the respect of the employees. They recognized that success is best when shared with others and were generous with their wealth, but they didn't tolerate mean-spirited behaviour.

The beer industry is very competitive. Because Steam Whistle is a small microbrewery competing against massive international companies with huge resources, Cam and Greg realized they must focus on their strengths. What Steam Whistle has that these big companies don't is the close-knit, family-like work environment. The corporate culture it's created is one of Steam Whistle's major strengths. Cam and Greg respect all of their employees, listen to their needs, and create a fun work environment; in return the employees give the company their loyalty and hard work.

I wasn't surprised when I saw that everyone in the office—including Cam and Greg—sat together in one big post-and-beam space with hardwood flooring. No corner offices here. This environment was more conducive to creativity and collaboration, reinforcing the sense of team. I experienced it first-hand in my interactions with the employees.

Brian had worked in the sales department for a little over four years. When I asked what his role in the company was, he refused to give me a definitive answer. He kept saying things like "I am Steam Whistle. This is my family."

I spoke with another employee, Chloe, about the work dynamic and this sense of company loyalty. She went on and on about how much pride she takes in her job. On bottling days, she told me, a crew of twelve to thirteen people will start at 8 A.M. and work a full day on the production line. Most of the people on the line have been with the company for five years or more. There's great camaraderie among the bottling crew; occasionally a few part-time employees will even take days off from their other jobs to come and work on the line.

"When I'm in the beer store and I see a case of Steam Whistle packaged on the day I worked, I'm like, 'That was me,' " Chloe said. "I helped put that together."

After some lake surfing off the back of Cam's 1974 motor yacht in the Toronto harbour, we sparked up the barbecue. Cam opened the cooler to find a couple of lonely bottles of Steam Whistle well past their due date—what he called "fallen soldiers"—likely left over from the previous summer. He reached in and held one up. The contents had started to break down, and the sunlight struggled to penetrate the resulting cloudy liquid with sediment floating about. Even though we'd brought a couple of fresh cases with us from the brewery, Cam cracked it open and took a swig. "I can't let a soldier die!" he said.

As it began to get dark, people started to realize that it was a Thursday night and tomorrow was another workday. Half joking, I suggested that we go for another rip in the boat. Cam smiled. "Just say the word."

I admire that no matter the environment—whether in a meeting with corporate executives, out surfing with buddies on his boat, or back at the office being interviewed in front of our video camera—Cam was always relaxed and completely himself. At the moment, this involved eating a large cucumber that his farmer friend dropped off while Cam answered my questions.

"One thing that I think a lot of young people don't realize is that it's not such a scary world out there. In meetings, you think, 'I gotta be perfect. Everything has to be perfect.' Then you go in and meet these executives and they're just human beings. At the end of the day, it's not as scary a world as people think it is, if you're relaxed and just being yourself.

"My advice is to get into the workforce, no matter what job you have to take or what you have to do. Because the day you start working is the day you start building usable real-world experience. If you can be positive about whatever job it is you're doing—even though it may not be your passion or what you want to do for your life—but if you can learn to be positive, then you're in a position where you're soaking up the experience."

At each one-week job I asked my co-workers what they liked most about their work. The most common answer I heard was the people they work with. Chloe loved to work on the production line because of her co-workers. They had fun, took pride in making a good product, and in turn the tough labour required became enjoyable. In thinking back on my different one-week jobs, I realized that my actual job duties had played a small part in whether I had a positive or negative experience. I knew that when my fifty-two weeks were over, it would be all the great people I met and the relationships I developed along the way that I would remember most.

Cam took another bite of his cucumber, then continued. "I'll never forget, Day One of business class at university. My professor said, 'The main objective of every business has to be the generation of profit.' And I sat there and thought, That's screwed up. None of us started this thing to make profit. We started it to build something. At the end of the day, we go out of business if we don't make money, but that's not our primary driving force. I think the companies that end up having trouble are the ones where their number one objective is growth and profit, rather than enhancing the customer experience, making a great culture for your staff, increasing employment, building something special—if those are your objectives, then profits come."

Cam and Greg had a wealth of knowledge about what it takes to make a successful business out of your passion—after all, they did it. They were living their dream, every day.

WEEK  JOB: **TATTOOIST / PIERCER**

LOCATION: **TORONTO, ONTARIO**

EMPLOYER: **NEW TRIBE TATTOOING AND PIERCING**

WAGE: **25–80 PERCENT OF TATTOO COST**

INDUSTRY IQ:

- The five most popular tattoo designs are tribal designs, stars, angels, crosses, and wings (surprisingly, hearts with MOM didn't make the cut).
- 18 percent of Canadians have a tattoo or have had some part of their body pierced.
- To become a licensed tattoo artist you need to apprentice and build a portfolio (perhaps even practise on yourself or some voluntary livestock). Raw talent helps too.
- Tattooing in the Western world became popular after sailors began returning home from areas such as Polynesia with body art.

WHAT I LEARNED: Never get a "normal" piercing.

Jonny, New Tribe's head piercer, was a big, bald, heavily tattooed, forty-one-year-old who'd been piercing at the shop for twelve years. I'd been hanging out with Jonny all afternoon, helping to set up, take down, and clean his piercing station. After I watched him put in a tongue ring, a nipple ring, and a nose ring, I asked, "What's the weirdest thing you've pierced?"

"Earlobes," he plainly stated.

"Earlobes?"

"Yeah," he said. "Once you've held a couple dozen penises in your hand, earlobes are just weird."

One of the perks of this job is you can look the way you want to look and you're not discriminated against. Most of us who work here are in this for the long haul.

—DAVE, owner, New Tribe Tattooing and Piercing

ALL THE EMPLOYEES at New Tribe were unique—Ian and I were the only ones in the shop not decked out in tattoos with full backs and sleeves (full arm covered in tattoos). I spent the majority of my week as the shop gopher—sterilizing and packaging equipment, setting up and tearing down stations, taking out the garbage, and going on coffee runs for the tattooists and piercers. It made me realize one of the obvious limitations of the project. A highly technical job, such as a tattooist or piercer, demands a specific skill set that I couldn't possibly develop in only one week. To be an accomplished tattooist requires years of training—well beyond my limited "paint by numbers" experience—not to mention an innate artistic ability.

That said, I was still happy with my decision to work at New Tribe. I got to experience the day-to-day world of an unusual profession and learn from people in the industry.

On my first day I worked with Joey, an eighteen-year-old with various piercings and a long Mohawk. He was apprenticing at the shop to become a piercer. He wanted to get his sleeves done but said that he first had to decide if this was truly what he wanted to do as a career. Understandably, having a lot of visible tattoos inevitably would limit his career choices. He mentioned that even though tattoos and piercings are becoming more common in the workplace, discrimination still exists when applying for jobs. "I've gone through a bunch of job interviews," he said. "Most times I'd take out my piercings, but if I didn't, I'd always notice a change in attitude. They just treat you differently."

Dave, the owner of New Tribe, had been heavily tattooed for seventeen years. "As much as you think it's acceptable, you still get looks, especially in more corporate or conservative environments."

I could relate. When I first got dreadlocks, I often noticed how people would acknowledge me, then whisper to the person next to them. I've had them for so long now that I don't notice anymore. Earlier in the year, I was asked if I thought that some companies wouldn't offer me a one-week job because of my hair. I imagined that the answer was yes, but I wasn't certain I'd want to work in an environment with individuals who would pass such judgment anyway.

If it's not preventing employees from doing their job, then I don't see an issue with being tattooed or having dreadlocks. But regardless of my opinion, discrimination in the workplace is real. In choosing the way we look, we may be limiting our options of potential careers or employers.

For many working at New Tribe, tattooing or piercing began as an interest or hobby that they later turned into a career. That was the case for tattooist Glenny, a smiley, heavily tattooed twenty-something I spoke to on her smoke break.

"When I was a young teenager and I first starting getting tattooed, I thought it was really badass, punk rock, and bitchin'—stuff like that," she told me. "Then I was like, 'That would be such a cool job,' but I just didn't really think of it in that context. When you're going through the mental inventory of career choices, it's not something that immediately comes to mind."

She took a drag off her cigarette, then continued. "It's a weird job and it's really hard. On one hand there's an artistic element involved—when someone's like, 'Draw me a mermaid,' you have to be able to draw that—but when you actually go to do the tattoo there's nothing artistic about it, it's very technical. You have to think about their skin, you have to think about your machine and how it's running. . . . Come to think of it, you might as well be welding."

Dave's first experience at New Tribe was as a customer. He walked up the stairs into the second-floor shop and decided to get a tattoo. It was the first time he thought of tattooing as a viable career, rather than just a distraction or a hobby. Now, several years later, Dave is the owner.

Dave had tattoo-covered arms, sported a full beard and, typically, a backward hat. "I'm doing something I like," he said. "I don't ever hate coming to work, unless I'm hungover or sick. But in terms of getting up every morning, I'm excited. I'm challenged by what I do."

He adjusted the brim of his hat and leaned back in his chair. "You look at all these people in university—they're changing their majors, they're doing a major/minor, they don't know what they're doing. They're just there for the experience. On one hand you could criticize that and say that they're wasting their time, but on the other hand it's good, because at least they're getting experience, they're getting exposed to stuff. I think exposure is so important. Right now you're being machine-gun–exposed to something new every week. I knew by waitering that I didn't want to be a waiter. I knew by making pizzas in a pizza shop that I did not want to do that either.

"Who knows, if I hadn't walked up those stairs that day, maybe I wouldn't be here today, an owner of this shop."

I'd never wanted a tattoo before, but each day when I walked up the stairs into the shop, I debated getting my first one. At the time it seemed like a sensible idea—working at a tattoo shop, almost halfway through my fifty-two jobs, a tattoo to commemorate the occasion—but in the end I chickened out.

WEEK 21 JOB: **CANCER FUNDRAISER**

LOCATION: **TORONTO, ONTARIO**

EMPLOYER: **PRINCESS MARGARET HOSPITAL FOUNDATION**

WAGE: **$158,075 YEAR (CEO, LARGE NON-PROFIT)***

[Source: Charity Navigator, 2009 CEO Compensation Study]

Princess Margaret Hospital is recognized as one of the top five cancer-research centres in the world and raises more than $60 million annually to support breakthrough research, patient care, and education programs.

INDUSTRY IQ:

- 10 percent of Canada's workforce is employed by non-profits.
- One in three people will be affected by cancer in their lifetime.
- Pleasure areas of the brain that are traditionally stimulated by food, sex, sweets, and social connection are also triggered by making charitable donations.

JOB DESCRIPTION: Helped promote the Ride to Conquer Cancer, a 200-kilometre two-day bike ride from downtown Toronto to Niagara Falls. I asked local businesses to help promote the event and attended meetings to sign up corporate sponsors.

WHAT I LEARNED: We work harder and more happily for things we care about.

Many of the employees at the foundation have been touched by cancer. I found that this personal attachment gave them a sense of pride in their role, an increased work ethic, and high job satisfaction. They believed they were making a difference.

I don't want to give the impression that we're all Mother Teresa. But at the end of the day, you feel like you're working hard for something that's really worthwhile. And isn't that what you look for in a job?

—SHERRI, vice-president of development, Princess Margaret Hospital Foundation

CONVENIENTLY, I'D FOUND myself in Toronto again. It would be my last week in the city, though over the next few weeks I'd still be close enough to spend some time with Danna. Ian and I had started to feel like locals. Even though I'd finished working at Steam Whistle over a week ago, we were still at Greg and Sybil's place (they were out of town), and sometimes after work we'd stop by the brewery to drink a couple of Steamys with the employees. Ian had planned on going back home after two weeks, but instead his wife decided to meet up with us. Karen was a computer programmer and typically worked from home, so she was able to bring her work on the road.

Ian and Karen are the model couple of the future: Wherever there is a wireless internet connection, they can pull out their laptops and work remotely. They're completely mobile. Ian, when he wasn't filming me on the job, was still doing freelance work, specializing in website design and search-engine optimization, and was also running an online travel magazine. I can't begin to explain Karen's job, but she's really smart and really good with computers. On the road, Karen worked from Greg and Sybil's house. She loves to cook, and so when Ian and I got home, typically she was happily whipping up some tasty new creation we were more than eager to try out. It was the closest thing to a routine I'd had in a long time. If Karen hadn't been there, we'd still have been eating pizza, frozen dinners, takeout, or when we felt ambitious, pasta.

• • •

While at Princess Margaret Hospital Foundation (PMHF), I had the opportunity to speak with some great individuals about what they do and what inspired them to work in the not-for-profit industry.

On my first day I went for a walk downtown with Steve so that he could show me the new signs promoting the Ride to Conquer Cancer. Steve, the keen high-school-PE-teacher type, was the CCO, "chief cycling officer"—responsible for managing and overseeing the event.

"I'm able to combine something I love—bike riding and athletics—with doing something meaningful and giving back to the community by raising crucial dollars for cancer research," he told me.

Having found a job that perfectly matched his skills and interests, Steve was a good person to ask for advice on choosing a career. "My advice is don't sell out, don't find a job that's a means to an end because it's a paycheque for you. Find out where your interests lie. Find something in your heart that you want to do. You may not get paid very well at the beginning, depending on what it is, but at the end of the day it'll work out. It's worked for me. I'm not going to be a millionaire, but it's about satisfaction and enjoying life. It's not about stressing on a Sunday night because you have to get up for something you don't want to do Monday morning."

Later in the week I sat down with Paul, the president and CEO of PMHF. Paul was an intelligent, articulate leader with a young face and white hair. He'd spent the majority of his career in the for-profit sector. He was the president of HMV music stores, president of BMG Music, and head of all Disney Stores in North America. Since then he had experienced how working for a cause he felt passionate about was more significant than he'd ever imagined.

"My mother died of breast cancer," he told me. "And that experience, for my whole family, it was something that totally changed my life. I felt that I wanted to do something related to cancer research, helping people with cancer. I was always in the private sector, and from a career point of view I've been blessed with having great jobs, but this is the best job I've ever had.

"One night I was describing my job to a friend. At the end, he said, 'You're working harder than you've ever worked, you're being paid less than you've ever been paid, and you work with people that have cancer, all day long. How can you love that job?'

"I told him that you certainly don't come into this sector to make a lot of money, but with all of the other benefits in the not-for-profit world, it's an amazing place to work."

After only one week at the foundation, I understood what Paul meant. When I visited local businesses to see if they would help promote the event, I felt as if my role was significant. I knew that the more stores I convinced to display our pamphlets, the more people would hear about the Ride to Conquer Cancer, and the more money would be raised for cancer research. It's truly special to have such a positive impact on the lives of so many. There's a sense of hope at the foundation, a profound belief in the work, and a shared commitment to achieving a common vision. Working there, I realized that it's important for me to find a career in which I'm making a difference. Since the start of the project, I'd raised $8,032 in donations from my employers to fight extreme poverty, and I felt proud of the accomplishment.

I asked Paul, "What advice would you give someone coming out of school trying to decide on a career path?"

After each question, Paul paused thoughtfully and responded deliberately. "It's not just people out of school looking for what they want to do," he said. "I know very successful people—people that have been presidents of companies, owned companies and sold them—a lot of people are still asking themselves the same question, 'What do I want to do with my life?' and 'What's a career all about?' And doing something that you love, I think, is the answer. My advice is while you're in high school, university, recently out of school, or even later on in your career, find something you can volunteer for. People that volunteer and who are on not-for-profit boards, they are leaders in their community, and you'll often find some great people who will mentor you. And for people in their twenties starting out, try to find some really smart, experienced older people—who aren't your parents, because I think your parents can only help you to a certain extent—but when you do find these people, listen to them, seek out their advice at the right time. They can help you see things that you don't see clearly."

Paul continually stressed the importance of self-knowledge—developing a strong sense of what you're good at and what you're not. He assured me that when the One-Week Job project was over, this knowledge would be the most valuable insight that I'd take away from the experience.

"This whole issue of self-knowledge and having a lot of experiences before you settle down is so important. My parents, they got married when they were seventeen, eighteen. Well, who's really ready to get married at that age? And how are you to know what career you want when you're twenty-one or twenty or nineteen and you're just starting out? But investing in that knowledge early on, as opposed to going to work and cranking away, buying a car, buying a condo, and getting the shackles on with all those mortgage payments—I think it's really responsible to find out what you really want to do with your life before you head down that road."

WEEK 22 JOB: **RADIO DJ**

LOCATION: **KITCHENER, ONTARIO**

EMPLOYER: **DAVE FM 107.5**

WAGE: **$39,360 YEAR (VARIES WITH SIZE OF CATCHMENT AREA)** **[Source: BLS]**

INDUSTRY IQ:

- *DJ* or *Deejay* stands for "disc jockey" and was first used to describe radio announcers who would introduce and play popular gramophone records.
- During World War I, armies had their own radio stations that would sometimes get ambushed by enemy forces and then be used to fool opposing soldiers.

WHAT I LEARNED: Socialize more, study less?!

Carlos, a Dave FM radio host: "You've heard it a million times—it's not what you know, it's who you know. Stay in touch with the people you go to school with, 'cause those are the people who are going to get you jobs. Get involved, volunteer, talk to people, make calls, make contacts. It's not so much about putting in a resumé. You get a million people putting in a resumé someplace, but what you gotta do is create a personal relationship with somebody—that's how you get a job. That's what's going to get you where you want to go."

Whatever that thing is that you do just for fun, see if there isn't something within that, or around that, that could actually be a job. If you fall anywhere near it, you're still going to have fun.

—SCOTT, program director, Dave FM

5:30 A.M. I rolled out of bed. Still half-asleep, I tossed on my Dave FM T-shirt and headed to the hotel lobby to wait for my ride. Shortly afterward, a black SUV with a large Dave FM logo on the side pulled up. I picked myself up off the never-been-so-comfortable lobby couch and hopped into the car.

When we arrived at the radio station, I was directed into the studio, handed a set of headphones, and told to have a seat. We were live on the air.

It's times like these when I wished I drank coffee.

I was barely coherent when the morning host, Jeff, probably working on his third cup, turned to me and said, "We're thrilled to introduce our most recent part-time employee, Sean Aiken. And he is the One-Week Job man. How you doing, buddy?"

How is it possible to have that much energy so early in the morning? I thought. I rubbed my eyes and gave an exaggerated tired look in an attempt to be funny. The dead air reminded me that facial expressions don't translate over radio. "Well, Jeff, I'm not used to waking up this early, but I'm doing pretty good and I'm happy to be here."

I'm told the key to radio is to try and make it as conversational as possible. To pretend you're talking to one listener and that's it. It should sound like a natural conversation between me and Jeff, and the listener is an unseen, silent person in the room. Even though there are many listeners, you don't want to address them as a group, or refer to them as "you guys" or "everyone listening." This helps the listener feel part of the conversation and makes it a more personal experience.

As the morning progressed, I got more comfortable. It felt as if we were a group of friends having a good time chatting about stuff.

"So, my softball team lost nine–nothing on the weekend," said Jeff.

"Ouch," said Gayle, the morning co-host.

"How's that even possible?" I piped in.

"I don't know," said Jeff. "Well, actually I do know. When you start cracking the 'soda pops' before you're even out of the first inning, chances are you're gonna have a rough go at it."

"That'll do it," said Gayle.

"Yep. Although I must say, we did have a good time," said Jeff.

It was weird to think how many people were out there listening, counting on us to drag them out of bed with a smile on their face.

Radio DJs always have something to say. They can talk about the most boring subject, but with their captivating voices and perfectly timed tonal variations, they somehow manage to make it sound interesting. Kind of like infomercials, I suppose. Growing up, I could watch those things for hours; then I'd run over to my mom to convince her that whatever was being pitched was something we absolutely *had* to have. I still hope to purchase that food dehydrater one day.

Time is extremely important in radio. The production, complete with commercials, traffic updates, weather reports, and scheduled talk breaks, must be organized right down to the second to avoid dead air. Five seconds of dead air is like ten seconds of microwave time. Not good. Especially to the listener stuck in rush-hour traffic with limited patience who's all too eager to hastily change the frequency. A majority of the audience can be lost in just a few seconds.

Before my week at Dave FM, I thought that radio DJs had a pretty comfy gig. Show up five minutes before they're on the air, talk about random stuff, answer a few phone calls, give out some swag, play some music, and call it a day. I was surprised to learn how much planning is involved. Each DJ that I worked with showed up at least one hour before the shift started. They went over the script for the day, got caught up on current events, and mapped out what they were going to talk about at each scheduled talk break.

That morning, the white chalkboard that outlined the topics of conversation read: *Sean, Baseball, Britney Spears, Joke of Day.*

"I find you can only prepare to a certain point," said morning co-host Gayle after we'd wrapped up. "When we come in here in the morning, we have to hit the ground running. We're not just sitting here listening to music. It's crazy busy for those hours in the morning. You have to eat, talk, prepare stuff, and take calls all at the same time."

The next day I was the co-host of *Big Afternoon Radio Show* with Carlos. We were live on location at a local golf course. Once every week Carlos took chosen listeners out for a round of golf in the morning, then he did his show outside the clubhouse in the afternoon. The company sponsor of the event was there with an alligator mascot costume. Being the new guy, I had the job of getting suited up, ripping around the course in a golf cart, handing out DAVE FM stickers, and making sure all the golfers were having a good time.

Back at the clubhouse, Ian brought out the camera and I asked Carlos how he'd gotten into radio.

"When I was a little kid, I didn't like being at home in the dark, it scared me, so my dad got me this clock radio. And the idea of someone being there and entertaining you just struck me from the time I was about five years old.

"I got my first job at a radio station in Toronto handing out condoms. It wasn't the most glamorous job, but I did everything I could. Six months later, I was on the air doing a number of jobs: filling in on mornings, filling in on afternoons. And eventually I got a full-time show."

"Could you see yourself doing anything else?" I asked.

"I can't imagine doing something I didn't love, because that's what I do every day. Some days I have to stop and ask myself, 'Is this real?' They pay me to go out and golf with listeners and then talk for five hours a day. I mean, it's crazy to think that someone actually pays me to do this." He glanced toward the golf course and smiled.

"The most important message I take away from what you're doing is to be proactive about figuring out what you want to do," he said. "If you don't know what to do, well, don't just sit around and wonder. Do something."

If he had only known me six months earlier. After graduating, I was so concerned with making the right choice that it prevented me from making any choice at all. I realize now that I've learned the most about myself by *doing* stuff—travelling, taking courses, joining clubs, volunteering. Anything that challenged me, caused me to step outside of my comfort zone, and offered a situation where I could learn something new.

"Even if you take a job at first that might not be the right fit, it's still a step in the right direction," continued Carlos. "Just like any failed relationship—you learn about what you liked and what you didn't. In the end, all of it helps you figure out what's going to make you happy and where you'll be most successful."

It was obvious that the employees at Dave FM valued a positive work environment. I noticed that even though they worked extremely hard, they never sacrificed their sense of play. They had fun and didn't take themselves too seriously.

For Scott, Dave FM's program director, this was one of the reasons he chose the profession. "I wanted to have a fun job," he said. "I thought radio was pretty cool, and the idea of introducing records and music on the air sounded like fun."

"Is it your passion?" I asked.

"My passion is the music," he said. "If you ask most people in radio where they started out, we're all kind of failed musicians really. Truthfully, we'd rather be the people making the music, but to be involved in music in some way—that's where the passion lies."

Even though Scott was not doing what he originally wanted to be doing, he loved his job. He worked in the industry, dealt with music people, and was still able to cultivate his passion for music.

I've been told that my generation has a sense of entitlement different from previous generations. Perhaps there's some truth to it, that we feel we deserve to be the CEO, the professional athlete, the acclaimed director, or the big rock star. That choosing anything else would be considered "settling." And so we seek celebrated titles with the assumption that happiness must be an inherent benefit in the job description. In reality, maybe we'd be just as happy being the person who rallies the extras on the Hollywood set, primes the stadium for a big game, or hands the rock star his guitar.

WEEK 23 JOB: HOTEL WORKER
LOCATION: KITCHENER, ONTARIO

MY EMPLOYER, THE Holiday Inn Kitchener/Waterloo, provided me, Ian, and Karen with a room containing two queen-sized beds. It was perfect—we wouldn't need to commute, and Karen could work from the hotel business centre during the day.

On Thursday, Ian and I sat in the staff lunchroom at a long table with several other employees on break. I'd just finished a shift in the laundry room, where I folded towels and ironed linen. On the lunchroom table there was a copy of the local newspaper. The cover featured an article about One-Week Job along with a picture of me back in the studio at Dave FM. An employee seated across from us picked it up and pointed to the picture. "Hey, is this you?" he asked.

"Yeah, it is," I said, thinking how seldom it is that you're reading an article about someone, then look up to realize that the person is right in front of you.

The employee agreed with me. "Wow, that's weird." He casually scanned the article, then asked, "So, you're working here this week?"

"Yeah, I'm doing a bit of everything—peeling potatoes, serving drinks to priority club members. Last night I helped set up for a banquet, and I just got back from working the laundry room."

"Where are you working next week?" he asked.

"I'm not sure yet," I said.

"Must be nice making the front page of the paper," he added. I detected a hint of sarcasm in his voice. The suspicion that I was doing this for the media attention rather than the jobs was at times hard to shake.

In reality, the media exposure had helped me attract job offers from curious employers, certainly more than I could have found on my own.

"You always manage to find a job?" the employee asked.

"So far," I replied.

It was always a last-minute decision. The offer would be too far away, or the timing didn't work, or perhaps it was a career that didn't interest me. Typically I'd receive more offers once I was in a city, and so I preferred to keep the options open. But it was now Thursday afternoon in the staff cafeteria, and still nothing had come up.

"It's kind of been like building a bridge as we walk," Ian explained. "We take each step not sure where we'll land but positive that it will work out."

Silence followed Ian's statement, which made it seem more profound than he'd intended. After a couple of reflective "I dig what you're sayin' " nods from all three of us, the employee shuffled the newspaper together and packed up his lunch. "Well, I got to head back to work. Catch you guys later," he said.

Back in our hotel room that night, I sat at my computer while Ian and Karen watched TV.

"So, where am I going to work next week?" I asked.

"Ha, I don't know," Ian said. "What are the options?"

I flipped through the few job offers in my inbox.

"There's a management trainee position at a hotel in Toronto," I said.

"Nah, we're already at a hotel this week," Ian said.

"Yeah, true."

"Here's one to be a hairdresser."

"That'd be interesting," said Karen.

"Oh, never mind. They say that the offer is not until the fall."

"Check out this one," I said, half joking. "Retro-Raw Boot Camp for Body, Mind and Soul."

"What?"

"I have *no* idea," I said. "Looks like it's in Hawaii anyway."

I opened another email from a couple of weeks earlier. "How about internal auditor?"

"Meh," said Ian.

Karen laughed. "There's no way I could leave it to the last minute like this. I'd have to have everything organized beforehand."

"That'd be nice," I said. "I need to figure something out pretty quick here."

I continued to sort through offers, but nothing grabbed me. I decided I'd send some emails out later to try and line something up.

I opened my iTunes, scanned my music library for a song that would liven up the dull mood. I located my favourite song at the time—"Starlight" by Muse, hit Play, turned the volume up to full blast, then leapt onto my bed. It wasn't long before Ian and Karen couldn't resist and joined in. Jumping on hotel beds with music blaring tends to boost any mood. We bounced up and down until the song came to an end.

I hopped off the bed to select another.

Hovering over my laptop, I swiftly compiled a new playlist—"jumping on hotel bed music"—then I noticed that I'd received an email. I sat down to read it.

"Hey, guys, check this out," I said.

I read the email aloud:

"Hi Sean, I heard you on Dave FM last week. How would you like to work part-time for one week at my vet clinic.Your title would be Veterinary Assistant. You would help hold animals for exams and treatment, assist with procedures such as dentistry, surgery, and radiology (with a lot of supervision, of course!) and perhaps help my receptionists as well. I am flexible about timing. You could start next week at 8 am if you like!"

I turned to Ian and Karen, still frozen as they'd been when the music ended. After a moment of consideration all three of us answered in a word: "Done."

I hit Reply. "Sounds perfect, Louise! I'll see you Monday morning at eight o'clock!"

I cranked the music, and the jumping resumed.

JOB: **VETERINARY ASSISTANT**

LOCATION: **CAMBRIDGE, ONTARIO**

EMPLOYER: **HESPELER ANIMAL HOSPITAL**
WAGE: **$12–$18 HOUR**

JOB DESCRIPTION: Held down the animals while anaesthetic was administered, monitored heart rates during surgery, lubed up thermometers and took temperatures (yes), prepared blood smears, polished teeth, assisted with X-rays, collected urine samples.

INDUSTRY IQ:

- Prior to the 1980s veterinarians were predominantly male. Today they are predominantly female.
- For those who love to work closely with animals but are unable to pursue a career as a veterinarian, becoming a veterinary assistant is a great alternative.
- About half of all households in Canada own pets.

WHAT I LEARNED: Eat before observing fatty lump removals.

Lizzy, a very sweet schnauzer, was in for surgery to have a fatty lump removed. I'd met Lizzy the day before. She sat nicely and didn't bark while I put eyedrops in her eyes, helped feed her, and took her temperature.

With Lizzy prepped for surgery, Dr. Langlais entered the room wearing surgical gloves and mask. She reached for her scalpel on the medical tray unit, then, before making the first incision, turned to Ian and me. "I hope you boys ate something this morning," she said. "'Cause you're not going to be hungry afterward."

WEEK 25 JOB: FILM-FESTIVAL REPORTER

LOCATION: TORONTO, ONTARIO

I WAS BACK in Toronto for one final week, which meant I'd get to see Danna. To make things even better, the job offer was one that I couldn't refuse—working for Roots, a major apparel/accessory retailer, during the Toronto International Film Festival.

One of the most prominent film festivals in the world, second only to Cannes, the festival is a huge event for Toronto every year, with more than three hundred films shown, private, star-studded parties every night, limousines and photographers everywhere. Roots sponsors the festival, and its flagship store in downtown Toronto would be a hub of activity during the week. On the second level of the store, a makeshift lounge had been constructed, next to which the American Movie Classics (AMC) channel had installed a set to interview the many celebrities—including several A-list actors—who would be in town for the festival.

My job was to cover the festival from a Roots perspective—take photos, write posts for the Roots Film Festival blog, and help out around the store. As usual, Ian would be filming me on the job.

My first day was at the Roots headquarters just outside of town. The office, with its modern, simple decor, had a great vibe, and all the employees we met were very welcoming, fun, and high-energy. They seemed more than happy to explain their jobs to Ian and me, and it quickly became apparent that the majority of them had been working there well over five years, some pushing twenty.

We finished off the day with a visit to the Roots downtown store, where I'd spend the rest of the week. As Ian and I walked through the front doors, we were spotted by the store manager, Brenda, who ran toward us and gave us both big hugs. She was kind, bubbly, as excited to have us there as we were to be there. She immediately gave us some Roots gear so we would fit in with the rest of the team and introduced us to the other employees. I took some pictures, Ian shot some video, and then Brenda led us upstairs to the temporary lounge area, where several leather couches, tables, and a small bar with a couple of stools took up one end of the store. Then we met . . . let's call him Richard. And our great day came to an end.

Richard was not a Roots employee; he was contracted to help organize media for events like this. But this week he'd be my on-site boss. He had just finished a conversation on his cellphone when we were introduced to him. As if careful not to waste too much energy, he gestured with a flick of his wrist for us to have a seat. "I'll be with you shortly," he said.

For the next ten minutes we waited while Richard appeared to search for ways to keep himself occupied. We sat and watched as he slowly made his way around the room—he had a couple of casual conversations, meandered to the spread on the table, grabbed a piece of fruit, then sat down in one of the leather chairs. It was as if he were purposefully passing time and wanted us to know it. Ian gave me a "What's this guy all about?" face. It later occurred to me: Less important people need to be made aware that they're less important and so must endure a mandatory waiting period in which to process their lesser importance. This also helps the more important person solidify in his own mind his greater importance. Note: This routine holds true even if the more important person is clearly not otherwise occupied.

We were finally summoned to join Richard. We sat down in the two seats across from him as he scrolled through his BlackBerry until it was once again clear that we were waiting for him. I didn't mind; I was keen. I even sat on the edge of my seat, leaning forward with my elbows on my knees to show just how keen I was.

"So, guys," he said, looking up at us. "How was your day?"

"Great," I said keenly. "We got a tour of the leather factory this morning, and everyone we met at the head office was awesome. It's funny—they all said how jealous they were that we get to be down here during the film festival, while they're stuck in the office. They said it's a really good time."

"Yeah. Well, you know, there's lots of stuff going on," he said, forcing a half smile. "That's why you guys are here—to capture it all on tape."

He told us about a campaign that Roots was affiliated with, Flick Off, which focuses on raising awareness about global warming. To promote the campaign, Flick Off was creating a video stringing together short clips of people answering the question "What do you do to lower your carbon emissions?"

"With the camera I want you guys to pose the question to celebrities in the store, shoppers, or people in front of the store, and I'm also going to send you to a music festival on Toronto Island," he said. "I'll get you media passes so you can film clips with band members backstage."

The thought of befriending celebrities on the red carpet at VIP parties and backstage media passes to a huge outdoor music festival was more than enough to keep my spirits high. "Okay, great!" I said. "We can totally do that."

"Good then," he said tersely, then turned his attention back to his BlackBerry. Silence followed. Ian and I looked at each other. Was that the end of the conversation? Then Richard, without lifting his head from the BlackBerry, slowly shifted his gaze up at us. We took the hint. Indeed, he was finished with us. We stood up, grabbed our things, and left the store.

I didn't get a good vibe from Richard, but he wasn't overtly a jerk. It was more a passive jerkiness, as if we weren't worth his time. But it didn't faze me. Nothing could faze me. It was a cool role with a big company, and I appreciated being offered the position. More than anything I just wanted to do a good job and make them glad they hired me.

Ian, Karen, and I were staying with a guy named Rob, whom we'd met through Craigslist. I was sure Greg and Sybil would have let us stay at their place again, but I didn't want to ask since we'd basically made ourselves at home there for close to three weeks. Besides, Rob lived downtown, so it only took twenty minutes on public transit to get to the store from his place. However, that convenience would cost us some sleep. Rob had a ton of space in his apartment, but there was nowhere to sleep except on the hardwood floor in the living room. Also, his apartment happened to be above a major intersection of street trams that ruthlessly screeched by every hour throughout the night. Being late August, it was really hot, so we had to keep the windows open, making it even more ridiculously loud. But again, no problem. Nothing could faze me.

On the first day of the film festival, Ian and I were on the subway heading downtown, both talking fast.

"Dude, this is so cool," I said.

"For sure. I wonder who will come by the store today," Ian said.

"Well, *eTalk Daily* is filming at the store. Maybe you'll finally get to meet Ben Mulroney." I laughed.

"Yeah, wouldn't that be great," Ian said sarcastically. "Maybe I could even get a signed poster for my bedroom."

"No, but really, I heard them say Don Cheadle has an interview with AMC. And I think that guy from *Jurassic Park*."

"Jeff Goldblum?"

"Yeah, him."

When we arrived at the store, there was a buzz of activity outside—people were everywhere. As we walked in the door, the entertainment talk show that would later broadcast from the store was setting up its stage and lights. With the bigger camera that Cam lent us, we felt official, important, and people took us seriously. We walked swiftly through the store with an extra bounce in our step and took the stairs to the second-floor lounge two at a time, excited to start the day.

We said hello to Richard, who generously threw us a nod, and then we got to work. Ian shot some b-roll for a video blog update, filmed the taping of *eTalk Daily,* then an intro piece of me in front of the store. I started asking employees, customers, and passersby what they do to lower their carbon emissions. And then we waited.

No one really knew when the celebrities were supposed to show up. There were vague rumours, but only those scheduled for an interview with the American Movie Classics channel were certain. On the first day, Jeff Goldblum, Don Cheadle, Aaron Eckhart, and the Arctic Monkeys dropped by. When a celebrity did come into the store, everyone would jump to their feet, energy filled the room, and people were on their best behaviour. Of course, Ian would turn on the camera. We'd give the celebrities some free Roots gear, then I'd take photos and Ian would shoot video footage of the celebrity holding Roots stuff, in the Roots store. Like *actually* in the store. Incredible. The celebrity would leave and things would quiet down. Then we'd wait again. Ian and I occasionally would leave the lounge, cruise around the store, check to see whether anything was going on outside. Oh quick! SpongeBob is outside! Standing on the curb, in front of the Roots store. Like *actually* on the curb, in front of the Roots store. Ian, did you get that? Oh, this is good.

We headed back up to the lounge to hang out with the other people who were hanging out waiting for something to happen. Richard was there. He turned his attention from his conversation to us. We made eye contact. I smiled and nodded. He shot back an unimpressed glare, then returned to his conversation.

The more I interacted with Richard, the more he demonstrated his uncanny ability to make others feel inferior. I realized he's the kind of guy who leaves you feeling diminished after each exchange, whether through a single comment or a quick unnerving look.

We hadn't been in the lounge more than five minutes, yet Richard shot us another glare from his repertoire. This one informed us that we should be off doing something. The only problem was that none of us—neither Ian, myself, nor Richard—knew what that something should be. We'd already shot enough footage to update the Roots blog with a video clip of the day's events. I'd written a post for the Roots blog with photos, and we already had countless street interviews. There was nothing going on in the store, yet we still weren't allowed to leave until well after 10 P.M.

The next morning Ian and I sat quietly on the subway. I'd been working at the store less than two days and I'd already built up an anxiety about going to work. Ian spent four hours that morning editing and publishing the video footage from the previous day. The VP at the Roots headquarters was impressed—he hadn't expected that we'd be able to post polished videos in such a short time frame.

But at the store Richard kept giving us the impression that we were lazy. He radiated the "I'm not paying you to sit around" vibe and never failed to make it apparent that we weren't doing a good job or weren't getting the right shot, even though he didn't know what the footage was for and how it would be used—the blog? Future Roots promotions? Richard's personal scrapbook of pictures of him with his arm around important people? Why were we filming this stuff? Although none of us really knew, we kept moving forward—and the tension built.

When we arrived at the store, our moods quickly changed. Upstairs in the lounge area, hip-hop artist Wyclef Jean was chilling at the bar by himself. The day before, whenever there was a celebrity in the store, there would be an entourage surrounding him. The celebrity would appear to be in a rush to keep on schedule. Not Wyclef. He was in no hurry. He sat so unassuming at the bar, I almost didn't recognize him.

Ian and I ventured a conversation with him. "Hey, Wyclef, how's it going? I'm Sean, and this is Ian," I said, motioning toward Ian.

"Hey, whattup guys."

It was a relief that nobody else was around and we could just relax, hang out, and talk normally without the feeling that we were any less significant than anyone else.

Wyclef noticed my Flick Off T-shirt and asked, "Yo, what-chu think about Al Gore's *Inconvenient Truth*?"

I started rambling about how I thought it was positive that he brought attention to the issue and put it in a context that people could understand.

"Man, Al Gore's a hustler," Wyclef said, to my surprise. "I tried to get him to do a talk—yo but I never said it was me, I got someone else to call 'bout it. The man charges like $250K a talk," he said, shaking his head. "I don't know, man, I question his incentive for starting this global-warming trend."

"Who knows if that was his original intention," I said. "At least there's an increased awareness about global warming. Companies are starting to notice, and people are more aware of their habits." I used the Flick Off campaign as an example.

Not effective.

"Man, Al Gore's *Inconvenient Truth* is like the George Foreman Grill—s'all packagin'," Wyclef insisted.

The topic then changed to One-Week Job, why I started it, and the various jobs I'd had so far. He then adopted a serious tone, and it appeared as if he was going to impart some profound wisdom.

"No matter what you do in these next fifty-two weeks"—he

put his hand to his mouth, took a look around, and paused in an exaggerated moment of reflection—"just make sure you work . . . in a high- . . . class . . . strip joint." We all laughed, then joked about all the interesting situations a job like that could get me into.

Before long, people started to notice that Wyclef was there. Word spread fast and a large crowd gathered. All of a sudden, I felt like we shouldn't be talking with him. Who did we think we were to just walk up and chat with Wyclef Jean, Rap Star?

Before he left, we managed to film Wyclef's career advice. "All my people in college, I'm gonna tell y'all like this, real talk. While you're in college, you gotta figure out what you wanna do. Don't be like, 'Yo, let me wait till I get outta college.' Cuz you're gonna be stuck. So my advice to you is, while you're in college, do like my homie right here." He put his arm on my shoulder and shouted into the camera like a rapper in a music video. "Get fifty-two jobs, you know what I mean, one job a week. Stop being lazy. You know what I'm sayin'. Let's get this thing going!"

I suspect taking a full course load *and* doing fifty-two jobs at the same time might be a bit much for one academic year . . . but hey, this was Wyclef after all.

He headed downstairs. Ian and I were pumped about the footage. "Dude, that was huge. Quick, put a new tape in," I said, just to make sure we wouldn't accidentally tape over the footage. Meanwhile, we heard cheering downstairs. Ian popped in another tape, and we quickly went down to check it out. At the front of the store they'd set up yoga demonstration mats, and Wyclef was balancing on his head. A large crowd had gathered to cheer him on. Ian had his camera in hand and we made our way to the front. Michael, one of the Roots co-founders, was anxiously standing by. He spotted us and yelled, "You're missing everything!" He looked around to locate Richard and called out, "Who hired these guys?"

Ian's face went red as he continued to move around the yoga mats filming different angles of Wyclef Jean, Rap Star, doing yoga.

I suspected that Michael had no idea why we were there. That I was offered the one-week job to report on the film festival with written updates and pictures posted to the Roots blog. And that Ian was there to film me performing the job. I'm sure he thought that Ian and I had been contracted out as third-party videographers. We were caught in the middle of the apparent miscommunication. But I can't blame Michael. During the film festival there's a ton of stuff going on, and he was also trying to run a company with more than one hundred stores throughout North America.

Once Wyclef left the store, things returned to normal. But now Richard wouldn't even look at us.

Later that night we joined some Roots co-workers and attended a party that Hilary Duff was throwing at a bar. Now we were able to be ourselves again. We could laugh, feel confident, and have a good time without someone there always ready to put us down. When the bar closed, Ian and I said goodbye to our friends and went to the pizza place a block over. We stood outside, had two slices each, leaned against the brick wall, and gazed out at the bar-closing scene downtown. Noise from the various clubs spilled into the street, cabs sped past, panhandlers stepped up their game, and scantily clad girls stumbled in their high heels, not looking as classy as they did when the night began. We felt like invisible spectators, taking it all in, eating our pizza, and intermittently trading profound observations.

"Man, if we had a big company, we wouldn't be jerks."

"For sure. If we were famous, we'd still be standing here, chillin', eating pizza."

"Yeah, man. We'd be doing exactly what we're doing now, just two guys, standing on the street after the bar, eating pizza, just being real . . . but we could press a button on our cellphone and a limo would pull up in like thirty seconds."

"Yeah, though we wouldn't even use it."

We finished our pizza, then began the forty-five-minute walk back to Rob's place. The hardwood floor was cozy that night.

The next day on the subway, Ian and I mapped out our plan. "We'll go into the store, get the media passes for the music festival, then get out of there as quickly as possible."

After shooting some video footage with the bands, we could stay at the music festival that night. The promise of seeing Smashing Pumpkins and the Killers live was the only thing keeping me going.

At the store, we went upstairs and spotted Richard sitting on a stool. I marched toward him. Ian elected to wait at the top of the stairs to reinforce our "not sticking around, we're here with purpose" message. Good call.

"Richard, just wondering if I can get the media passes for the music festival?" I hoped he could hear my dislike for him in my voice.

"I couldn't get them," he said, then, like an arrogant businessman tossing a beggar a dollar, handed me two regular tickets. He suggested that we try to talk our way backstage by telling them that we were with the Flick Off campaign. Then he added, "Oh, and once you get some footage there, we have the private event for Norman Jewison tonight that you'll have to film."

I was pissed. I was pissed that it had nothing to do with reporting on the film festival for the Roots website *or* the Flick Off campaign. I was pissed because there would be absolutely no future use for the footage we'd shoot. I was pissed that in the store I had to listen to Cody Chestnutt sing "Look Good in Leather" on repeat all week. But most of all, I was pissed because my light at the end of the tunnel had vanished—we'd have to miss the two main bands at the music festival.

We left the store and headed for the subway in silence. Not only had Richard successfully made us feel inadequate all week, but now we felt exploited. What made it more frustrating was that every time we went from one event to another on the subway, it cost us $5, not to mention the cost of videotapes with the extra footage. Fine, maybe it wasn't much money, but when we were sleeping on a hardwood floor in the Grand Central of Chinatown, choosing to walk forty-five minutes to avoid a $20 cab fare, and yet were being asked by a multimillion-dollar company to shuttle around the city on our own dime, it felt a bit much. Then again, we didn't ask to be reimbursed either.

This week had been my most challenging since I began the One-Week Job project. It wasn't until my last day that I realized the issue was communication. I was being judged by different bosses with different expectations. For one person I was doing a great job, and for another I was completely off track. It put us in a difficult situation because we were never sure what was expected of us, and worse, we felt scrutinized all the time.

I'd never quit anything, but right then I felt like walking away. The weird thing was that we met many great people who worked at Roots who were very kind and welcoming to us, but Richard had been our main point of contact. It's amazing how it can take only one person to ruin things, especially if that person is in a position of authority.

As we sat on the subway on our way to the ferry docks, I turned to Ian. "I don't want to go back, man. Why should we go back to a place that's going to make us feel like crap? I don't want to do it."

"You want to quit?"

"I don't know. I just don't want to go back there." I stared out the subway window and watched blankly as another few stops passed by.

"The thing is, they don't even know that there's an issue," I said. "If I quit, they're going to be surprised and I'll have to explain the situation. I don't know. I don't feel like making a big issue about it with only one day left."

"Yeah, but it's the principle."

"Yeah, I guess. I just don't want to be all dramatic, like we couldn't hack it or something. Anyway, how can I justify quitting a job, where I'm not getting paid, I'm only there for a week, and they were nice enough to offer me the job in the first place?"

I also realized that it was partly my fault. I hadn't said anything. I'd kept quiet, letting the tension and bitterness build inside of me all week. If I'd said something from the beginning, perhaps we could have clarified our roles early on.

We arrived at the ferry docks. At the ticket window, it quickly became apparent that we wouldn't be allowed to board. With the larger video camera that Cam had lent us, we appeared too official—we'd need media passes. They wouldn't let us in unless we left the camera outside.

With no clearance to get into the concert, it was impossible for us to perform what was expected of us. If we'd brought the smaller camera, perhaps we could have snuck it past the gate, but even then we'd have had to figure out a way to get backstage.

We walked away from the crowded entrance, crossed the street, and sat down on the curb. The environment screamed fun, but at the moment it was just background noise. We watched as streams of people passed by, laughing, full of anticipation, heading over to Toronto Island to enjoy the concert. It was weird to think that just over a month earlier we hadn't been too far from there—out on Cam's boat having a barbecue and drinking Steam Whistle beer with the crew. Things were much different then. We'd been in friendly company, loving life, feeling like anything was possible. People were good. Now, as we sat bummed out on the curb, it seemed like a distant memory.

As I watched the procession of concertgoers across the street, I suddenly felt angry about the whole Richard situation again.

Then two things occurred to me.

First, I was being really lame. And second, why was I allowing this guy to make me feel this way? I chose to take it personally, to feel down about it. I can learn from this, I thought. I will never forget how he made me feel, and I will always be conscious to never make someone else feel less important. I don't care how busy I think I am, there's always time to treat others like equals. I also learned that I could never work for someone who puts others down.

I looked over at Ian sitting next to me surely struggling to put the situation in perspective. His eyes were fixed on the pavement between his feet, elbows on his knees, his hands hanging lifeless toward the ground. His face was slack; a stranger walking by might have assumed he was exhausted. But I knew otherwise. It takes a lot to get Ian down—he's always so solid and can come through with an appropriate Buddha quote when needed. Right now we were in desperate need of one, but I'd never seen him so deflated.

I jumped to my feet. "Screw it," I declared. "I'm scalping these tickets."

Still seated, Ian watched in disbelief as I ran across the street and disappeared into the crowd.

Ten minutes later I emerged, cash in hand. I jogged back to Ian and looked down at him with a triumphant smile. "Let's go grab a couple Steamys!"

Ian laughed and shook his head. He grabbed my extended hand, pulled himself up, and we started walking toward the nearest bar.

My last day at the film festival was much of the same, except I felt a lot more like I did the first day—unflappable. I suppose it was like the last day of many regular jobs—nothing was really expected of us, and we counted down the hours until we could get the heezy out of there. We were able to see it from an outside perspective and laugh at the ridiculousness of it all.

At the beginning of the week, I'd never been more excited to begin a One-Week Job. Now, at the end of the week, I'd never been more happy to finish one. On the surface, this job seemed unbelievable—going to this huge film festival, interacting with celebrities, and being part of all the excitement in the city—but we weren't able to enjoy it because of the constant tension underlying the experience. In hindsight, I would have preferred to work at the Roots headquarters with all the great people we met the first day.

As we walked out of the store for the last time, we wore wide grins on our faces—the kind of grins worthy of an impromptu pause in the street for an overly exaggerated high five—"Yeeaah!"—before proceeding to the subway station.

Soon we were back at Rob's place gathering our stuff and waiting for Danna to pick us up. My next job, with an advertising agency in Montreal, started that night.

WEEK 26 JOB: **ADVERTISING EXECUTIVE**

LOCATION: **MONTREAL, QUEBEC**

EMPLOYER: **COSSETTE COMMUNICATIONS**
WAGE: **APPROXIMATELY $35,000 YEAR (ENTRY LEVEL); $100,000–$150,000 (AFTER 10 YEARS)**

INDUSTRY IQ:

- Over $1 trillion is spent on advertising each year in America.
- The cost of a thirty-second commercial during the Super Bowl is $2.7 million.
- Cars are the most advertised product on television.
- Advertising dates back to the Egyptians, when it was used for political campaigns, lost and found, or local happenings.

WHAT I LEARNED: Two perspectives = two outcomes.

At the advertising agency there were a lot of people who talk big and throw some wild ideas on the table, but the impressive thing is, they actually make them happen. On a couple of occasions I thought to myself, Yeah, right, that can't be done. Though when I looked around the room, there was never any doubt on the faces of the advertising team about whether these ideas could be pulled off. Instead of wasting time coming up with excuses, they asked, "What steps do we need to take to make this happen?"

Working at Cossette Communications, I learned that there are two perspectives you can have when trying to achieve a goal. You can focus on the barriers that could prevent you from attempting it, or you can focus on how to make the goal a reality. The perspective you choose will make all the difference.

WHEN I THOUGHT of an ad agency, I imagined people sitting around eating Gummi Bears in a room filled with bean bag chairs, foosball tables, and whiteboard walls, tossing out ideas about how best to manipulate a target market. Everyone would be the fun creative type with an abundance of energy. I hadn't actively sought out a One-Week Job since the first few weeks, but advertising executive was one job I really wanted to try. I emailed a few ad agencies asking if I could work there for a week, and the largest one in Canada, Cossette Communications, offered me a position. Turned out they'd be producing a commercial for Molson that particular week, and so my first shift began with a midnight shoot on set.

Danna arrived at Rob's place in Toronto. I ran outside to meet her and gave her a big hug. Danna, Ian, and I packed up the car and hit the road. I was happy to be leaving Toronto. I was even happier to be leaving Toronto with Danna. I hadn't seen her at all during my week at Roots. But now, with some time off work, she decided to make the five-hour drive to Montreal with us. Karen, who hadn't been too excited about our hardwood-floor sleeping situation the previous week, had opted to go to Montreal after the first night. We had a couple of friends, Kyle and Dom, with a great place in the city, and they were happy to let us stay with them. Kyle and Dom are the young, fun married couple that are hard to keep track of because they're always off on another adventure—the type of people who trade a red paper clip up to a house and then write a book about it (seriously, Google it).

We arrived in Montreal shortly after 2 A.M. and dropped Danna off at Kyle and Dom's place. Then Ian and I went directly to the commercial shoot located on the roof of a seven-storey building downtown.

We met with Marie-Claude, the director of the Molson account, whom I'd be shadowing that week. Marie-Claude had a strong presence and directness that was softened by her great sense of humour, long curly brown hair, and warm smile.

"Good morning, boys," she said in her slight French accent. "You must have a long day?"

"Yeah, it's a been a long week," I replied.

We followed Marie-Claude through the old apartment building, which was being renovated. We stepped out of the elevator on the seventh floor, then made our way past various props, electrical cords, and big black equipment boxes to a narrow stairwell that led to the rooftop. On the roof, bright white stage lights projected onto the set. It appeared to be an outdoor basement scene with a couch, two La-Z-Boys, and several university-aged guys and girls positioned for the next take. They all faced the flat, windowless brick wall of an adjacent building located a small parking lot away. On the wall was a huge projection of a hockey videogame.

"This is really cool," I said, checking out the scene.

"Yeah, we are happy with how it's going," Marie-Claude said.

"So, what's the story behind the commercial?"

"Our client, Molson, has a campaign in which their beer drinkers write in with a wish they want to be granted. Then the spokespersons for Molson—three of those guys you see over there, symbolic of three average good guys—they choose different wishes to grant," she said. "This request was from a group of friends who loved videogames, but didn't have a very good setup in their basement. So the three average good guys set them up on top of a high-rise building with a couple of La-Z-Boys and beers, with that building there acting as a screen for their videogame."

Marie-Claude told me that this was a great point to join the development process of the advertisement. They were several steps into it, but there remained a lot more work before they arrived at the finished product. I'd get to watch the initial filming of the commercial and the postproduction work, meet with the clients to get their input, make the appropriate adjustments, and, finally, see the end product.

Typically the process starts when the client comes to the

agency with a new product or campaign to launch. The director of the account acts as the main contact with the client. She'll then take the project to the creative department. Much as I imagined, the creative department will then congregate with Gummi Bears at the bean bag chairs and come up with various concepts and make sketches, prototypes, or whatever is necessary to translate their vision. The director then takes the developed concept back to the client. Once the concept is approved, it will go to another department, called Blitz, which organizes all the logistics. In the case of the beer commercial, they had to scout an adequate location to film—a building that had a flat clean wall and that was adjacent to a building with enough roof space to accommodate the set. They also had to contract out a production company and sound technicians, organize film permits, and rent the building, among other details. According to Marie-Claude, this is the department that "makes it happen."

For the most part, I stayed behind the scenes with Marie-Claude and observed the filming process. They wrapped the shoot just before sunrise, which allowed Ian and me to beat the morning rush-hour traffic back to Kyle and Dom's place.

We quietly slipped into our room, where two double beds held Danna and Karen, sound asleep. It had been an incredibly long day and an even longer week. But now a comfortable bed that Danna kept warm awaited me. I was happy.

On Tuesday morning we arrived at Cossette's head office well rested and ready to go. I was told that the advertising industry tends to attract young, dynamic, creative people. The type of people who like to travel and are open to the world. It's an industry where everyone becomes your friend. Sounded a bit euphoric, even for me. But when I arrived, the first person I met appeared to fit the mould perfectly.

His name was Marc. VP of group account services, Marc was the hip, nerdy type. He had short hair and sported rectangular glasses that, by design, bumped him up a notch on the creative scale. He was supposed to be my boss for the week, but there was a last-minute change in plans and he had to leave for Toronto in twenty minutes for an important pitch meeting.

"You know, Sean, at first I wanted to set up an interview with you. Then I thought, What, am I kidding? If this guy can be doing what he's doing, then of course he can work here!" It was early Tuesday morning, but he had a ton of energy and was incredibly animated, bouncing off the walls as if it was the Friday afternoon before a long weekend. He quickly spat out ideas, managing to emphasize each point.

"Number one, you have to understand that we are the clothes that the corporation wears—the image this company is going to be in public. And a brand of a product is no different than you. You are a brand. Your name says something, and what you stand for says something."

Veins protruded from his neck as he stretched every breath until he was forced to take another. He threw both arms up and exclaimed, "We sell freakin' ideas!" Then he straddled an imaginary line on the carpet. "We have one foot in a boardroom with product managers and marketing vice-presidents who have a very high fiscal responsibility, and the other part of our day is with creative guys. And the best creative people, they're like a bucking horse." He pretended to mount his spirited bronco. "And the more creative they are, the harder they buck, the more they push the limit." He tried to stabilize the steed. "And us, we're just trying to control them and keep their ideas within the brand box, make sure they're communicating what we want to say about the product."

He dismounted, took a breath, and changed direction. "Right now the job you're working on is with our Molson account, and the big idea is 'a true beer for the average guy.' Who is speaking for the average good guy? It seems that all we talk about is the fifty-million-dollar athlete or the freakin' loser who shoots everybody. There're still a lot of good guys out there. And they drink our beer."

His assistant entered for a third time and insisted that he leave that instant or he'd miss the flight. He wished me luck and hurried out the door.

I was left in his office wondering what had just happened. He had twenty minutes and he used every second. After speaking with him, I felt motivated, like I wanted to go out and do something. I wasn't sure what, but something. I wanted to be active, accomplish things, make stuff happen. I didn't speak with Marc again, but I'll never forget him. I guess that means he's got a good brand.

We met up with Marie-Claude, and she took me on a tour of the office. More than five hundred people worked there, and the environment on each floor catered to the department. When the elevator door opened on the sixth floor and immediately revealed a foosball table, I knew we'd arrived at the creative department. I didn't see any bean bags, but I did spy simple, comfortable-looking chairs that you'd expect to see in an IKEA showroom.

An hour later, we hopped into a taxi with Marie-Claude and headed to the editing suite of the production company that was responsible for the Molson commercial.

We met with two VPs from the marketing department at Molson to view the initial cut of the commercial. Everyone had suggestions and input for the editing team. One of the representatives liked the fast-paced loud music, whereas the other questioned it. I found it fascinating that two people from the same company had different views of what best portrayed their brand. Inevitably all the viewers at home would have their own take on it. The challenge, in advertising speak, was to find the best possible means to communicate the message in a way that would resonate with the target audience.

The production company noted all the feedback and suggestions, then went back to work on the commercial. The deadline was very tight, with the commercial's air date set for that weekend. It was incredible to see how much work went into making a thirty-second ad. There was a lot of discussion, and tweaking of sounds, colours, images—while keeping the client and target audience in mind.

"Each department in the agency has a very different role," Marie-Claude said. "But we all must work together in order to keep the concept moving forward, and to ensure that the client will be happy with the final product."

A few days later we were ready for the final viewing with the Molson VPs. We spent most of our time going back and forth to meetings—from the office, to the editing suite, to the sound studio—showcasing the commercial to the clients throughout the process. As Marie-Claude said, "The key is to keep the client involved as much as possible. This way we can avoid a situation where the client is completely surprised by the final product, it's not at all what they wanted, and we're forced to start all over again."

Even with the tight deadline, every day we found time to enjoy remarkably relaxed lunches. Generally in the corporate world, people tend to eat on the run, at their desk, or perhaps at a scheduled business lunch. I'm not sure if it was the French culture, the ad-agency culture, or a bit of both, but every day without fail we stopped everything, left work at the office, and had an amazing sit-down lunch with some great conversation. When we returned to work in the afternoon, I found there was a sense of calm in our interactions despite the looming deadline. I felt more focused, more relaxed, and ideas flowed better.

Back at the studio, the client was happy with the finished commercial. It was sent to the television network that afternoon and would air the following night.

I enjoyed the fast-paced, creative atmosphere at the ad agency, and I could definitely see myself working at one. I liked the idea of focusing on a project with all of my energy for a period of time, seeing it through to fruition, then moving on to the next one. I'd find it easier to keep motivated knowing that it wouldn't always be the same kind of work—that when a project was finished, it would be time to move on to something new.

Walking out of the studio, I asked Marie-Claude, "So, do you guys celebrate when you complete a project?"

"There's no time to stop and celebrate," she said. "Monday it's on to the next one."

Now, at the end of Week 26, the halfway point of One-Week Job, I could relate. My next job awaited in a couple of days.

Back at Kyle and Dom's place, Danna packed up her car to return south to Toronto, while Ian, Karen, and I loaded our rental car to head twelve hours east to Halifax.

"Is that everything?" I asked Danna as she closed the trunk.

"Yeah, I think that's it."

She stood hesitantly, then reached for my hand. "So . . . I guess this is goodbye?"

"Yeah, just for now," I said.

"When are we going to see each other again?" she asked bashfully.

I had no idea. I was surprised that I'd already seen this much of her. But now my jobs were taking me much farther away than a six-hour hitchhike. I fidgeted with my car keys and looked at the ground, uncertain how to respond. Danna noticed my reluctance, and reality kicked in—we might not see each other until the end of the project. Her eyes welled up as she fought back tears.

I pulled her close to me. "We'll make it work," I said, trying to assure her as much as myself.

"I know," she whispered.

I clutched her tighter. "I'm happy we've been able to spend so much time together over the past two months."

"Me too," she said, her head buried in my chest. "I'm definitely starting to realize how much patience everything is going to take."

"Well, you know what they say, right?" I drew back from the hug and smiled. "Good things come to those who wait."

"Yeah, right!" she said, through laughter and tears. "You're the one waiting for me!"

We kissed goodbye, piled into our respective cars, and drove our separate ways.

WEEK 27 JOB: **BARTENDER**

LOCATION: **HALIFAX, NOVA SCOTIA**

EMPLOYER: **GUS' PUB & GRILL**

WAGE: **$20,460 YEAR** **[Source: BLS]**

JOB DESCRIPTION: Served drinks, interacted with customers, and cleaned up the bar at the end of the night. The clientele at Gus' Pub was quite eclectic. During the day, they had customers who had been going there daily for twenty to thirty years. Then at night it was a much younger crowd of students with popular bands playing Wednesday through Saturday.

INDUSTRY IQ:

- Typically more than half of a bartender's earnings comes from tips.
- Flair bartending is where the bartender performs tricks with the liquor bottle while making the drink. There are major flair-bartender competitions around the world, with typical prize money of $20,000 or more.

WHAT I LEARNED: Being a bartender requires patience.

While I enjoyed trading stories with patrons, by the end of the night my feet ached and my patience dwindled. Being a bartender is like going out for a night on the town with friends as the designated driver. As the night wears on, you watch the people around you become more intoxicated and more difficult to communicate with. Their demands get more obscure. And scarfing down fast food at three in the morning is not nearly as enjoyable when you're sober.

JOB: ROCK-CLIMBING INSTRUCTOR (INDOOR)

LOCATION: **VICTORIA, BRITISH COLUMBIA**

EMPLOYER: **THE BOULDERS CLIMBING GYM**
WAGE: **$12–$15 HOUR**

JOB DESCRIPTION: Helped out with the adjacent high school's climbing teams, organizing warm-ups and a training program at the end of each practice. I also helped with a kids' birthday party, cashed out and closed the gym, and, on the last day, learned how to build anchors when climbing outdoors.

INDUSTRY IQ:

- Bouldering is a style of climbing that doesn't require ropes. For this reason routes are usually less than five metres high.
- Acrophobia is a fear of heights.
- North America's highest mountain is Mount McKinley (a.k.a. Denali) in Alaska, at a height of 6194 metres.

WHAT I LEARNED: Often, activities are merely a pretext for being together.

There was a great atmosphere at Boulders. The kids loved the sport, but it was obvious that the friendships, sense of community, and team spirit played a huge part in bringing them back to the gym every day.

FROM HALIFAX, IAN, Karen, and I flew back to Vancouver, where I'd spend one night at home before continuing on to my job in Victoria.

After I graduated, I'd always felt a sense of apprehension before I returned home. I no longer related to it as I once did, but I wasn't sure where to leap before fully letting go. I was never at home long enough to justify getting my own place, and so, in my prolonged state of transition, I simply returned to my parents' guest room in the basement—"temporary" quarters since high school graduation.

Upstairs, my childhood bedroom remained untouched. My stuffed animals still sat well behaved on the floor in the corner, while old photos, dusty trinkets, and toys lined the bookshelves. It was a time capsule of worn posters, sports trophies, and tacky wallpaper—relics from my youth that I hadn't been able to throw away for fear of losing part of myself with them. For years it provided something of a foundation, confirmation of who I was. A distant past, which when I returned home didn't feel so distant.

My mom arrived at the Vancouver airport to pick me up. Ten minutes later she turned to me in the passenger seat. "Now, don't get mad, Sean, this is what mothers do, but . . . do you make your bed when you stay at all these people's houses?"

The next afternoon, Ian and I jumped onto a bus headed to Victoria. At the terminal that night, we were greeted by Kimanda and her dog. Kimanda was the chair of the non-profit that runs the Boulders Climbing Gym. The gym offered adaptive recreation programs, a youth climbing team, rehab programs for stroke and brain-injury victims, and autism programs.

"Hey, guys, you made it!" said Kimanda. Not wasting any time, she turned to lead the way. "All right, let's head to the car."

We followed her to her car. She walked so fast that Ian and I struggled to keep up as we lugged our laptops and luggage.

Ten minutes later we arrived at the underground parking garage where her car and the car that she'd rented for us were parked.

"You guys aren't insured to drive the rental car yet, so tonight you can just drive my car," she said, then tossed me the keys.

"Sure, where is it?" I asked.

She pointed to a brand-new Mercedes-Benz hardtop convertible.

"Well then, glad that's settled," I said. "I guess we'll follow you?"

We hopped into our new ride.

It was late evening and the mid-fall temperature had dropped considerably since we'd boarded the bus that afternoon, but we didn't care—the top had to come down. Ian reached for the bright pink iPod sitting on the dash. "Let's get some tunes going," he said, flipping it on. We paused, fixed in anticipation. Suddenly Barry White set the evening breeze alive with "Can't Get Enough of Your Love, Babe." We both laughed, Ian cranked the volume, and we pulled out behind Kimanda's four-door family-sedan rental car.

On the way back to her house, I caught Kimanda glancing in her rearview mirror to see Ian and me having way too much fun with the top down in the freezing cold, rocking out to Barry White. She smiled and shook her head.

Kimanda helped run the climbing gym, but her day job was being a political lobbyist. A sense of competition and fight was instilled in her early in life. When she was a kid, she remembered, her dad conducted a midnight mission to deface the sign of a rival political party on a neighbour's lawn (an act she quickly assured me was never repeated). She loved his passion and wanted to get into politics from a young age. Kimanda was driven, enjoyed a heated debate, and was always eager to prove her capability.

I'd never spent so much time in a kitchen as I did at Kimanda's place. Each night when Ian and I came home from work, we'd drop our bags and set up shop for a few hours in the kitchen, chatting with Kimanda, having some drinks, and dancing around to nineties pop music. It was just that nice of a kitchen—and the floors were heated too.

I stayed in the guest room in the basement. Every morning, the first thing I'd see when I opened my door was an indoor climbing grip hanging from the ceiling. One night during a lengthy kitchen talk, I confessed that I'd tried to complete a couple of pull-ups but hadn't been too successful.

"Oh yeah? Well, you should hit the gym, big guy," said Kimanda. "I can do pull-ups using only one finger on each hand."

"I'd like to see that!" I said, a hint of doubt in my voice.

At the time, Kimanda's arm was in a sling, as she'd had minor shoulder surgery earlier that day. We continued to chat, dance, and drink in the kitchen. Then, during a lull in the conversation, Kimanda made a dash for the basement door, a determined look on her face. Ian and I quickly followed, warning that it was probably not the best idea. But there was no stopping her. Kimanda took off her sling and lined up in front of the two grips hanging from the ceiling. At first she had difficulty raising her arm, then managed the pull-up anyway, using three fingers instead of one. Given her surgery that day, we let the extra two fingers slide.

Kimanda had an infectious zest for life that I won't soon forget. Later, back in the kitchen with an ice pack on her shoulder and her unyielding smile on her face, she said, "I'm going to be paying for that tomorrow."

WEEK 29 JOB: TRADE-SHOW SALESPERSON

LOCATION: ATLANTA, GEORGIA

AS THE ONEWEEKJOB.COM website was passed around the internet, I received more offers from around the world. I was invited to be a counsellor in Israel, an English teacher in China, a *panchakarma* assistant (whatever that is) in India, a shrimper in Mexico, a promoter of male grooming products in London. I'd also received various offers throughout the United States, but I was uncertain if my monthly sponsorship money could cover out-of-country travel costs.

Then a friend's dad offered me a position with his innovation technology company. The company was presenting its latest product, the FIFO bottle, at a trade show of food-equipment manufacturers in Atlanta and offered to pay for me and Ian to fly there. I thought it'd be a great opportunity to accept some of the other offers I'd received in the area.

One-Week Job was now international.

The trade show was absolutely massive—even with a great parking spot we had a fifteen-minute walk to our booth in the Georgia World Congress Center. My boss for the week was named Ian. With his furrowed brow and serious tone, Ian appeared stern, but this first impression was quickly overturned once he cracked a joke. While we were setting up our booth, Ian explained the FIFO bottle to me. "It's sauce dispensing reinvented," he said, holding one up to show me. It looked like any red ketchup squeeze bottle, except that it had an opening on both ends. "The FIFO bottle is based on the first-in, first-out (FIFO) concept," he said, then unscrewed the cap on one end of the bottle. "When you refill the bottle, the sauce goes in one end, but when the sauce is dispensed, it comes out the other end—meaning the sauce that has been in here the longest comes out first." In a traditional one-sided bottle, the sauce on the bottom is never entirely used up before the bottle gets refilled. He handed me the bottle. "Plus, when you take off both caps, it makes it easier to clean."

The FIFO bottle is one of those things that's so simple and such a good idea that you wonder how it could not have been invented earlier. Today every Subway fast-food restaurant in the world uses them.

I quickly learned that trade-show life can be tedious. You're on your feet for long consecutive days, saying the same thing over and over again—and each time you say it, you must show as much energy and interest as you did the first time, because for the potential customer it is the first time.

Salespeople are often negatively stereotyped. The perception is that they are always trying to sell you something you don't need. During my week with the FIFO crew, I found that it wasn't about selling people something they didn't need. Rather, it was about finding the people who would genuinely benefit from the product and connecting with them. That was the idea, but with my limited knowledge I could only do so much. I knew enough about the FIFO bottle to get people interested and highlight its benefits, but when I got more serious questions (such as price or location of distributors), I had to pass them on to a more knowledgeable coworker.

Ian had been an entrepreneur his whole professional career. Before he developed the FIFO bottle, he invented Table Shox, a successful product for preventing wobbly tables. As an entrepreneur, Ian earned his money through innovation and perseverance. He had been able to identify unmet needs and apply the capital and know-how to turn those needs into profit. In turn, he spent his wealth on the good things in life: a fantastic house on the water, a boat to explore the coast, and the free time to enjoy it all with his family. If there's a secret to living well, Ian had come close to finding it: Work hard, don't take things too seriously, and have fun.

There's a lot of risk involved in being an entrepreneur, yet Ian continually pushed through that to find success. I asked him, "What is the number one challenge of being an entrepreneur?"

Immediately he responded, "Fear. It's real simple. If you're afraid to fail, you fail. And we all have fear, but you can't let that fear paralyze you."

"How do you overcome that fear?" I asked.

"There's one line in a famous book that I always remember—'What would you do if you weren't afraid?' " He paused, as if expecting a response. "As soon as you put that fear aside, compartmentalize it, then you can move forward.

"I've met so many people who have ideas, but very few who have executed those ideas," he continued. "If you're a glass-half-empty-type person, frankly, it's not a good idea to be an entrepreneur. But for people who want to go down this path, I think it's really important that they study what's out there. Read lots—read magazines that you'd never pick up at a newsstand, read biographies of people who have done really well, read psychology on how *you* do well, ask people questions—find out how to get into that mind space, not only the creative aspect, but having the inner fortitude to take those creations to the next level."

I admire the freedom that Ian had created for himself. He was able to control the projects he takes on and was ultimately responsible for their successes and failures. His simple definition of success—"doing what you want to do."

After meeting Ian, I wanted to learn more about being an entrepreneur. Also, I enjoy hilarious T-shirts, which is why I accepted my next one-week job.

WEEK 30 JOB: SMALL-BUSINESS OWNER

LOCATION: ALPHARETTA, GEORGIA

I STROLLED THROUGH the warehouse of SnorgTees, a young, hip company that sells funny T-shirts through its website to customers all over the world. The company was started by three friends in their early twenties in the basement of one of their parents. By the third month in business they were profitable and had recently moved into their own office/warehouse space.

The warehouse held about seven rows stacked high with inventory of more than two hundred T-shirt designs. I picked up a green T-shirt featuring the image of a fat jolly Buddha that said, I HAVE THE BODY OF A GOD. The one next to it bore an image of the moon having a conversation with Pluto: IT'S OKAY, PLUTO. I'M NOT A PLANET EITHER. Others referenced movies: THAT'S WHAT SHE SAID, I LOVE LAMP, I AM MCLOVIN'.

Matt, president and co-founder, said that starting the company was a huge undertaking, and what allowed him to keep moving forward was breaking it down into small achievable steps. First step? Learn how to print T-shirts.

"When you come in and look at a business, you're like, 'Oh, this is how things work.' It just seems that everything flows smoothly," he said. "In the first few months, we put up the website, then thought we were going to run a few ads and stuff would just start flying off the shelves. Well, that didn't happen." He smiled, shaking his head. "The key was to keep the bigger vision in mind, then focus on the smaller steps that would eventually lead us to that end goal. Every month it gets better and better. It becomes more comfortable, more fun, and starts to feel more like what you expect."

There was a casual atmosphere at the office—except for "Formal Fridays," when employees dress up in business attire. People often write to them with T-shirt ideas, and so once a week the staff will get together in the boardroom to judge the ideas based on the very efficient thumbs-up, thumbs-down rule.

"The idea can't be *too* clever," Matt said. "It's gotta be something that will make people laugh when they first hear it."

If an idea receives a thumbs-up majority, the concept is forwarded to one of their designers. The designer creates the artwork, and then it's sent to the printer. As a thank-you, the person who sent in the idea gets $150 plus a choice of a free T-shirt.

In the previous thirty weeks I had had the opportunity to work with many people who owned businesses. Most of them said that they love the freedom, they wish they'd done it sooner, and that they'd never again work for someone else. I can appreciate that, but with that freedom comes more work and pressure. I found that most small-business owners work very long hours and don't have much time for themselves. It's true that they make their own schedule, but since their input is directly related to their bottom line, it's a challenge for them to ever stop thinking about work.

Most nights Matt worked at home, trying to stay on top of everything. I imagine it must be difficult to simply relax, take a vacation, enjoy a movie or a book, when there's always something that could be done. It must become even more difficult when you actually love the job.

"We're raised thinking that we'll end up working for someone else," Matt said. "So when you work for yourself, you're kind of like, 'Well, where's my paycheque?' But you pay yourself, so it's all up to you."

Being a small-business owner takes a certain type of personality. It requires a lot of hard work, long hours, and the ability to manage risk and put off short-term gain for the potential of long-term freedom. It's not for everybody, but Matt's positive that it's for him. "Having had a taste of owning my own business and working for myself, I can say that it's definitely what I want to do the rest of my life."

As for me, I'd like the challenge and opportunity to create a successful business. But I question if I'd be able to manage the same risk and commitment required if a family was involved. All of a sudden, the outcome of my decisions would affect not only me but the future of my family. The challenge is finding that healthy balance.

WEEK 31 **JOB: AQUARIUM HOST**

LOCATION: ATLANTA, GEORGIA

EMPLOYER: GEORGIA AQUARIUM

WAGE: ABOUT $30,000 YEAR

JOB DESCRIPTION: Helped out at exhibits and touch pools; shadowed another worker who answered questions about the animals. I also greeted visitors upon entering the aquarium and handled the aquarium's mascot, Deepo, a smiley clown fish.

INDUSTRY IQ:

- The Georgia Aquarium is the largest in the world, with more than thirty million litres of water and more animals than any other aquarium.
- By 2050, 90 percent of all species of wild seafood will be depleted.
- Scientists believe that there are nearly 20,000 species of fish, of which nearly 5,000 are yet to be discovered.
- A whale shark's mouth can span more than a metre in width, though its throat is only about the size of a quarter. It also has three hundred rows of teeth.

WHAT I LEARNED: Aquariums provide a glimpse into a world few of us experience.

At the Georgia Aquarium there's a strong focus on educating visitors about the conservation of marine life and how our actions can negatively impact their environment. The hope is that once visitors are able to view the beauty that exists beneath the ocean, they will be more aware of the consequences of their actions; we tend to care more about things with which we have developed a relationship.

When you look back on your life, it's like the branches of a tree. You can see all the twists and turns you took, the interests you followed, to get to where you are today. To help guide you, try and understand where your interests are leading you, while you are being led.

—Ray, director, Georgia Aquarium

I WAS SITTING across from Ian in the Georgia Aquarium's cafeteria eating lunch when my phone rang.

"Hello, Sean speaking."

I liked answering the phone, especially with my phone number available to anyone on the website. Every caller was a surprise—kind of like opening up a magical present of infinite possibility. Maybe it was a devout Roman Catholic who wanted to talk about my spiritual beliefs and my "well-suited personality" for a prosperous career as a bishop. Or maybe it was someone with an offer to be a horse trainer, a frumple maker (I don't know what this is either), a celebrity matchmaker, or a gymnastics coach in Kansas. Or another stay-at-home mom who wanted a vacation from the kids. Or a career counsellor looking to chat about stuff.

Or Bianca.

"Hey, Sean, my name is Bianca. I'm a producer at *Good Morning America.* We heard about your project of fifty-two jobs in fifty-two weeks, and we'd love to have you on the show to talk about it."

My eyes opened wide. This was huge. Ian responded to the hugeness of my expression with an inquisitive look.

"I'd love to be on." I looked at Ian, then pointed to the phone and whispered, "*Good Morning America.*"

They wanted me on the show sometime in the next few weeks. This is big, I thought. With a daily audience of six million, the show could bring me a lot of job offers.

Later that afternoon I got another phone call. It was a producer at CNN. They wanted to interview me live in the studio on Sunday morning. Only a few days away. I couldn't believe it. This could really change things.

On my last day at the Georgia Aquarium, the VP of communications, Dave, booked me a room at one of their partner hotels so that I could be downtown the night before my CNN interview. It was a far cry from where Ian and I had stayed that week, an older house with leaks that unfortunately sometimes found our faces at night. Ian and I didn't have high expectations, having both slept in many train stations or park benches while backpacking overseas. All we needed to be happy was a warm place and a roof over our heads. However easy to please, when presented with the choice of spending my last night at the leaky house on the floor or at the downtown Hilton on the aquarium's partner account, I opted for the latter. It was too bad Ian couldn't appreciate the drastic improvement to our living arrangement. After my job at the aquarium, he went home to be with Karen for a few weeks.

CNN weekend host Betty Nguyen shuffled her papers, signalling that we were coming to the end of the interview. "So, Sean, it's Sunday. Tomorrow's another workday. Where are you heading to next?"

"Well, that's a very good question," I said. "After the interview I have to figure that out. Chances are I'll be on a fifteen-hour bus ride tonight to Miami, but I'm really not sure."

Then I awkwardly added, "Maybe at CNN?"

I hoped that she'd exclaim, "What a *glorious* idea! You start tomorrow!" with high-fives ensuing.

That didn't happen, but at least she indulged me with a chuckle.

Then she turned and looked into the camera, her expression instantly became serious, and as news anchors often do throughout the course of a broadcast, she began to speak about an entirely different subject. I took this as my cue to leave. Besides, I had to find myself a job that started the next day. And, more important, a place to sleep that night.

I went downstairs in the CNN building and stared up at the big screen they had in the food court. Wow, I was just on *that* TV, I thought.

I guessed I also appeared on many other people's TVs across the country. Moments later a man walked up to me and asked, "So, have you figured out how you're getting to Miami yet?"

I laughed. "Nope, not yet. Not sure what I'll be doing when I get there either."

"Can I buy you breakfast?" he asked.

I never pass up a free meal. "That'd be great. Thanks a lot!" We took a seat.

Another man walked up with a wrinkled receipt in his hand, then flipped it over. "Hey, man, can I have your autograph?"

Shortly afterward, a Starbucks worker passed by the table. "Hey, you work at Starbucks yet?"

The man who bought me breakfast was named Jake. He worked across the street at the Georgia World Congress Center with all the trade shows that came to town.

"Over at the Congress Center, they always have CNN up on the big screens. But when your segment came on, that was the first time that I've ever bothered to stop and watch," he said. "Yeah, well, ya know, I quit my job on Friday. Never did like it much. I got two more weeks left, then I'm finished."

"Oh, yeah? And what's next?" I asked between bites.

"I've always wanted to work for the military, but I never have. So now I'm going to give it a try."

I'm always inspired to hear stories of people going after what they want in life. For Jake to make such a drastic change took a lot of courage. I learned that he'd entertained his idea for a long time and had made many excuses for why he shouldn't make the change. Now he'd finally decided to go through it and was excited about what lay ahead.

After we finished eating, he emptied the loose bills in his pocket and put them on the table. "Here's a little something to help for the road."

"Oh, no no," I said, waving my hand. "Thanks, though, that's very kind of you."

"No, I want you to have it," he insisted. "It's not much."

I suspected that it might become awkward or that he might think I was rude if we went through the process again, so I took the cash off the table.

"Well, thanks so much, Jake," I said, then shook his hand. "You're very generous."

"Don't mention it," he said. "I hope you find what you're looking for, Sean."

"Same to you."

I hurried back to the hotel to figure out my next step, as I was dangerously close to going from the Hilton to homeless in less than twenty-four hours. I pulled out my laptop and checked my emails. I had mentioned Miami in the CNN interview; I already had a couple of offers in my inbox for the Miami area: call centre, mobile dog groomer, exterminator.

My cellphone rang.

"Hello, Sean speaking."

It was a man named Andrew. "Sean, caught you on CNN this morning. Love what you're doing." He spoke really fast yet quietly. "Can't talk long—at a PodCamp conference in Boston. Want to be a stock trader in Fort Lauderdale? I'll be back there tonight. I'll pay for your flight. You can start tomorrow. This will be one of your best weeks, I assure you."

"Yes." I tried to be as efficient with my response as he'd been with his offer.

"Great. Call you when I step out of the conference."

I heard back from Andrew a half-hour later. He had checked with his wife, and she wasn't on board with the idea. We decided we'd try for the following week, after she had more than several hours' notice that a stranger travelling around the continent doing a different job each week would be staying at her home.

He still insisted on paying for my flight from Atlanta to Miami, but I said, "No, thanks."

Ten minutes later, I received an email with a confirmation number for a flight that left in three hours.

I packed my suitcase, confirmed one of the offers in Miami, then headed toward the airport.

The next morning I'd be starting as an exterminator.

WEEK **32** JOB: **EXTERMINATOR**
LOCATION: **MIAMI, FLORIDA**

EMPLOYER: **TRULY NOLEN PEST CONTROL**
WAGE: **$31,040 YEAR** **[Source: BLS]**

JOB DESCRIPTION: Helped fumigate a house, accompanied a sales rep out in the field to inspect other houses, and watched all their training videos about proper inspection, safety procedures, and how to identify infestations.

INDUSTRY IQ:

- There are more than 94,000 species of pests in the United States.
- The collective weight of all the ants in the world is about equal to the weight of all the human beings in the world.
- If a choice had to be made between eliminating the medical industry or the pest-control industry, we'd prevent more disease by eliminating the medical industry. (My source: an executive in the pest-control industry.)

WHAT I LEARNED: Being an exterminator is a pretty good gig.

I enjoyed showing up at the house with the truck and all of the equipment, then putting on the protective jumpsuit and facial mask, grabbing the spray gun, and helping the customer solve their infestation problem. If I were to do it on a permanent basis, though, I'd need to find a way to break the incessant loop of the *Ghost Busters* theme song playing in my head.

WEEK 33 JOB: STOCK TRADER
LOCATION: FORT LAUDERDALE, FLORIDA

DURING MY WEEK as an exterminator, I heard from Andrew, the stock trader who purchased my plane ticket to Miami.

"Sean! Andrew here."

"Hey, Andrew."

"Look, I spoke to my wife, and we're on for next week."

"That's great!"

A New York City stockbroker at heart, Andrew is now a 40-SPF local on the beaches of Fort Lauderdale. He spent most of his life in New York City, and it's evident in his accent and the fast-paced work style he brings to laid-back Fort Lauderdale. He left because he hated the cold and wanted to be the big fish in a small pond. Whether managing over $70 million of client assets with his investment firm, Horowitz & Co., writing books, updating his money blog, or producing a successful investment podcast, Andrew always had something going on.

"How many hours a week do you work, Andrew?" I asked, curious how he found time to deal with everything.

He laughed and said, "You don't want to know. It's zero to one-twenty in ten seconds with me. Strap in!"

After we got off the phone, I wasn't surprised to see an email from Andrew a couple of hours later, outlining my homework for the week as well as the dress code. He gave me a few resources, then asked that I be prepared with the list of companies that would be reporting earnings on Monday and Tuesday. Also, he wanted me to find out the important items that would be reported regarding the economy. He added, "After you do this, then I'll show you what really matters."

The job of a stock trader is to make money for clients. The more money they're making, the better job the trader is doing. I wondered if this relationship would alter a stock trader's perception of success. To Andrew money is just the means of keeping score—it's the challenge, excitement, risk, and decision making that attract him to the profession.

"Success is all within yourself," he said. "Be happy first, make sure what you're doing is making you happy. There is nothing worse than getting up on a Monday and saying, 'Ugh, I don't want to be doing this.' There is an amazing number of things out there that you can do—you just have to go for it. You always have to go for it."

In university, the stock market really excited me. For a while I thought that I'd get my trading licence and become a stockbroker. In the end I decided not to. I figured it was something that I could always do for myself on the side without having to do it full-time.

I had noticeably more energy this week. Even though I didn't get much sleep, when the market opened and there was money on the table, I got a jolt of energy. The job demanded it. There was a lot at stake. A day trader—a trader who buys and sells stocks within the same trading day, so that when the market closes, he has no stocks left—must be engaged constantly or risk losing a lot of money in a matter of minutes. Over the first two days, we had a total net profit of $5,500 and handled approximately $1.75 million. Whenever I hear about such large sums of money, it doesn't seem real. I can't help but think of the board game Monopoly.

Andrew set me up with a computer next to him that had the same live trading program he used. I could see everything that happened in real time and make real trades. To find stocks of interest, we'd look at lists of the most active on the NASDAQ and NYSE to see what was "making noise." We'd check on a particular stock; if Andrew liked what he saw, he'd call out a price and number of shares, then I'd feel the pressure to type it as fast as possible, click the Sell or Buy button, and hope that I heard him correctly and didn't make a typo. Brokers would normally do this themselves, but Andrew brought me in on the action.

On the screen, I could see all the buy orders (in green print) and sell tickets (in red print) from other investors. Andrew told me that when there is an increasing number of buy orders coming in, that could mean that the stock is going to climb. Similarly, if there are a lot of people selling, looking to unload some shares, the stock price is likely to come down.

With a detailed graph on the screen, I could see the stock's movement minute to minute as it slowly drew a line across the monitor. "What about these graphs?" I asked. "How can we use these?"

"One thing we can do is use support and resistance levels to help us decide when to buy or sell," he said, pointing to the computer screen. "For example, let's say a stock is selling for twenty-one dollars, and that over the course of the day it's been trading at a twenty-one-to-twenty-three range. Every time it approaches the twenty-three price, it seems to plateau and back off slightly. And whenever it approaches the twenty-one-dollar range, it holds its ground and doesn't seem to dip below. We could then set our support level at twenty-one dollars and our resistance level at twenty-three. This would be our range. When buying comes in from investors that begins to breach these resistance points, we'd look to either buy or sell."

"Okay, seems simple enough."

He laughed. "Well, there are a few other factors to consider. Did you bring the information I asked you to find?"

"Yeah, I did," I said, pulling the papers from my computer bag and handing them to him.

"The reason why I asked you to do this is that typically when a company reports earnings, there's going to be more activity with the stock price," he said. "And when there's more movement in the stock price, there's more opportunity to make money on the margins."

He flipped through my findings and continued, "Likewise, if there are important items reported regarding the economy, we can watch to see how the market is responding to the news. If some stocks are fast-moving, breaking out, we might want to get in there, pick up some shares, and ride it for a bit."

I enjoyed the excitement of the markets, but I don't think I could handle all the ups and downs on a daily basis. It requires tough nerves, discipline, and the ability to recover quickly after a big loss or gain. Andrew admitted, "While you have control of what you do, the market and the prevailing economy have the ultimate control. And unfortunately with the incredible amount of stress involved, it sometimes is very overwhelming."

On my last day, I felt I had a good grasp of everything—I read the charts, predicted where a certain stock would go, and decided on what would be good buy and sell points. After I made the right choice on a few hypothetical trades, and after I could have been, hypothetically, $5,000 richer, my confidence grew.

The stock that I analyzed was Crocs, the shoe company. Overall it was a bad day on the market and the stock was down, and I thought for sure that it was a good buy point.

I turned to Andrew. "Hey, Andrew, can I put a buy order in for five hundred shares at thirty-eight dollars?"

He took a look, then said, "Sure, go for it."

I bought in.

I leaned closer to the computer. My eyes fixed on the screen, I tried to read the graphs based on what Andrew had taught me. Now it was up to me to decide.

Immediately the stock began to look positive.

"That's right, keep it going, you can do it," I egged on the Little Shoe That Could. I thought about selling but decided I'd hold on a bit longer.

My phone rang.

It was a reporter from the local Fox News affiliate. They wanted to interview me.

"Sure, no problem," I said as I tried to concentrate on the direction of the stock. "But you'll have to meet me at the airport." I paused. Many sell orders appeared on the screen. "We have to leave for the airport within the hour."

"Okay. We'll meet you out in front of the departure terminal," he confirmed.

"Good. Bye."

My attention shifted back to the stock. It started to creep downward. I glanced toward Andrew. He was busily trading. I sat there in silence as I anxiously watched the stock drop below my purchase price.

If I sold, I'd be down. It would mean that I'd made the wrong decision to buy. But if I held on? Maybe the stock would turn around; maybe it would come back up and I could break even. It couldn't *possibly* go down any further.

It did.

All of a sudden it wasn't black-and-white after all. I was no longer looking at graphs, hypothetically making trades. I wasn't hypothetically rolling dice, moving around the board in my silver race car, casually picking up prime real estate, building some hotels, jacking up rent, emptying out the bank's supply of $500 notes, then tossing all my paper money into the air. A quick calculation and I realized I was dealing with some serious money, the real kind. Close to $20,000.

An alert popped up on Andrew's computer because the price had hit a certain low point. "Ah, you watching Crocs there, Sean?"

"Yeah. It's not looking too good," I said. "I don't understand. It shouldn't be down this much." Crocs had released some good news that morning, though I hadn't taken into consideration that the whole market was down.

Andrew got up and stood over my shoulder. The stock trickled down further.

"Are you going to just sit there and watch it go down?"

I stared at the computer intently and begged it to change directions.

"This is real money, Sean," he said with urgency in his voice.

The screen lit up red with another string of sell tickets. It has to turn around, I thought. I didn't know what to do. I didn't want to accept that I'd lost the money. It wasn't my money to lose. Now that Andrew was watching the stock too, I thought, Okay, he's got my back on this one. How much could he really be willing to lose to teach me a lesson? The stock continued to dip.

"The stock doesn't care about you, Sean. You must decide when to cut your losses."

I got my answer: "Enough."

I put in a sell order, it quickly went through, and just like that, it was over. I'd just lost $1,000. I felt terrible.

We watched the price drop further.

"This is getting ridiculous," said Andrew.

I was just glad that we got out when we did. I felt even better that the attention was now focused on the abnormal movement of the stock and off the fact that I'd just lost a thousand bucks.

"Sean, go back in for another two thousand shares," Andrew quickly said.

"What? Really? Are you sure?" That was four times the number of shares that I'd originally purchased. At $34 a share, we'd be in for $68,000.

"Yes, do it now!"

I tapped the keyboard, clicked the mouse, and we were back in the rapids.

Then the Little Shoe That Could, unhindered by its different appearance, started to climb.

We both stood and cheered on the stock as if we were at the racetrack urging our bet to push further. I had to be at the airport in twenty minutes in order to have enough time to check in. We had to leave. But the stock still climbed, then climbed higher, then passed my original purchase price.

"You should hang on to it," I suggested. With the good news released that morning and the market upturn late in the day, it'd surely climb higher.

Andrew put in a sell order. And within seconds all the shares were sold. Then, as if it was part of his lesson plan all along, he calmly said, "Number one rule: A day trader never holds a stock overnight."

I exhaled deeply. "That was the most stressful forty-five minutes of my entire life."

Andrew smirked. "Welcome to my world."

We quickly gathered up our stuff and rushed out the door to the airport. In the end, we were up $5,000 on the day, with an invaluable lesson learned—no matter how many models and techniques you have to help predict what direction the stock *should* go, the bottom line is that the stock market is unpredictable.

Andrew ripped into the departure terminal and abruptly stopped in front of the sliding glass doors. I spotted the news van parked outside, the reporter and camera guy waiting on the sidewalk. I ran past them with my luggage. "I'll be right back."

I made my way to the check-in counter, got my boarding pass, and checked my luggage.

"How much time do I have until they start boarding the plane?" I asked.

"They should be starting to pre-board any minute now," she said.

I ran outside the terminal. Andrew was with the news crew.

"Okay, let's do this," I said.

"We've just been told by an airport representative that we're not allowed to film on the premises," said the reporter, in no hurry at all. "We'll have to go off the property."

"I can't. My plane is boarding soon."

"It'll only take five minutes," he calmly assured me.

I looked at the ground, then glanced toward the airport terminal, then back at the ground. "Fine. Let's go."

Andrew and I hopped into the back of the van. There were no seats, only various equipment and cords strewn about, so we were forced to crouch. The driver pulled around the loop.

"How about there?" I suggested. "Pull over there."

He slowly pulled over on the grass at the side of the road. I quickly hopped out of the car. "All right, here we go."

The camera guy pointed the camera at me, and the reporter asked, "So, how did this idea come about?"

In one go, I spewed out all the answers to every question that I imagined he could ask. I explained how I'd started the project, my promise to seek passion, how employers offered me jobs, where I stayed while on the road, how I travelled from city to city.

"My favourite job so far was probably at a brewery, or as a cancer fundraiser, or at an ad agency, or maybe when I was a yoga instructor—I don't know, they're all so different [my answer changed every time]. My worst job was working twelve-hour days in a smelly swamp in the scorching heat. The biggest thing I've learned so far is that the real world is not such a scary place after all." I exhaled and smiled.

"Okay, let's go. I got a plane to catch."

We piled back into the van and made our way around the loop back to the departure terminal. As we arrived at the sliding door, I turned to Andrew, both of us crouched down holding on to the back of the headrests for support. "Thanks for a great week, Andrew. You were right, it really is zero to one-twenty in ten seconds with you."

He laughed. "You're going to need that speed to catch this flight." The van stopped.

"Till next time," I said.

I grabbed my computer bag, hopped out of the van, and ran through the sliding glass doors toward security. They called my name over the intercom as the departure gate came into view. I stepped onto the plane, and the flight attendant closed the door behind me. I jostled my way down the aisle, then tossed my computer bag into the overhead compartment. My heart raced, in stark contrast to the calm setting of the airplane. I sat down, exhaled deeply, and took in my new surroundings. I couldn't help but wonder how the other passengers had spent their last few hours. Some people quietly read their book, or listened to music, or watched television, or slept. Some sat motionless, staring at the back of the seat in front of them, while others passively attempted conversation with the person next to them.

One scene ended as quickly as the next had begun.

I was off to New York City.

WEEK  JOB: **BAKER**

LOCATION: **BROOKLYN, NEW YORK**

EMPLOYER: **ONE GIRL COOKIES**

WAGE: **$25,020 YEAR [Source: BLS]**

INDUSTRY IQ:

- Although many colleges offer programs in culinary training, being a baker does not require formal education, just a knack for baking and on-the-job training.
- A pastry chef is a baker, but a baker is not necessarily a pastry chef. *Chef* means "boss," which means that a pastry chef is in charge.
- A "baker's dozen" is thirteen. It began in the thirteenth century when bakers would sometimes give thirteen pieces for the price of twelve to guard against being punished under the Assize of Bread and Ale, which protected customers from being shortchanged. Baking thirteen items also allowed a baker to lose one item to damage and still end up with a dozen.

WHAT I LEARNED: If it's not right, try something else.

One Girl Cookies co-owner Dawn worked in the fashion industry before she decided to open up the bakery and focus on her passion for food.

"Don't get too wrapped up in what you're about to do. Nothing is permanent," she said. "When you start doing something, you might find out that you love it and you want to continue down that path. Or you might discover it's not the right thing. And that's okay, you can change your path and try different things until you find what's right for you."

I ARRIVED IN New York City on a Friday evening. Ian flew in on Sunday. Danna was also in town for a few days visiting a friend.

The week before we'd arrived, we had no place to stay. Given the difficulty of finding a room in the city for under $200 (and with our budget more around the $20 mark), Ian emailed several hotels along with a couple of bed-and-breakfasts to see if we could stay there in return for a mention on the website. A few responded, expressing interest but no offers. After a couple of days we got an email from Anne, the owner of East Village Bed and Coffee on the Lower East Side of Manhattan. She wrote, "I'm totally up for it. Though I don't want anything in return." Having owned Bed and Coffee for twenty-two years, she didn't want any attention that would attract American tourists. According to her, they're accustomed to more luxurious lodgings and have different expectations.

Her place catered to the European budget-traveller crowd. The rooms were small, each with a decor theme. There was the French Room, the Dutch Room, the Treehouse, the Beach, the Flight Room, and the Zen Room, among others. Each floor had a shared bathroom, a small kitchen, and a living room. It felt more like an apartment than official accommodation. I took the "E.R. Room"—a sofa bed in the downstairs living room that could be enclosed with a hospital curtain at night. Ian stayed above the kitchen in the fort resembling that of *Peter Pan*'s lost boys, built of rough-hewn wood, with a low ceiling, and accessed by a ladder.

It felt great to be in New York City, with people everywhere and its vibrant character. I couldn't help but feel alive, as if in the centre of it all. The city was an artistic, capitalistic, fashion-conscious, multicultural mélange. We took in the gated grass park for viewing pleasure only, dog pooh in the streets, deadline-driven, walk-when-you-please pedestrians, and met genuinely kind people. It was a seething microcosm of humankind yet had a small-town charm.

For the first time in my life I didn't feel like I was missing out on something. This was the place to be.

Tuesday afternoon at One Girl Cookies in Brooklyn, an articulate little girl sat in the café enjoying her first bite of a freshly baked apple pie.

"My, the apple pie is particularly good today," she remarked.

It sure is, I confirmed to myself rather smugly. Kids are tough critics, and this one knew what she was talking about. She was a regular at One Girl Cookies and always had a piece of apple pie when there was a fresh one on the counter. Dave would say the level of "deliciosity" must be quite high to warrant such a remark. I had to agree. But then again, I'd made it.

Dave and his wife, Dawn, are the owners of One Girl Cookies. Dawn is the business brains behind their cookie enterprise, while Dave is the head baker. "We love what we do, but it's hard work," said Dawn. "We take our work home with us, so it's a challenge to balance the business with quality time together. We take only one day off a week. It has been hard to let go of the reins, but we're working at it."

Their hard work has paid off, and their gourmet, handmade cookies are well known throughout the city.

This week I worked alongside Dave in the kitchen. I made all sorts of things: pumpkin cookies, pumpkin bread, cupcakes, caramel-fudge-square thingies, and of course, an apple pie. There's a real creative element to baking. We'd start with a bunch of ingredients that weren't much by themselves, then we'd mix them in a certain order, shape them, toss them into the oven, and they'd come together to create some tasty goodness. I found there was also a meditative aspect to it, working with my hands, creating, concentrating solely on the task before me.

Dave had fallen into baking almost by accident, then quickly climbed the dough ladder. He started as a bread bagger, then became the muffin man, then the cookie guy, then the head baker. Every task and every day in the bakery offered him a new challenge: how to bake a better cookie, how to further motivate his employees. But mostly, he's passionate about baking.

"It's a tangibly satisfying career," he said. "To come into the bakery each morning with nothing on the shelves, and then when you leave, there're people in the café eating cakes that we made that day, and there's forty pounds of cookies flying out the door to some party in downtown Manhattan. I think people want that satisfaction, that feeling that when you leave work, you've done something interesting, different, or helped people."

Dave was a soft-spoken, unassuming, and generally calm guy. I couldn't imagine him getting upset about a pie knocked to the floor or a spoiled tray of cookies. He appeared always able to put things in perspective.

"When I was looking to go to college, my father said to me, 'You've got to get out of the house.' He wanted me to go out and experience some different things, to get away. And it doesn't mean you have to leave your house; that's just his way of saying 'Be adventurous, try some things that you want to try.'

"When you're doing something a little bit different than you're used to, you challenge yourself. And when you challenge yourself, that's when you'll learn the most about yourself."

On my last day at the bakery, Ian and I boxed up a batch of freshly baked goods, then said goodbye to Dawn and Dave. We hopped onto the subway back into Manhattan and met up with Danna and her friend to explore the city.

JOB: FASHION BUYER

LOCATION: **NEW YORK CITY**

EMPLOYER: **GLOBAL PURCHASING GROUP**

WAGE: **$60,000–$100,000 (ASSISTANT: APPROXIMATELY $35,000)**

INDUSTRY IQ:

- Clothing sales in the United States is a $250 billion industry.
- More than 4 million people in America work in fashion.
- No specific qualifications are required to become a fashion buyer, but many schools offer programs in fashion and specializations in fashion merchandising, which are recommended.

APPLICATION PROCESS: Vocation Vacations, a company that provides individuals the opportunity to try out their dream job, contacted me and offered to set up this position.

WHAT I LEARNED: It's surprisingly difficult to dress a mannequin.

MY FIRST DAY on the job, I didn't have time to contemplate my wardrobe. I tossed on the most accessible items in my suitcase—jeans and a long-sleeved collared brown shirt—and hurried out the door. I was a little concerned about how it would go over under the trained critical eyes of a professional fashion buyer, but it was too late.

Construction on the New York City subway put Ian and me back another five minutes, and we arrived at the office, in the

Flatiron District of Manhattan, fifteen minutes late. As we got in the door, we were greeted by an assistant, who immediately escorted us through the ninth-floor office. In the next room, I saw two young designers with their collection laid out on the table already waiting for me. Followed by Ian with the video camera, I was led into the office of Mercedes Gonzalez, my boss for the week. She wasn't impressed. "Nice to see that you dressed up for your first day working with a fashion company," she said, nose turned up.

Mercedes was of Cuban descent, with dark straight hair and big brown eyes. She maintained a serious demeanour and a direct tone, yet always finished with a wry smile that softened her edge.

Apologizing for my lateness and inadequate wardrobe, I took a seat across from Mercedes at her desk. She quickly explained her business.

"It's not a business about fashion really; it's an information business. Basically the company is broken into three divisions. The first division is retail—if you want to open a store, we'll work with retailers from concept to opening day. The second part is working with the young designers who need help understanding the business side of the industry. And the last part of the business is working with established retailers who are in a distress situation to help them streamline or grow their business."

I glanced around the office and took in a few racks of clothing, each wall a different colour, with eccentric pieces of artwork. On her desk sat a framed picture of her two Yorkie pups, Gucci and Prada.

My attention shifted back to Mercedes, who was still throwing information at me.

"When a designer calls me up and is like, 'I have something that's *so* out there and *so* new and *so* . . .' you know what that means to me? Not sellable. 'Oh, but I'm an artist.' You know what? Art belongs in a museum. This is fashion; fashion goes in retail."

I'd yet to catch my breath from running to the office that morning, and it looked like I wouldn't get a chance to all week—Mercedes meant business.

She finished her information blitz with a polite caution: "We take this business very seriously. We have a lot planned this week; it's going to be . . . intense." She paused, awaiting my reaction.

In its silence, the room felt different, offering me my first moment of reprieve since I'd arrived. My bewildered expression informed Mercedes that she'd succeeded in intimidating me. The corner of her mouth pulled back in a wry smirk. "You ready?" she asked.

I'd always wondered who the people were who sat in a room somewhere and chose what would be the next fashion trend for the upcoming season—deciding what it is that people want but don't realize they want yet. There's always some new style that keeps the industry thriving. After all, who wants to be caught wearing something that was "so last year"?

An hour later, Ian, Mercedes, her assistant, and I were racing in a cab on our way to visit a company where such trends are born.

Mercedes took me to the global headquarters of Stylesight, a trend-forecasting company. Here I'd learn what designers, buyers, and retailers pay big bucks to find out—what would be "on trend" the following season. On the way, Mercedes explained the process. "When you look at the runway collections, it seems like all the designers got together, had a cup of coffee, and said, 'This is what we're going to do.' But what they actually do is subscribe to all these trend-forecasting companies, and a lot of designers get their inspiration from this."

We arrived at the office, Ian following closely with his camera. I felt like everyone was whispering, "Why's the camera here?" "I wonder what network this show will air on." "Who's that guy with the dreads and no fashion sense?"

With all eyes in the room directed at me, the vice-president/creative director explained the concept of trend forecasting and taught me what trends to look for next spring. "Reporting comes from correspondents all over the world, feeding us information about what people are wearing and the different styles that are surfacing. We filter that and decipher what the code is and what it means to make new product."

"So if I was a designer, and I came to you guys, what information would I receive?" I asked.

"You would have the analysis as to what would be important going forward analyzed from the collections, street and retail, organized in such a way that you could see the future for design." She directed my attention to the couple of photos in her hand. "What we're looking at in the new millennium is what we've been looking at since the beginning of this decade—we're looking back before we really feel confident to go forward and create something that's truly original and modern."

If it goes through such a calculated process, I wondered, how can anything truly be "original"? It seemed like it would always be an updated or modified version of something that we'd already seen.

Even trend-forecasting companies look at what others are doing to determine how we should dress. Somebody will start to do something different, people take notice, it may catch on, then it influences future fashion trends. We decide whether someone is fashionable or "on trend" based on this set of predetermined guidelines that were derived by gathering information from those around the world who choose to do something new. So the risk is, if you dress differently and come up with your own style, you could be seen either as a trendsetter or simply as someone with no fashion sense. Choose wisely.

At the forecasting company, I had more interest in the social implications of the industry than in the specific trends to watch out for, though with all the attention focused on me and knowing that I'd be expected to use this information throughout the week,

I took diligent notes and asked lots of questions. They took me through the styles and colour combinations that we'd expect to see the following spring season. My vocabulary expanded to include industry buzzwords like "body con," "retro," "architectural style," and "asymmetrical deconstruction."

Back at the office that afternoon, Mercedes immediately put me to the test.

"Okay, a new designer is coming in; he should be here any minute now," she said. "I want you to handle this meeting on your own. I want you to see the new line, get updated, get the delivery dates, get the price points, and figure out which of the clients will fit the bill for him."

I figured that I'd take the lead but she'd be there to help guide me. In the previous thirty-four weeks, I'd often questioned whether my employer really expected much out of me. There was often a sense that no matter how much I messed up, I couldn't do more damage than simply embarrassing myself with my apparent incompetence. Not this time. It was up to me to take care of the whole meeting from start to finish—learning about what stage the designer was at, taking a look at the products, and giving my opinion on what the next steps should be.

The first of my two meetings was with a designer named Andres Stickney. He'd recently designed a dress for Whoopi Goldberg and showcased it on the nationally televised morning talk show *The View.* Then there was me, first day on the job, giving him my opinion as to whether I thought his uniquely designed rubber belts, priced around $200, would sell. I fumbled my way through as best I could, but my knowledge of the belt market was limited—unfortunately my all-determining trend-forecasting training hadn't extended to accessories.

The second meeting was with a middle-aged mother who had a dream of designing a kids' clothing line. She'd employed Mercedes to help her get there. She seemed as clueless as I was, and so we both did our best to pretend. The logo that she'd designed involved several monkeys hanging out intertwined between the label's lettering. A few of the monkeys held bananas. One of them sat with his back against the last letter, which granted a profile view of the curious smile on his face. Cute enough. Except with his hands clasped together, he held the banana in a rather delicate position between his legs, which only made his already curious smile even more curious—and creepy. I made the executive decision that parents probably wouldn't find it nearly as funny as I did.

Next it was time to experience the other aspect of the business: retail. The following day, Mercedes took me to a designer's showroom to look at next season's women's collection. "So, Sean, everything that you learned yesterday about colour, function, style, body, you're going to apply because we're actually going to place an order for one of our stores, a boutique in Las Vegas."

We met with the showroom manager, Beatrice, then took a seat while she brought out the spring and summer collection. "Okay, Sean," Mercedes said. "I want you to pick out the pieces that you don't like so that we can narrow down the collection to the few pieces we'll order."

I stood up and walked toward the articles of clothing that lined the wall. "Can I pull out the ones that I *like*?" I asked.

"No. Pull out the ones that you *don't* like."

There were about fifteen pieces to choose from: pants, shorts, dresses, tops.

I had no idea where to start. I'd pull a couple of items off, then try to gauge Mercedes's reaction before handing them to Beatrice.

At one point, Mercedes was quick to comment on two pieces I pulled off the rack. As I handed them to Beatrice, Mercedes turned to look at Ian with the camera, "That dress was really a winner; so was that tuxedo shirt."

Defending my interpretation of "on trend," I stepped up and reaffirmed my preference. "I don't know, I still don't like that dress."

"Well, let's ask Beatrice." She turned toward Beatrice. "Beatrice, how has that dress been selling for you?"

As if they'd planned it, Beatrice immediately responded, "This has been one of our bestselling dresses."

With $250 billion spent every year in the United States on clothes, there's a lot of potential in the fashion field. But at the same time, it's a tough industry.

"Just because you always liked to dress your Barbie doll or everyone tells you that you're a good dresser does not mean fashion buying/retailing is the field for you. It's a lot of work, and people need to be realistic about what to expect," Mercedes said.

She told me that nine out of ten new boutiques don't survive. It takes a certain personality to be successful. Since Mercedes had started her business nine years earlier, she had helped clients open seven hundred stores, only one of which had closed.

"It's a tough business," she admitted. "You'd better be aggressive, assertive, proactive, analytical, and good with math."

Once you place an order, you have to be good at numbers to price the merchandise correctly and consider what your bottom line will be if you need to reduce the price.

"If you think this life is all about Paris runways, you'd better adjust your expectations. But if you understand that this is a business like any other and work hard and smart, it can be very profitable."

Mercedes knew exactly what she wanted and how to get it. At first she appeared hard-nosed, though the way she easily switched to all smiles made me think that sometimes the toughness was just a show. She was so kind that I'm not sure she was capable of being genuinely angry; rather I suspect she felt the need to put up a front for fear of being taken advantage of in such a competitive business. It's how she got things done. Mercedes embraced that fear and used it as motivation instead of letting it paralyze her.

"At any age, you can make a change," she said. "I think the biggest thing preventing people from making a change is fear. I live with it every single day. I wake up and I'm like, 'Oh my God, am I going to be able to make payroll this week? Are we going to be able to find a new client? What's the next retailer? What's the next designer?' But that fear is what keeps my passion alive and keeps me moving forward."

I concluded my fashion buyer training in the small town of Margaretville, in rural upstate New York. Mercedes owns a retail store in town, and so I was able to practise my new knowledge in a retail setting—the front line of fashion.

As it was also Thanksgiving that week, Mercedes and her husband, Aldo, invited us to stay at their cottage in Margaretville for a home-cooked turkey dinner. And so, along with Gucci and Prada, we loaded up the car and headed north.

That night I'd find myself in a charity fashion show—the only guy among a pack of sixteen-year-old girls strutting my stuff down the catwalk.

Mercedes's friend owned a vintage clothing store and was hosting the event. She needed a male model, so she asked me to be in the show. The clothes fit, and I figured that opportunities to be in a fashion show in rural upstate New York don't come around too often, so I said yes.

The fashion show was held in a hotel conference room they'd spiced up with harvest-themed decor and bright colourful spotlights that splashed the catwalk. The raised wooden runway stretched down the middle of the room, with the enthusiastic audience members seated close by on either side. As I was the only male backstage, my designated change room was a small closet out of view. I put on my first of three vintage outfits—a grey wool sweater, green cargo pants, and construction boots—and then soon, a funky electronic backbeat loudly played and the show was under way.

With each outfit I modelled, the emcee, a comedian from New York City, kept making comments about my butt. On my last tour of the runway, she stopped me once again. "Here comes our hunk, Sean," she hollered. "Sean, turn around a moment for us, show us that beautiful backside!"

I paused. All eyes in the room were aimed at me. Typically in these situations, my discomfort would manifest as me singing a random yet somewhat appropriate nineties pop tune (in this case, I'd likely go with Sir Mix-A-Lot, "Baby Got Back") or I'd simply dance awkwardly in an attempt to redirect the attention.

The loud music eliminated my singing option, so I did the only thing I could do in such a circumstance: I resorted to a spirited booty shake, to the delight of the elderly women in the front row.

WEEK 36 JOB: PHOTOGRAPHER

LOCATION: **NEW YORK CITY**

WHEN IAN AND I had first arrived in New York City only two weeks earlier, everything seemed foreign. It's amazing how you can get comfortable in a city so quickly. I recognized street names, saw familiar faces, had my favourite grocery stores, knew where to find a great sandwich. The Bed and Coffee had become our home, and Anne our friend. We'd chat about the art of pie baking or wow her with our knowledge of fashion-industry buzzwords. And she'd encourage us to learn more than the first line to all the random songs we'd sing. If it got late and guests hadn't arrived, Anne would go home and leave it up to us to check them in, show them their room, give them a tour and the list of recommendations for nearby places to eat. It was comfortable and exactly what we needed. Whenever the door closed behind me, everything would become quiet. As if entering a library, I couldn't help but take a deep breath, switch gears, and begin to relax.

It was through Anne that I found my last job in the city. I'd mentioned that I'd like to try being a photographer, and she happened to have several friends in the business. She gave them a call and set us up with her friend James, who lived a few blocks away. James was a photographer/filmmaker who has worked all over the world, shooting commercials, film shorts, documentaries, and features.

James, Ian, and I met for coffee one night during my week as a fashion buyer. Immediately he struck me as an intriguing character. I got the impression he viewed the world from an alternative perspective, as if he spent a lot of time in the creative space in his own mind, and that his creativity is not constrained by societal norms.

James told us that a freelance photographer must be motivated to create his own work. Typically this requires an ongoing investment of time and money. If James has an idea for a photo shoot, he must scout the location, apply for permits, contract out the models, find the props, rent extra equipment, prepare the sketches, conduct the shoot, and perform post-shoot work on the photos, all before he knows the pictures will sell. Hopefully the shoot will be a success.

James agreed to work with me and suggested several tasks that I could undertake to help with a photo shoot.

On Monday morning, he explained my first task—scout out locations for the shoot, take pictures of the spot, write down its location, and then report back. He wanted "a modern, simple, sleek, clean look, with some depth to it." He handed me a map of Manhattan and suggested some areas to start.

Ian and I debated taking the bikes from Anne's place, until we pictured Ian with one hand on the bike and the other on the camera trying to capture the shot while navigating a swift yellow current of taxicabs. We opted for the subway instead.

We spent the majority of the day walking around the midtown area, and I took pictures of various locations I thought somewhat resembled what James had in mind.

Back at the apartment, James flipped through my findings in silence. Turns out I'd misinterpreted his vision and didn't do a very good job. He liked a couple of them, but because those spots were in busy public areas, it'd be difficult to set up a shoot without acquiring various permits.

The other important task James gave me was to purchase the props needed for the photo shoot that Friday evening. He envisioned businesspeople, typically seen in serious roles, put into a more playful setting. "You always think of businesspeople being so serious, giving press conferences and having board meetings," he said. "I'm trying to show how they are just regular people. They were children and they had fun and played with rubber duckies—so there is always a way that you can have access to that part of their personality."

The shoot would be a fun multitasking theme. The model, dressed in full business attire, would be in the shower trying to manage his entire morning routine—eating breakfast, reading the paper, writing emails, hailing a cab—all at once. That would be contrasted with the model, still in business attire, being playful in the bathtub with various toys, as if a child again.

James handed me a long list of random items for the shoot: three men's suits, ties, dress shirts, newspapers, a rubber ducky, shower cap, nightgown, umbrella . . . the list went on.

The same day James gave me the list, an article about One-Week Job was published in *The New York Times.* I received calls from publishers asking if I wanted to write a book, production companies who wanted to create a reality show, agents who wanted to represent me. My email inbox filled up with various job offers, media requests, and letters of encouragement. Suddenly, my role as a photographer became secondary as I tried to stay on top of everything else: organize future jobs, respond to emails, answer my phone. At the end of a long day, we passed a secondhand store and I managed to find three full suits in the size James wanted. I thought this would be the hardest part. I'd easily have time to get the rest of the props before 3:30 P.M. the next day, when we were to meet at James's apartment.

The next morning I woke up, had breakfast, then sat at the kitchen table with my laptop to catch up on emails. Ian worked on his computer across the table.

Before long, it was 1 P.M.—still plenty of time to go shopping.

Moments later I received an email: "Hey, I think it's great what you are doing, but I can't see your website. It seems to be down."

I typed in "oneweekjob.com." Sure enough, it was down. I looked across the table at Ian. "Hey, the site's down. Do you know what's going on?"

Ian tapped at his keyboard, then looked up at me. "Hmm, I don't know," he said.

Then I received another email. "I saw your project on Yahoo.com. Way to go!"

I went to Yahoo.com and saw the *New York Times* article about One-Week Job featured on the home page. My jaw dropped.

"Ah, Ian? Go to Yahoo.com."

"What? Why?"

"Just do it."

Ian tapped at his keyboard. I awaited his reaction.

"No way!"

"Yeah."

My cellphone rang. "Hi, is this Sean? I'm Paul from Texas."

"Hi, Sean, it's Wendy from California."

"Sean, if come you to Mexico City, I have a place for you to stay."

As soon as I hung up from one phone call, the phone rang again, and again. I looked at my inbox and saw emails trickling in one after another—84 . . . 85 . . . 86 . . .

"Dude, we need to get the site back up."

Ian hurried to put up a basic site that could handle the amount of traffic it received. It included the basic information about the project, how to offer me a job, my contact information, and the latest episode Ian had edited, from my week at the Georgia Aquarium.

And my phone kept ringing. Some called to offer me jobs, others to talk about their career journey, some just to see if I'd actually answer the phone. More book editors, more film people, more agents. It was surreal and exciting—I felt important.

Before I knew it, 3 P.M. came. I had a half-hour to get the props I needed, or at least enough of them to give the impression that I had made a respectable effort. The phone rang again. This time it was James. "Sean, how's it going with the list I gave you?"

I hesitated and looked around the room to see what items I could find at an initial glance. Vaguely I responded, "I'm not sure about the inflatable tube, but pretty good, I guess."

He kept asking me specific questions. I continued to be vague and asked questions in return to clarify details about the objects he'd requested. He finally asked me straight out, "Sean, do you have any of them yet?"

"Yeah, I found the business suits. Umm, I also have the newspapers . . ." I looked around the room. Nothing. "I'm really sorry, James, it's been a crazy day, but I'm heading out now to get the rest of the stuff."

It was too late.

"Sean, I want you to get in a cab and pick up a couple of apple crates I rented. Then come straight to my apartment and we'll prepare for the shoot."

"What about the rest of the props?" I said, not yet willing to admit defeat. I wanted to come through with the items and get to his apartment. I still had time.

"I'll have someone else do it."

There was disappointment in his voice. I felt terrible.

James didn't mention anything about my failure until the next day. Ian and I went to his apartment to film an interview and say goodbye. Just before we left, he stopped me. "Sean, I want you to know that I was very disappointed in you yesterday. I had a lot planned. I was counting on you and needed you to come through."

I explained how crazy the last few days had been with the media exposure the project had received. I dropped names like CNN, *Good Morning America, The New York Times,* BBC, and other media outlets around the world who deemed my project worthy of covering.

He wasn't impressed.

I explained the important phone calls I received, the significant people who wanted to meet with me, and how much the project had grown since the beginning. But something didn't feel right. My spiel had become routine. Somewhere in the midst of all the noise, I'd gotten away from my original intentions. I started to base the success of the project on the media coverage it received. When I'd gotten a call from *Good Morning America* a few weeks earlier, I told friends and family about it and remembered my proud sense of accomplishment when they congratulated me. It had felt good.

Now, as I stood there rambling, I saw myself through James's eyes, and I looked transparent. I felt like a fraud.

Back at Anne's place, Ian made toast and eggs for brunch while Anne worked at her desk next to the kitchen. The place was silent. I sat at the table, stared blankly at the plate of food in front of me, then slowly picked up my fork and began to eat.

"Are you okay?" asked Ian.

I looked across the table at my best friend.

An emotion buried deep inside began its ascent. My throat was constricting, and I felt like I was suffocating. I couldn't speak. I quickly got up and went to the living room.

All that I had set out to accomplish with the project seemed to have changed. I felt empty, lacking foundation, in search of myself yet again. I'd forgotten my initial reason for setting out on this journey. During my week with James, I'd been so worried about fielding calls and responding to emails from various media, agents, and production companies that I didn't care so much about the job and only attempted to make it appear as if I was into it. James had kindly agreed to let me work with him, to show me his profession, and trusted me with important tasks to help with the photo shoot, but all I wanted to do was catch up on emails and make it through another week. Another down, sixteen more to go.

It hadn't started that way. I had set out to find what made me happy. A journey far away to make me feel comfortable in my own skin at home. But no matter how many jobs I tried, cities I visited, people I met, or miles I travelled, the one thing that I could never escape was myself.

I took a couple of deep breaths, then returned to the table.

I sat down and slowly reached for my fork, but within moments emotion overtook me once more. I rushed from the table, grabbed my coat and scarf, and headed out the door into the street. I hurried down the busy sidewalk, around the corner, and turned to face a brick wall. I imagined strangers pretending not to notice as they briskly passed behind me in the street. I pulled my scarf over my head, looked down to the pavement, put my hands to my face, and bawled.

The next day we woke up at six, packed our bags, and stole out into the crisp Manhattan morning. I hailed a taxi, and we rode out to LaGuardia Airport as the sun rose behind billowing grey clouds. Our plane was scheduled to depart for Atlanta at 9 A.M. From Atlanta we'd take an overnight bus to Fort Walton Beach, Florida, where I'd be a firefighter.

We arrived at the airport with plenty of time. Having booked the tickets, Ian confidently stepped up to check us in. Fighting to keep my eyes open, I stood beside him and imagined myself fast asleep on the plane, waking up to the sound of "Please return your seat to its upright position."

Agitated that it was taking longer to check in than usual, I returned from my daydream. It seemed that the ticket agent couldn't find our names in the computer. There must be a very good reason, I thought. I looked at Ian. "Ian, why can't she find our names in the computer?"

I could see him rebooking the ticket in his head as he dug out the confirmation number from his bag and handed it to the ticket agent. Moments later she found our reservation.

My sleep would have to wait. We were two weeks early.

After the initial surprise, we tried to rebook our tickets for later that day. They were $200 more than we had paid. Any chance of getting on standby? *Nada.* Well, at least we could get a fare credit for future flights, right? Nope. Turns out there was a $100 charge to change a ticket (the tickets themselves were only $90 each).

There was nothing we could do. We walked through the airport and tried to find a place to sit down and figure out our next move. I didn't want to discuss it with Ian. I didn't even want to look at him. I was tired and angry. We'd just wasted $180 plus the cost of a cab, we had no way of getting to Florida, and I had no job for the week.

It had already been a difficult few days. I felt like giving up. And this situation was about to put me over the top.

I opened up my laptop and went through my various job offers. I came across an email I'd received just over a month earlier from Irene and Darren, a married couple who owned a pizza place on Cape Cod called Sweet Tomatoes. They invited me to their small village of Osterville, Massachusetts. Osterville is only a seven-hour bus ride north of New York City, and the ticket was in our price range. I dialed Irene's number.

"Hello?" answered a woman on the other end.

"Hi, is this Irene?"

"Yes."

"Hi, Irene, it's Sean Aiken. You emailed me over a month ago about the possibility of coming to work at your pizza place, and I'm wondering if the offer is still on the table."

"Of course!" she said. "That's great! When would you like to come?"

I explained our mishap at the airport, then asked, "I realize it's the last minute, but I'm wondering if I could start tomorrow? There's a bus leaving New York City at three-thirty, and we could be there shortly after ten tonight."

"Perfect. We'd love to have you!" she said without hesitation. "We can pick you up at the bus station, and we'll have a room ready for you guys when you arrive."

Her enthusiasm was a welcome surprise and reminded me that it'd been a while since I last smiled.

When I'd dragged myself out of bed that morning on the Lower East Side of Manhattan, I thought that by the end of the day I'd be in Florida preparing to start working as a firefighter. But instead, in twelve hours I'd be in a town called Osterville, in the state of Massachusetts. The next day I'd be slinging pizzas.

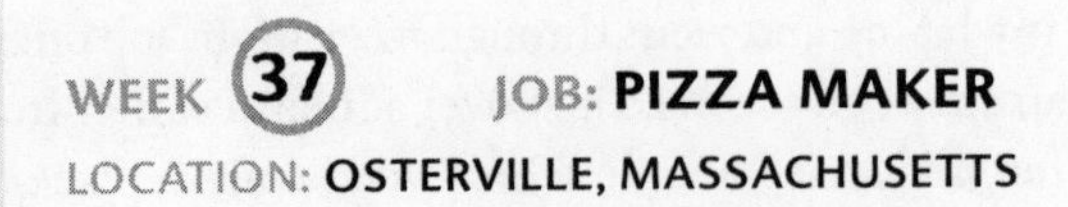

A FEW HOURS into our cold, snowy ride in the pitch-black night, I once again felt like we were venturing into the unknown. It felt good to be going somewhere.

I like travelling. I often find it difficult to be content where I am. But when travelling from one place to the next, I have no choice but to stay put. I can't make time pass faster, and there are no other possible choices. So, I might as well accept it and enjoy the ride.

But the bus ride to Osterville felt more like time at the office than a period of much-needed reflection.

At the bus station in Hyannis Port, Ian and I were the only ones around. The station was locked for the night, and we stood waiting outside. I was on the telephone with an agent from Los Angeles when Irene and Darren arrived to pick us up. A jeep quickly pulled into the parking lot, then abruptly stopped at the curb twenty feet in front of us. Irene and Darren jumped out of the car. It was as if we were returning home after being away at summer camp, our parents excitedly running toward us. They gave us both a big hug.

"Oh, I hope you guys weren't waiting long," said Irene.

In sync, she and Darren recounted the story of their evening; while one paused to take a breath, the other added details.

"No, not at all," Ian got a word in. "We only got here about five, ten minutes ago."

"Here, lemme get your bags," insisted Darren.

Still on the phone, I smiled, waved in acknowledgment, and made an apologetic face. Then we all made our way to the jeep.

I finished my phone call with the agent, jumped into the jeep, and closed the passenger door. Darren drove, Ian sat behind him, and Irene behind me.

"Sorry," I said. "It's been a crazy week."

"No problem," said Irene, as if she hadn't even noticed.

On our scenic drive through town, they went on with enthusiasm about the pizza shop, their kids, Dakota and Callum, their four dogs, the town of Osterville, Hyannis Port and its relationship with the Kennedy family, how they'd heard about the One-Week Job project, and their decision to email me.

"When we heard about what you're doing, we thought, Now,

that is just so cool, we need to email this guy," said Irene, placing a hand on my shoulder. "We've been following your journey closely ever since."

We were all quickly caught up in the excitement of one another's company. The telephone conversation I thought too important to finish when Irene and Darren arrived now seemed trivial.

With a smile, I turned to the backseat and looked at Ian. Nothing needed to be said—we were supposed to be there, and we both knew it. The emails and phone calls could wait.

On my first day at Sweet Tomatoes, Darren gave me a lesson in pizza making—how to roll out the dough, spread the secret sauce, sprinkle on the cheese, arrange the toppings, and toss it into the oven.

I can eat pizza at any time of the day, and it always tastes good. Pizza is especially fun to make. With a piece of dough in front of me, I felt like an artist staring at a blank canvas. Except my canvas was a ball of dough, my hands brushes, and the array of toppings my colours. If I found the right combination, I could create a masterpiece. Well, it wasn't quite that dramatic, since making pizza mainly required following instructions correctly, but when your go-to dishes are pasta with bottled sauce, hot dogs, fajitas, or any frozen food that is microwavable, you take pride in the most simple of chef-like tasks.

Things got a bit intense during the lunch rush; a lineup of hungry construction workers had formed, orders came in quickly, toppings spilled on the floor, the pizza out of the oven stuck to the large wooden spatula, my once-red apron became white with flour. I no longer had time to leisurely toss the dough in the air while singing *Mamma mia, we makin' some piz-za.* I traded off pizza-making duties and packaged slices for customers.

I'm a bit of a perfectionist. At times I'd get too focused on placing each piece of topping in just the right spot to ensure that the first bite was as good as the last. I'd definitely have to speed things up if I wanted to work there full-time. Darren and Irene were polite about my slowness because we got along so well—or maybe because they knew I'd be out of there in a few days.

On my third day, the Cape Cod newspaper came into Sweet Tomatoes to interview me. The reporter assumed that I was related to Irene and Darren based simply on the ease of our interaction. I guess a few late nights of gourmet dinners, beers, and spirited games of Rock Band have a way of bringing people together fast.

Irene and Darren welcomed us into their family and provided us with a much-needed home away from home. Ian and I stayed in their guesthouse above the garage, which couldn't have suited us more perfectly. Two beds, wireless internet, unlimited long-distance. When we arrived, our small fridge was full of cookies, orange juice, and beer. There was even fresh fruit in a basket on the table.

Irene and Darren had made a conscious choice to be where they were. For them it was a question not so much of "What do I want to do for a living?" as of "What kind of life do I want to live?" They decided what was important to them and built their life around that. As Darren said, "I live two minutes from work, I have the flexibility to make my own hours, I get to connect with my community on a daily basis, and it allows me to come home and put my kids to bed at night."

This life also includes sharing their king-sized bed with their four dogs and sometimes young Callum. One night after several beers and a couple of hours of Rock Band, I said to Irene, "I have to see this to believe it. How could you possibly fit three people and four dogs in one bed?"

"I'll show you," she said.

We left Ian and their other son, Dakota, in front of the Xbox to continue jamming and made our way upstairs. Darren had gone to bed earlier and was fast asleep. Irene gently pushed open the door. Sure enough, there they all were. Darren snored. Callum slept horizontally, his head on Darren's stomach. The dogs were interspersed among them, sharing the leftover bed space. Irene would have to wedge her way in, with no room to reposition.

"You must have some sleepless nights?" I whispered.

She smiled and surveyed her crowded bed. "Yeah, for sure, but how lucky am I? I'm surrounded by the people I love." She turned to face me. "I would trade much more than a few sleepless nights for that."

When it was time to leave our new friends, Darren and Callum drove us the hour and a half to Providence to catch a train back to New York City.

At the train station, we gave Darren a big hug. Exhausted from a week of staying up late, working during the day, and somehow managing to find time to sightsee on the Cape, he said, "Thanks for reminding me what it's like to be a twenty-five-year-old again."

My experience on Cape Cod reminded me why I'd started out on this journey—meeting these people, learning about their lives, enjoying one another's company—this is what was important; this is what made the experience special.

In the streets of New York City, with my scarf over my head and tears streaming down my face, I realized that for years I'd based my decisions on what other people thought. The fear of wasting potential was the primary motivation behind many of my accomplishments. Society had painted an image of success in my mind that I tirelessly tried to emulate, and I could no longer discern where this image I'd constructed ended and the real me began.

Within the last month, I'd fallen into the same trap. I sought validation from others in the external success of the project, which would alleviate any sense of failure I might feel about not accomplishing what I'd originally set out to do—find what I needed in a career to be happy. If I never found it, I could still go home feeling that at least the project was a success in the eyes of others. But the bouts of emptiness like I experienced in New York would never end—my sense of self would be forever reliant on the perceptions of others.

What mattered most was that I continue to pursue my passion regardless of what others thought. In the end, I'd be the one who would have to live the life I'd chosen.

I might not have been certain who I was, but I knew who I wanted to be. And I decided I must never compromise that for anything, especially for a fleeting fifteen minutes of fame.

The next morning Ian and I sat in the departure terminal at JFK waiting for our respective flights. Christmas was two weeks away, and Ian was returning to Vancouver to be with Karen. I waited for my flight to Seattle, where I'd connect to Yakima to spend a week as a winemaker.

We'd just spent every day of the last month together, and over the years we'd grown comfortable with sitting together in silence. Yet as other passengers on Ian's flight boarded, Ian asked, "So, you're going to be a winemaker this week, eh?"

"Yeah. It should be cool. I'm working at a small family-owned winery in the country."

"Cool."

"Yeah. So, you excited to see Karen?" I asked.

"Yeah, I am. It's going to be good to be home for a bit," he said. "You're coming back for Christmas, right?"

"Yeah. I'm going to work at a martial arts studio in Vancouver next week."

"Cool."

"Yeah."

We glanced toward Ian's departure gate. Only a few people remained in the line to board the plane. As we heard the final boarding announcement, we both stood up.

"You got everything?" I asked.

Ian casually surveyed his baggage. "I think so."

"Well, I'll see you back at home then."

"Just over a week, I guess."

"Cool."

"Cool."

"All right," I said. "Give me a hug."

Ian hugged me with the arm that didn't hold his backpack. I'd always tried to get Ian to hug with both his arms, like he means it. But Ian's a one-arm shoulder-hug kind of guy (though that isn't to say he doesn't mean it).

He walked toward the departure gate, handed the agent his ticket, then turned to face me. "Bring back some wine!"

WEEK 38 JOB: **WINEMAKER**

LOCATION: **YAKIMA VALLEY, WASHINGTON**

EMPLOYER: **TWO MOUNTAIN WINERY**

WAGE: **$96,000 YEAR** **[Source: *Wine Business Monthly's* Salary Survery Report 2008]**

Two Mountain Winery is located in the Yakima Valley wine region, where there are more than sixty wineries.

JOB DESCRIPTION: The owners/brothers, Pat and Matt, taught me about the many duties of a small winery, such as managing the "topping" process, testing the sulfite levels in the wine, and tasting to figure out blends for this year's fresh pick.

INDUSTRY IQ:

- Grapes are the world's number one fruit crop, with 8 million hectares planted worldwide.
- Crushing wine grapes with your feet is very effective, as it doesn't crush the grape's seed, which can release bitter flavours. However, today all commercial winemaking has been mechanized.
- The wine industry generates more than 145,000 jobs in California alone.

WHAT I LEARNED: During harvest time, Matt told me, it's not unusual for them to work eighteen-hour days. When I was there, it was the time of year when they taste previous vintages and compare them to see how they're aging. On a table, we lined up several varieties from the previous four years and went to work. It was a lot of information to absorb, though my liver handled it considerably well.

WEEK 39 JOB: MARTIAL ARTS INSTRUCTOR

LOCATION: VANCOUVER, BRITISH COLUMBIA

WHEN I ARRIVED at the bus station in Vancouver, my mom was there. She has always been there. During the long winter soccer seasons, bundled up on the sidelines braving the cold and rain. In the gymnasium, sitting in the stands at every basketball or volleyball game. It's when she wasn't there that people would notice.

She cares. That's what she does; it's who she is.

When I worked as a radio DJ on the East Coast, she asked what time I'd be on the air. I hesitated to tell her that I was scheduled for 7 A.M. She was three hours behind on the West Coast, and I knew that she'd set her alarm for 4 A.M., crawl out of bed, put on her robe and slippers, then quietly make her way downstairs in the dark, flip on the computer, and listen to me on the radio station's website.

When we arrived home, I dropped my bags in the living room. Then, out of character, my mom asked me to have a seat at the kitchen table.

My mind immediately recalled the email I'd received a few weeks earlier in New York City. It was from my dad. He said that he was very proud of me. I'd read it, then looked at Ian. "Something's wrong at home, and they're not telling me."

"Really? What do you think it is?"

"I'm not sure, but there's something they're not telling me."

My mom and dad share an email address, but my dad had never written me an email before.

Now that I was home, I could see that my mom had something to tell me. We sat down at the kitchen table, and she told me that during a routine mammogram, they'd found a lump that needed to be tested. They expedited the typical wait time, and she'd had the biopsy the week before Christmas.

"I'll get the results back next week," she told me.

I tried to process what this meant, but it somehow felt surreal. "So, they're testing . . . for breast cancer?" I asked.

She nodded.

My chest became heavy. I stared at the kitchen table, I don't know for how long.

"It's nothing to worry about," she said. "Truly, I feel healthy. I don't know why, but I feel in my gut that everything is fine."

I wanted to believe her.

On Monday morning at Dojang Studios, my first class, seven 9-year-olds, kneeled on the mats in front of me. "Who knows what they want to be when they grow up?" I asked, then listened as each child confidently answered. I need to get my act together, I thought.

When I had arrived an hour earlier, the co-owner and founder, Robert, taught me the warm-up routine that starts each class. Halfway through I fought to catch my breath. "This is only the warm-up?" I asked. At home I'd regularly exercise, but now I felt the result of being on the road for so long.

Dojang means "a place to study the way." It combines different forms and styles from the traditional and modern combative arts. "We're not trying to turn every student into one type of martial artist," said Robert. "Everyone is his own martial artist—what we like to do is just bring that out."

There's a strong focus at the studio on making sure the kids have fun. I think we accomplished that, especially when it was time for me to put on the protective sumo suit and the kids were allowed to go all out punching and kicking me, then tackling me to the ground.

Robert and his wife, Emma, Dojang's other owner/founder, are a driven couple motivated to succeed at all levels—developing a healthy body and mind, caring for the environment, continually educating themselves, and, most important, leading by example. Before they made the decision to open the martial arts studio four years earlier, they asked themselves what they could do that was worthwhile. As Robert said, "Martial arts for us is a respectful sport—a means of mutual respect between human beings. The feeling that you're benefiting the world in some form is important to me; it's important to my family. It's important for my kids that they go out there and do something productive in the world."

Most weeks I found myself in somewhat intimidating positions, always learning something new. This week I was constantly humbled.

One example came in the form of a nine-year-old girl who was mock sparring with me. She had me backing up in circles around the studio as I attempted to avoid her high side kicks directed at my face. It was Kate, Robert and Emma's daughter. The whole family participates in the sport; their son Aidan, age fourteen, had just put out his first DVD designed for kids. This was not a household you'd want to mess with.

Emma said that she had the best job on the entire planet. They designed it that way. "We wanted a change in lifestyle; we wanted to spend time with our kids. And we wanted to show people that a different style of life was possible. What I try to impart to my kids is that if you love something and you work really hard at it and you're good at it, then all the other pieces that you're looking for in terms of fulfillment will come."

It was encouraging to meet a couple like Robert and Emma.

They set out with a vision of the life they wanted to create and the positive impact they hoped to have. With some hard work they managed to build a successful career that achieved both.

The studio was closed Christmas Eve and Christmas Day, so I was able to spend the holidays with my family. I'd never missed a Christmas at home. This year was no different, yet now an unavoidable significance accompanied our typical routine.

The day I was supposed to leave for my next job, the doctor called. The results were in. My mom's appointment was scheduled for 5:15 P.M. We'd have to leave for the bus station at 6:45. I started packing my bag not certain whether I could—or should—go.

I came downstairs surprised to see my dad sitting on the couch reading a golf book. "What? Dad, you didn't go with Mom?"

"Go with her? I didn't even know where she was going until she was out the door."

"Mom would never ask you to go with her, Dad. You *know* Mom."

Mom had always tried to protect us. Often that meant not revealing the seriousness of a situation, or simply taking it on alone. Still, I was angry at Dad for not going. I stormed out of the room and returned upstairs to continue packing.

Sorting through my clothes on the bed, I tried not to think that a positive result would mean cancer. But I couldn't shake the thought.

I threw down the shirt in my hand and looked around my childhood bedroom with its various memories. They reminded me of a time when life's chief injustice was that during summer my bedtime came before sunset—forcing me to lie in bed and listen to the older kids outside having fun in the late shadows of twilight.

Now life wasn't quite so simple.

I was still upstairs when I heard the garage door open and my mom's car pull in to the driveway. The back door clicked. The house was silent. I listened closely for a sign. I heard car keys hit the carpet and what I thought might be my mom crying. Please let me be wrong. As I slowly came to the top of the stairs, the sound became clear. My mom was weeping. It felt like a movie. My muscles went numb. The book and pen in my hands dropped to the floor. I delicately walked downstairs. The weeping grew louder, the dreaded reality more certain.

I came around the corner into the family room and saw my mom in my dad's arms. He noticed I'd entered the room and looked up at me. "It's bad news," he said. I didn't know what to do. What was I supposed to do? In the movies, they would have changed scenes at this point.

I glanced at my mom, her superhuman powers gone. I walked over, held her in my arms, and cried hard but silently into her shoulder. My dad left the room. He came back minutes later, sat down on the couch behind me and Mom, and went back to reading his book. I'm not sure what I expected him to do. I continued to hold her for a long time.

Eventually she pulled away. "Sean, have you finished packing yet?" she asked. "You better hurry up if you're going to make that bus."

She wasn't thinking about herself and the inevitable struggle that lay ahead. She'd already focused on her family, how the news would affect us. She wouldn't want to inconvenience anyone by being sick.

We went upstairs and she helped me pack. I was going through the motions, somberly tossing clothes into the suitcase.

"Don't even consider staying, Sean," Mom said, seeing my hesitation. "You have to finish what you started."

I wished time would stand still, but my mom kept moving me forward as if I was thirteen again and late for soccer practice, reminding me to pick up my cleats, handing me a granola bar as I hurried out the door.

Now we hurried to the bus station.

She walked me to the platform. Still, I wasn't sure if I was going. If I stayed, she'd feel bad that her situation caused me to stay. And if I left . . .

"If you plan on taking this bus, you'd better get on it," the bus driver informed us.

I turned to face my mom.

"Go, Sean."

She had tears in her eyes. I gave her a hug. And left.

WEEK  JOB: **CHIROPRACTOR**

LOCATION: **BANFF, ALBERTA**

EMPLOYER: **DR. SHAWNA B.**

WAGE: **$81,340 YEAR [Source: BLS]**

JOB DESCRIPTION: Assisted with client exercises, shadowed the owner and head chiropractor, and learned about the philosophy of rehabilitation.

INDUSTRY IQ:

- The human body has 300–350 bones at birth. As the infant grows, some of these bones fuse together, making a total of 206 bones in the adult body.
- A four-year bachelor's degree, followed by a four-year program at a chiropractic school to receive the Doctor of Chiropractic (DC) degree, is typically required to become a chiropractor.

WHAT I LEARNED: The importance of finding balance.

I'd received an email a couple of days earlier that asked, "Sean, does it *all* have to be in the career?"

The author was implying that we can reasonably fulfill our passions outside of work. Previously I would have wanted to say yes. That if I were able to choose, I wouldn't sacrifice the majority of my time at an unfulfilling job so that I could spend my minimal time outside of work doing something that I enjoy. But I wasn't so sure anymore. Shawna did a great job identifying the many things she loved doing, like skiing, rock climbing, hiking, and then satisfied these through a combination of her professional and social life. It's about finding a balance in there somewhere.

DANNA HAD MOVED to Banff in October for the winter ski season and was working at a restaurant in town. Part of the reason I'd organized a job at the chiropractic office was so that we'd be able to spend New Year's Eve together. Located in a national park in the Rocky Mountains, Banff is a dramatic setting where enormous snow-capped mountains tower over the town and living space is shared with an abundance of protected wildlife. It was great to be there with Danna, but my thoughts were with my mom.

I wondered if my dad would be there for her, go to all the appointments, take care of her and support her when she needed it, even though she'd never ask him to.

Sitting with Danna in her living room, I expressed my concern.

"Of course he'll be there for her," Danna assured me. "They've been married for, what, like thirty years?"

"Yeah, but I don't know," I said. "My mom needs a lot of positivity right now, and my dad can be so negative sometimes—as if the world's against him or something."

"Do you feel bad for not being there?" Danna asked.

"What could I do, right? Maybe, I don't know," I mumbled. "I just want to make sure she's getting the support she needs."

At the chiropractic clinic, Shawna explained her philosophy on patient care. "I like to use a holistic approach," she said. "I'll often incorporate different elements such as physiotherapy and acupressure, and I've also studied a lot of Eastern medicine, which I like to integrate into my practice too. Every client is different, so I try my best to design a treatment that works for the individual."

I'd previously thought that chiropractic care was mainly joint manipulation and bone-cracking stuff, whereas physiotherapy was more about muscle strengthening and a softer approach to rehabilitation.

For several years I had wanted to be a physiotherapist, and I entered university with that intention. The profession generally involves working with people with active lifestyles and helping them get better through problem solving. Having been involved in sports my whole life, I thought I'd enjoy it. But in my sophomore year, all of the science requirements turned me off to the idea and I chose to major in business instead.

Each day after work, Danna would meet me at the clinic and we'd walk back to her apartment together. At the clinic on Friday, we both said goodbye to Shawna, then embarked on our final commute together.

"How was work?" she asked.

"Good," I said. "This one girl came in on Monday who had injured her back snowboarding. Shawna treated her Wednesday and today too, and I helped her with her exercises. By today she was slowly getting better. How was your shift?"

"I need to get out of this industry," Danna said, exhausted. It wasn't the first time I'd heard her say that. Danna had been a server for a few years, as she worked on her degree. But she wanted to find a full-time career.

"What do you think you want to do?"

"I don't know, maybe go back to school," she said, not sounding convinced.

"Why don't you come on the road with me?" I said, half joking.

"I can't, Sean," she said, slightly agitated. "My life is here. I just can't take off from work all the time. I have bills to pay." She stopped herself. "Gosh, I sound like I'm middle-aged with three children."

Her mindset felt familiar. It was the challenge faced by many graduating students, buried under the weight of mounting student debt and the rising cost of housing. I was fortunate enough to attend school while living at my parents' place. They were happy to have me around, and I was happy to save some money.

Danna sighed. "I don't know, I'm kind of realizing that I can't have it all instantly. You know? Like I need to clock my hours today for what I want to do tomorrow."

"All the more reason you should come on the road," I said. "Maybe try and figure out what that tomorrow looks like."

She shot me a glare. "Not all of us are lucky enough to have a sponsor to cover our expenses, Sean."

The next morning we said goodbye, and I hopped on a plane to Los Angeles, where I'd meet up with Ian. As much as I enjoyed spending time with Danna in the snow and mountains, I was excited for some warmer weather. I was certain that Ian and I would be the only ones in L.A. at the beach in January.

WEEK  **JOB: REAL ESTATE AGENT**

LOCATION: **BEVERLY HILLS, CALIFORNIA**

EMPLOYER: **VICTORIA, COLDWELL BANKER**

WAGE: **$54,410 YEAR (VARIES WIDELY BASED ON AMOUNT OF SALES AND COMMISSION)** [Source: BLS]

INDUSTRY IQ:

- Even though Victoria works under the umbrella of a large real estate branch, she's more or less running her own business—she sets her own hours, is responsible for her own paycheque, and must prospect for clients.
- The majority of a real estate agent's time is not spent visiting houses and meeting with clients. Victoria spends most of her time researching online listings for properties that match her clients' needs.

WHAT I LEARNED: "Ooh-la-la-ing" skills will make or break you.

Apparently, in Hollywood Hills, the "ooh-la-la-ing the family pet" selling technique is a valuable one to master: "This just might be the deciding factor that will help you win over a potential client," Victoria said. "So I don't care how ugly the thing is, or that it's rubbing up against you and covering your pant leg in fur. You smile, bend down, and pet the thing."

WHEN I HAD spoken to Victoria on the phone the previous week, she'd said, "I have some big clients that we'll be prospecting for, so it's a great week for you to join me."

There was no way that I could have fully grasped what she meant by "big" until Monday afternoon when we walked into our first open house in Beverly Hills—a mansion listed at over $13 million. It had a movie theatre and a two-storey den with a fireplace, a library, and a pool table. Outside was a waterfall that spilled into the beautiful pool with a large deck. In one of its wings there was a fully licensed nightclub complete with stage, dance floor, and grand piano. A very different reality from mine. I was happy to be scraping by on the $1,000 a month that NiceJob gave me for travel expenses.

Fortunately, each week I'd been able to stay at my employers' houses, or with a new friend who contacted me through the website. With the money I saved on accommodations, I was able to put that toward flights, buses, and food. My hosts had also been incredibly generous to me, at times offering to pay for travel, and often welcoming me at their dinner tables.

After spending the day prospecting million-dollar homes in the Hills (the cheapest one we checked out was $4.5 million), Ian and I went back to our temporary home for the week—our high school friend Mike's three-hundred-square-foot bachelor apartment. Mike is a drummer attending music school in Hollywood; Ian and I slept on the floor next to his bed and drum kit—a cozy weeklong slumber party.

Victoria became a real estate agent by accident. Like many in Los Angeles, she had wanted to be an actor. She had spent some time doing voice-over work for cartoons when a guy she was dating happened to buy a house. "I found that I really liked the process and so decided to pursue it. Sometimes I work sixteen-hour days, sometimes I work five-hour days, but I love all of it."

Being a real estate agent requires a lot of self-motivation.

Victoria told me that when the market is slow, she will often go door to door to try and sign up new clients. "We're supported by the branch with referrals and training seminars," she said. "But ultimately it's up to us to make the sale."

Victoria was a spunky, attractive thirty-seven-year-old going on twenty-five. We spent as much time talking about her love life and giving her dating advice as we spent talking about the real estate industry. At lunch one day, Ian and I came up with a variation of One-Week Job for Victoria to meet guys. She'd date a new guy each week, then blog about her experience: "One-Week Stand: Searching for some action, not a relationship."

She loved it.

The job of a real estate agent appealed to me. I liked the entrepreneurial spirit and the idea of connecting a family with their future home. The ultimate goal is to help someone complete what is, for the majority of us, the biggest financial transaction that we'll make in our lives. It's a huge decision, and people can become somewhat emotional about it. As a result, Victoria often takes on a therapist role as she coaches clients through the process.

"It's important to take the time to know the clients and what they're looking for in a home," she said. Once she does that, the payoff is the best part. "The most rewarding thing is when I walk into a house and I know that it's the perfect house for someone, that they'll raise their family and have memories there."

JOB: HOLLYWOOD PRODUCER

LOCATION: HOLLYWOOD, CALIFORNIA

IAN RODE SHOTGUN, while I drove. We pulled up to the studio's gate, staffed by a security guard in a glass booth. I reached for the volume control, lowered Tupac's "California Love," then rolled down the window.

"Name?" asked the security attendant.

I felt like I'd arrived at a VIP party, hoping that there hadn't been a mix-up and that my name had in fact made it onto the guest list.

"Sean Aiken. We're here with Emmett/Furla Films," I said, overly polite, as if it would help my chances of getting in.

"Sean Aiken, hmm." He flipped through the sheets of paper attached to his clipboard.

Past the wood barrier in front of our rental car, I could see hints of movie magic—large buildings with stage numbers, a cluster of wardrobe racks with clothes hanging from them, props being unloaded out of the back of a truck, and people walking around wearing headphones like the ones they wear at fast-food drive-throughs.

"Dude, we need to get some of those," I said, pointing them out to Ian. He nodded, though he seemed unconvinced.

"Okay, found you," said the security guard. "Sean Aiken and Ian MacKenzie." He highlighted our names with a neon marker, then handed me a parking pass. "Make sure this is on your dash. And when you leave, return it at the gate."

"Sure thing."

The wood barrier rose. Ian cranked the music, and I pulled forward into the lot. We were in.

We parked the car, then walked through the studio grounds in search of the offices of Emmett/Furla Films. We turned a corner, and in the distance, perfectly situated on the forested hill, were the large white letters that spell HOLLYWOOD. I'd seen them so many times in movies. Now I was actually there. And I was a Hollywood producer.

We arrived at the fifth-floor office where I'd meet Randall Emmett. Randall is a top Hollywood producer and co-founder of Emmett/Furla Films. The company has more than forty movie titles to its credit, including the last Rambo film and *Righteous Kill,* starring Robert De Niro and Al Pacino.

As we opened the glass door, I heard a very loud, animated conversation. I peeked into the office to see Randall behind his desk, yelling into his phone as if it were a walkie-talkie. He put up his index finger to acknowledge he'd seen us, then resumed his rant.

Greg, Randall's tired-looking assistant, greeted us. "Hey, guys, just have a seat here. Randall will be with you in a moment."

"Thanks," I said.

Ian and I sat on two of the chairs just outside of Randall's office and scoped out the framed posters that lined the wall, of various films that he'd produced.

"Okay, Randall is ready for you guys," Greg said.

We stepped into Randall's office. He stood up and flashed a big grin one would typically reserve for old buddies. "You're an animal! I love it, I just love it!"

He continued with enthusiasm: "When I heard about your project, I thought, I need to get ahold of this guy. It's such an amazing idea. I could sell this thing in a second."

The telephone rang. Randall's assistant put the call through. "Just a second, guys," Randall said. As he spoke on the phone, his attention alternated between his computer and the person on the other end, while his fingers incessantly fidgeted with his BlackBerry.

Something on his BlackBerry caught his attention. "Hold on a sec," he said to the caller. "Greg!" he yelled at his assistant in the other room. "How could you not remind me to call George? What the hell are you here for?"

Randall is the stereotypical Hollywood producer—he's arrogant, loud, and flashy when it comes to overt examples of success (nice car, photos with celebrities, name-dropping). He's like a hyperactive little kid with a large ego.

Randall hung up the phone and directed his attention back to me. "So, this week we're going to try and give you a little insight into what a Hollywood producer does—an overview. Basically I'm responsible for buying the script, deciding who's going to direct the movie, who's going to star in the movie. It's also my job to secure those actors, and to do the budget, make sure that we have the money. We like to make big commercial movies here. We like big action stuff."

Randall knows how to get things done in L.A. He bullies, whines, yells, and demands until he gets his way. When he's behind a project he believes in, he is a fighter. He won't take no for an answer. A true Hollywood success story, he worked his way up with his own sweat and hustle, from gopher and assistant to Mark Wahlberg to movie mogul.

One of the two cellphones on Randall's desk rang. He picked it up and started into a rant about One-Week Job. "So get this. This guy in my office graduates from college and doesn't know what he wants to do with his life. So he starts up a website to do a different job each week for a year—fifty-two jobs in fifty-two weeks! Is that not sick?"

Ian and I sat on the couch as Randall paced around the room, arms flailing, making noise for the sake of making noise.

"He's travelling all over the place, sleeping on couches. . . . Yeah, he's working with me this week. . . . I know! It's the greatest concept on the face of the planet!"

He hung up the phone and immediately picked up where he'd left off. "So I'll have you read scripts this week, and actually be my eyes and ears for stuff we're looking out for—unfortunately/fortunately, we get fifty to seventy-five scripts a week. I have a very small staff, I like to keep it tight. Everyone is involved in the company, so I'm going to look to you to find me a good screenplay, something we can option. If it's something that's exciting and interesting, we can go after the option and then try to make it."

Randall explained that to purchase an option for a screenplay means purchasing the rights to make the film for a set period of time. If within that period they decide to make the film, then they will pay the screenwriter the agreed-upon purchase price for the screenplay, significantly more than the option price.

If within the set time period (usually eighteen months) Randall chooses not to make the film, then the rights will revert back to the screenwriter, who can then sell the option to another company.

"When I look at a script, I have to ask myself, 'Is this something I think everyone would want to go see?' So from the very beginning, I have to think about how the whole thing would come together—who would star in it, who would direct it. Sure, there is some glitz and glamour to the life of a Hollywood producer. But you know, we go to work every day, it's a lot of business, a lot of negotiation. The other side is you get to go to the premieres, and that's a perk of the job. But for me the passion is making good films so I can take an audience on a journey."

I'd entered into a very different reality again this week, a reality far from our slumber parties at Mike's place. Some of the conversations seemed to be straight out of an episode of *Entourage*—talking about celebrities on a first-name basis, organizing top directors and actors for a new feature film, discussing a new production company that Randall was starting with rap star 50 Cent.

At one point he was getting quotes for flying Sylvester Stallone around the world for premieres of *Rambo*. With stops in four cities, the final quote for the private jet came out to $500,000. A different reality indeed.

Like Randall said, I learned there's a lot of work that goes on behind the scenes. There are many aspects he must oversee to keep things moving forward before they can even start to shoot.

Turned out I'd also get to experience some of the perks of the job. The world premiere of the new Rambo movie was in Las Vegas the following weekend, and Randall promised us two tickets. Ian decided to go home and be with Karen for a couple of weeks, but there was no way I was going to miss out on the chance to see a major red-carpet premiere in Las Vegas, with the likes of Sylvester Stallone and Arnold Schwarzenegger.

With an extra ticket to the premiere, I immediately called Danna.

"Hey, babe, how's it going?"

"Good. Aren't you at work?"

"Yeah, I am. But just wanted to see if you had any plans for next weekend?"

"Plans? No, don't think so. . . . What? Why, what's up?"

"Well . . . I was just wondering if you would like to accompany me to a red-carpet world movie premiere in Las Vegas next weekend."

"What! Seriously?"

"Well, I am a Hollywood producer this week, you know."

She laughed. "Okay, in that case I'll have my people call your people. . . . And by that I mean, I'll beg for the time off work and let you know if I can find a flight that won't cost me a couple months rent."

"Done."

And so it was decided. After my next job, in Denver, I'd fly to Las Vegas for the weekend and Danna would meet me there. From Vegas, I'd continue to my next job, in Idaho. I figured that while I was a Hollywood producer, I should at least do my best to try and roll like one.

On the day I left Los Angeles, I received a call from a different kind of producer.

"Hello, Sean speaking."

Ian claims that I have different tones when I answer the phone and that he can differentiate whether or not I know who is calling depending on my tone. I probably answered in my "Who's calling me at ten on a Sunday morning?" tone.

"Is this Sean who is doing the different jobs?" asked the man on the other end.

"Yup, that's me."

"Great. I have a job offer for you. But first I want to know, is there anything you *wouldn't* do?"

Now, when someone asks that question, it's a sure giveaway that you're being set up. I didn't take the bait.

"Well, I don't know. I guess that depends. What did you have in mind?"

"Porno," he answered abruptly.

I laughed, thankful that I didn't have to retract an "I'll do anything" statement. But this was too good. I had to find out more.

"What would the job entail?" I asked.

He hesitated, then said, "Acting out a few scenes in a gay porno."

I paused for dramatic effect.

"Well, I appreciate the offer, but I'm going to have to pass."

"I'll donate five thousand dollars."

"Sorry, but thanks anyways."

WEEK 43 JOB: **MOTIVATIONAL SPEAKER**

LOCATION: **DENVER, COLORADO**

EMPLOYER: **GENERATION WHY INC.**
WAGE: **$5,000–$25,000 PER PRESENTATION**

Generation Why is a training and consulting firm that helps organizations recruit, train, manage, motivate, and retain the emerging workforce—me. Eric, the founder/president, delivers around sixty-five keynote presentations and training seminars per year to major organizations throughout North America.

INDUSTRY IQ:

- Eric was inducted to the CPAE Speaker Hall of Fame in 2004, an honour shared by less than 2 percent of all professional speakers.
- In 2008, former president Bill Clinton earned nearly $6 million in speaking fees.

WHAT I LEARNED: You must be willing to start at the bottom.

Eric, gen-Y expert: "If you think you want to be in television, don't go in saying, 'I want to be the star of the show.' Go in and say, 'I want to clean toilets, I want to make coffee in the morning. I just want to be around here to find out what it's really like.'

"You want to be a lawyer? Don't just start applying to law schools—do a little job shadowing. Be willing to make photocopies, be a courier. Just get into the profession, and see it from a different view to find out if it's something you're really passionate about and if you're willing to pay the price to get there."

Young people need to realize that finding a career is not an easy thing to do. The expectation that I should be able to just hop into something that makes me feel good and that gives me the kind of money that I want is unrealistic. Finding your true career passion takes a lot of work.

—ERIC, speaker/consultant, Generation Why

WITHIN FIVE MINUTES of picking me up from the airport in Denver, Eric turned to me and asked, "Sean, what do you see yourself doing five years from now?"

Eric's a passionate guy. Sports enthusiast. People enthusiast. Life enthusiast. He's easy to talk to. Engaging. Educating. Inspiring. Somewhere in his forties, he's built like an ex-bodybuilder and uses words like *bro* and *dude* (though I'm not sure if that was just for my benefit).

"I'm not entirely sure," I said. "But I know that I want to effect change. I want to know that what I'm doing means something. And I know that I don't ever want to be defined by my career or title."

Eric explained the concept of organizing our lives in distinct boxes: a learning box (where we acquire knowledge), a work box (where we pay the bills), a play box (where we have fun). I told him that I wanted a sandbox. I was never allowed to have a sandbox as a kid. My mom said it would become a toilet for all the neighbourhood cats.

"Would you like to be a TV host, an author, or maybe even a professional speaker to share your experience with others?" he asked.

"Hmm, that doesn't sound so bad," I mused.

He continued, "So there's not necessarily anything wrong with being defined by your career or title; you just have to make sure you have the right one."

Eric had only one week with me. We were ten minutes into it, and my first lesson had already begun.

• • •

I was surprised to learn that Eric is often required to work sixty-plus hours a week in order to deliver 65 one-hour presentations a year. He must market himself to potential clients, negotiate presentation fees, prepare a tailored presentation, then follow up with each client after the fact. There's a lot of travel time, and he must also manage the administrative tasks that come with any small business.

This week Eric had three presentations. The first was in Boulder, Colorado, in front of more than two hundred teens from fourteen high schools in the area—all members of their respective student councils.

When we're young, our high school years seem to last forever, but Eric demonstrated how quickly they pass and how precious that time really is. He asked for a volunteer, then stretched a tape measure the entire length of the large hotel conference room. The tape measure signified an average person's life span, and he showed how the years spent in high school made up only a small fraction of its length. He spoke about the importance of making the most out of these influential years, as they help form the foundation of our future.

Eric spoke about visions, decisions, and collisions. We first must develop a vision—what we want to achieve. This causes us to make decisions—choices that provide the means to achieve our vision, which then allow us to make meaningful collisions—the actions required to make our vision a reality.

About halfway through his program, he surprised the audience and introduced me as the "One-Week Job guy." I was then given the chance to share my story with the students and to experience first-hand what it's like to be a motivational speaker—to feel the nervous rush of standing in front of a large group, with all eyes directed at me, and deliver a meaningful message—something that would cause the audience to think and act in a way they might not have before they walked into the room.

At the office that morning, Eric had given me a few pointers on professional speaking. "Before the presentation, you must own the room. When you walk in there, make sure that it's set up the way you want it. Check that there's nothing on the tables blocking the audience's vision, test the microphone and audiovisual equipment. Then, when you begin your presentation, the first task is to break the audience's assumptions. A lot of them are thinking, Why do we have to listen to this guy? You have to give them reason to listen. These first few minutes are very important and will set the tone for the entire presentation."

Eric suggested that I jump right into an engaging story that at first might seem completely off topic. Then five minutes later, when they're all listening attentively, interested in where the story's going but wondering what it has to do with anything, you surprise them by relating it back to the presentation topic.

"So, what is your message going to be?" Eric asked.

"My message?"

"Yeah. If they only take one thing away from your presentation, what do you want that to be?"

I thought about it a moment. I'd learned so much over the past year, but how could I decide which message was the most important, especially when my choice would likely be different from theirs? What one thing would I have liked to have known when I was their age?

I finally said, "My message is, don't beat yourself up worrying that you don't know what you want to do with your life. It's okay not to know. But at the same time, it's not okay to do nothing about it."

"So your message is, 'Just do it'?" Eric said with a grin.

"Yeah, I guess that one's already taken."

He thought for a moment. "What about 'Be proactive about your search'?"

"Yeah," I confirmed. "Let's go with that."

• • •

Just before the presentation, Eric assured me, "Sean, you have an important message. People want to hear what you have to say."

And he was right. Many of the students came up afterward to meet me and ask questions about my different jobs. It was really special to see their faces light up and to hear how my story resonated with many of them. Some spoke about pressure they felt from their parents, some expressed how they too were committed to finding something they're passionate about, and some asked, "How do you get your hair like that?"

Eric's favourite aspect of the job is the ability to inspire and change lives. "I'll get letters from people who were in my audience years ago telling me that something I said made an impact in their life. They made a change, it altered their course, and they still remember and appreciate whatever wisdom or piece of advice they may have gleaned from my presentation."

Earlier in my year, I had learned that we often don't realize the impact we have on others. I found this becomes even more true when you're a professional speaker. Your role is to move the audience, to motivate them to make tough decisions. It's obvious how much pride Eric took in this role and how well he understood the associated responsibility. He knew that the stakes are high. As Eric said, "Standing up and speaking to a group is a privilege, not a right. What you're saying better be true and be something practical that they can incorporate into their own life, no matter what background or home situation they're coming from."

On Thursday afternoon, Eric and I went to lunch with his longtime friend Lee. We talked about One-Week Job. Lee was pensive throughout the conversation. Lee was fifty years old, with a young face and greying hair. President and majority shareholder of a company that does $20 million in sales a year and employs three hundred people, he owned two beautiful homes, nice cars, had a good family and a loving wife. I'm not quite sure if he had the white picket fence, but in modern-day terms of success, this guy had made it.

Lee was very drawn to what I was doing and the idea of trying out different jobs at a young age. After a reflective silence in the conversation, he finally spoke. "I wish I could just be a coach," he said with a faint smile. It was if he imagined himself on the sidelines, clipboard in hand, cheering on his team. He spoke of the excitement and buildup to a big game day, the interaction with kids, morning practices . . . He trailed off, his daydream cut short. With a gleam of hope in his eyes, he said, "Someday."

It's not that he hated his job—it was simply "fine."

"If I could do it all over again," he said, "I wish I would have acted without the fear of what others thought."

He turned to me. "Sean, I applaud what you're doing," he said with sincerity.

"Thanks, Lee," I said.

On the car ride back to the office, Eric made a point to tell me, "I've known Lee for a very long time. He meant what he said.

"The problem is, Sean, not a lot of people are happy in their careers. If they were, no one would be interested in what you're doing—no one would care. They'd say, 'I'm happy, what the hell is his problem?' "

In New York City, I realized that for a long time I felt as if I needed to prove to others that I was succesful first, and *then* I'd be able to do what I really wanted. I had always thought that I'd be happy as a teacher. But then I'd remember a saying I'd once heard: "Those who can't do, teach." That haunted me. I needed others to know that I could do.

The reality is that many people, like Lee, make these huge life-changing decisions based on their perception of what others think. I often thought, What are my friends doing? What will make my parents proud? What title will allow me to confidently answer the question "What do you do for a living?" I was cultivating a life built on fear, not conscious choice.

During the year, many people told me that they had fallen into their career. That it wasn't a conscious choice but rather the path of least resistance. Initially, they accepted the position. After a while, they got used to it. Soon it was "the way things are." Eventually, it becomes "the way they've always been."

Still, in the car ride back to the office, Eric mentioned that for Lee to make a big change at this point in his life would be more difficult than me coming out of university looking for my first career. Without the same responsibilities, I was "lighter."

"When you're young, try and stay as light as possible," he said. "And by 'light,' I mean unencumbered. It's a lot easier to make choices when you don't have a huge car payment, a family to support, or expensive habits. When you're light you can make economic choices very rapidly."

"Yeah, I suppose," I said. "But that's a lot easier said than done. Especially if you're graduating with a huge student loan to pay back."

"I agree. But like I said, finding your true career passion takes a lot of work."

We stopped at a red light. Eric turned to me, not wanting to miss an opportunity to teach me another lesson. "My dad used to tell me that anything worthwhile is not easy, and anything easy is not worthwhile. I think that people, given a choice, would aspire to do great things with their life, and yet greatness does not come without a cost. It's something you need to work at. And between wherever you are and whatever you visualize as greatness, there are going to be some obstacles, there are going to be some challenges, and there are going to be people that tell you, 'You can't do it.'

"You're going to run into a myriad of problems that at one point or another you might think are insurmountable. But if you have the will, the desire inside, and there is belief in your heart that you can move toward that, you'll find a way to overcome those obstacles and get to where you want to go."

Eric glanced back at the traffic light—still red, still time. "I think it's that grittiness to hang in there, and that never-say-die spirit, that separates the people who ultimately achieve their goals and find success in whatever career path they've outlined for themselves and those that wind up living a shallower existence, hating what they do on a day-to-day basis and fantasizing about doing something else."

The traffic light turned green, and we continued toward the office.

Once we arrived, I set up my laptop across from Eric at his desk. He'd asked me to write an entry about my first speaking experience for his blog.

In the room's silence, I reflected on what Eric had said in the car.

"I have a pretty good idea of the type of lifestyle I'd like," I said. "I'm just not sure what specific career that would be. I think it's probably going to be a combination of things."

Eric looked up from his computer. "You may have an idea of what you want now, Sean, but when a family comes into the picture, what you want may become selfish."

I thought about my dad, arriving from Jamaica with his expectant wife and $5,000 to their name. I wondered what path he would have chosen if he hadn't had a young family to provide for.

"Life is tough, Sean."

"I don't know," I said. "I think life is ultimately what you make of it."

Eric paused a moment before responding, contemplating how he wanted to go about teaching me this final lesson.

"You're going to tell the eight-year-old with terminal brain cancer that 'life is what you make of it'? Or the man who's been hit by a drunk driver and is forced to breathe from a tube for the rest of his life? Unfortunately, for some, life has little to do with what they've made of it, and has more to do with what has been made for them by conditions or circumstances beyond their control. Life is hard and uncertain, brother. Sometimes it can kick the crap out of you when you least expect it. You never know what tomorrow will bring."

As he hit me with example upon example, I sank lower and lower in my chair. I thought about my mom's unexpected battle with cancer. Certainly that was never part of her plan. For the first time, I began to question whether "Sean's world" was simply the product of a naive, sheltered, and privileged upbringing.

The following afternoon I said goodbye to Eric and hopped on a plane headed for Vegas, where I'd be attending a red-carpet Hollywood movie premiere.

Danna's on my arm. We strut down the Las Vegas strip toward the enormous Planet Hollywood hotel, where two huge spotlights beckon us as they twist and turn, lighting up the night sky. Danna's wearing a stylish grey-and-black striped sweater dress with black leggings. She's beautiful. I'm in jeans with a blazer over my One-Week Job T-shirt and black dress shoes to finish off my nifty casual-yet-if-needed-can-pass-as-not-so-casual hip look.

In my back pocket are two tickets to the world premiere of *Rambo,* along with another two tickets for the VIP party following the film.

We arrive at the theatre. A large crowd is gathered on either side of the red carpet as the stars begin to arrive. Sylvester Stallone, Arnold Schwarzenegger, Jason Biggs, Sean Aiken, Danna MacLeod—the usual crowd. Cameras flash, stars seem to exude a glow as they stop to talk with reporters and pose for pictures with fans. It feels like I'm watching an entertainment talk show that immediately starts after the news hour. I'm quickly sucked into the fast pace, the constant stimulation, and I can't help but keep watching.

Eventually, everyone slowly begins to file into the theatre.

Danna and I casually take our seats, trying our best to maintain a no-big-deal, just-another-premiere demeanour, so as not to look like we don't belong.

Stallone gets up onstage to introduce the film and to thank some of the people who were involved. "We worked really hard on this film," he says. "I think you're going to like it." He makes a couple of jokes about having the Terminator and John Rambo in the same building. We all laugh because we don't want to get beaten up. And then he finishes with a salute to Arnold: "I'll be back."

We wait for the movie to begin. Danna and I sit silently as we take in the surreal environment and subtly try to locate the various celebrities seated around us.

As the lights in the theatre dim, I turn to Danna. I want to acknowledge the once-in-a-lifetime occasion with a witty remark. But I stop. Danna smiles knowingly.

The curtain rises, and we proceed to watch the most violent movie ever created.

PIZZA
SANDWICHES

WEEK 44 JOB: **PRESCHOOL TEACHER**

LOCATION: **MERIDIAN, IDAHO**

EMPLOYER: **NATURE'S CHILDCARE**

WAGE: **$26,610 YEAR [Source: BLS]**

JOB DESCRIPTION: Led four-to-five-year-old children in hands-on educational projects such as art, cooking, reading, and math.

INDUSTRY IQ:

- To become a preschool teacher you need to study early-childhood education at a postsecondary institution.
- The average income of a preschool teacher is around $25,000, while a kindergarten teacher earns $50,000.

WHAT I LEARNED: Be careful what you say in front of your kids.

When the kids first met me, they were scared, shy, staring at me with blank faces. Five minutes later, we were best friends and they wanted to tell me everything. I'd sit on the ground, then they'd all huddle around me and pull at my hair and clothes, each one firing off random stories in an attempt to get my attention. "Um, I went for a walk, um, with my dog. And, and, he found a stick." "My dad drives a truck. It's green."

Some of the things the kids would say were hilarious, and I wondered if some of the parents realized just how much their kid was absorbing at home.

If you're in a career that you're not happy with, that will affect every aspect of your life. As a parent myself, I've found happiness. And now my family is happy because of that—so happiness trickles down.

—KEN, director, Nature's Childcare

WE PULLED INTO the parking lot of Nature's Childcare. On the front window, I spotted a colourful cartoon painting of myself in which I was giving a thumbs-up. Above it in multicolour print read, "Welcome Sean Aiken!"

I smiled to myself. I'm a preschool teacher.

Nature's Childcare opened in 2006 and had about 150 children enrolled. The director, Ken, greeted me and gave me a tour. Ken was not your typical child-care worker. For one thing, child care is a female-dominated industry. And with his six-foot-six, three-hundred-pound frame, he more resembled an NFL linebacker than a child-care worker. But before he even said a word, his kind face and gentle smile were a dead giveaway—he was the big teddy bear type.

It's unfortunate that we tend to stereotype careers into being more female- or male-oriented. There are not many male figures in child care, and Ken had been discriminated against as a result. This is something he worked hard to change as he recognized how important it is that children have both positive female and male role models. The school was lucky to have him.

After the tour, a local news crew arrived and wanted to get some footage of me with the kids. I hadn't been there fifteen minutes, but I found myself in front of a class of five-year-olds reading a story aloud. Knowing that I had to keep the attention of a roomful of harsh critics demanding to be entertained, I mimicked voices of the different characters, added big "wow" facial expressions, asked leading questions. And it worked. They sat quietly in front of me, stared intently at the pictures, and even started to add their own sound effects. As I grew more comfortable, my voices got more spirited and my expressions bigger.

Everyone at Nature's Childcare loved what they were doing; they were clearly in the profession for the right reasons, as Ken kept reaffirming, "We're poor in our pockets, yet rich in our hearts." It takes a certain type of person to work with kids. The job demands a lot of patience but comes with great rewards. No matter what's going on in your life, or how bad traffic was on the way to work, this is a job where it's difficult to start the day in a bad mood. The kids are always so happy to see you. How can you not smile when, as you enter a room, your adoring five-year-old fans run toward you, shout your name with excitement, and give you a big hug?

I enjoyed it so much that I'd make the rounds of the classrooms in order to re-create the group hug as often as possible. I'd stay with a class long enough to play some games, get the kids all excited and worked up, then move on to the next room. I was like the fun uncle—"Mr. Sean's here!" "Time to play games and have fun!" I'm not convinced the other teachers, left with a hyper class to settle down, appreciated my rounds as much as I did.

As I sat across from Ken in his office, he was pumped. "I love coming to work! It's a great feeling to walk into a room and have twenty kids cheer, 'Mr. Ken!' It's pretty much love at home and love at work. I've seen so many children learn how to tie their shoes, climb the monkey bars for the first time, or learn some sort of new activity. And to know that I'm helping is amazing."

Ken has a great vision for the centre: He wants to bring attention to the importance of providing quality child care and positive role models, and aims to make Nature's Childcare the best child-care facility in the state of Idaho. I have no doubt he will.

I never realized the extent to which daycare is involved in a child's upbringing. Some of the kids spend close to twelve hours a day there, five days a week. I'd guess that in many cases the teachers know the child better than the child's parents do. By the time some parents pick up their kids at the end of the day, there's only enough time to have dinner, spend a couple of hours together, then put them to bed—only to drive them back to the school the next morning. I learned that kids are incredibly impressionable, and so these teachers play a huge part in their growth and development. It's something they take a lot of pride in and is a major factor in their job satisfaction.

A common theme I noticed throughout the year was that the people who were the most passionate about their jobs felt they were contributing to something greater than themselves. They genuinely believed in what they were doing and understood the significance of their job in the bigger picture. It *matters* that they show up to work each day, because they give something valuable, whether to the company, the community, or the world.

I thought back to my week at the martial arts studio. Robert and Emma focused on developing a strong sense of community, getting the kids active, and leading a healthy lifestyle, making the world a better place by empowering their children.

When I worked with George on the organic dairy farm milking eighty cows twice a day, at first I was just milking cows and dealing with dung, until George explained to me that it was much more than that. To George, he was providing food for thousands of people in an eco-friendly way. It's what got him out of bed before sunrise every morning.

The people I worked with at Princess Margaret Hospital Foundation were passionate about achieving the vision of the foundation—"to conquer cancer." They knew that the better job they do, the more people they help.

And I saw it again during my week at Nature's Childcare.

It reminded me that in many instances the best way to help ourselves is to focus on how we can help others. It can be any job, but the important thing is that we're working toward something we feel is significant. And I learned that if we can relate whatever that job is to the bigger picture, we'll be much happier.

WEEK 45 JOB: **ASTRONOMER**

LOCATION: **HILO, HAWAII**

EMPLOYER: **UNIVERSITY OF HAWAII INSTITUTE FOR ASTRONOMY**

WAGE: **$99,730 YEAR [Source: BLS]**

JOB DESCRIPTION: I shadowed Gary and Kenyan as they visited classrooms around the island to educate the kids about the cosmos and introduce them to a profession often overlooked. The highlight of the week was a trip to the top of Mauna Kea, one of the most important land-based astronomy sites in the world, where I met other astronomers exploring the galaxy.

INDUSTRY IQ:

- It's predicted that the high school students of today will be the astronauts of tomorrow who walk on Mars for the first time.
- Light travels at the speed of about 300,000 kilometres per second. It would take 14 billion years travelling at the speed of light to get to the edge of the universe.
- The light from the sun takes eight minutes to reach our eyes. This means that when the sun is within eight minutes of the horizon, in reality it's already set.

WHAT I LEARNED: We are really, really small.

If you're able to find something that allows you to express your interest, your creativity, and that you're passoinate about—to me, that's success. Not how big your bank account is, not how happy and proud your mom and dad are, but that you're doing it for yourself and that you're getting something out of it through which you're continuing to grow.

—GARY, University of Hawaii Institute for Astronomy

AT 9:30 A.M., we loaded up our 4x4 truck and ascended toward the summit of Mauna Kea, one of five volcanoes that formed Hawaii's Big Island. Kenyan, our guide, was at the wheel. He informed us about the significance of the mountain's spiritual and cultural history to the Hawaiian people.

"When the Polynesians originally made their voyages to the Hawaiian Islands, they landed on this island first, likely guided by Mauna Kea rising above the clouds as they neared land," he said. "Because of its height the Polynesians thought of Mauna Kea as the connection between earth and sky, the land and the heavens, and the area where they could communicate with the gods.

"During ancient times only the highest of chiefs and priests were allowed to the uppermost areas on the mountain, and only for short ceremonies that occurred a couple of times a year."

I imagined the spiritual trek to the summit to pay tribute to the gods must have taken days, maybe weeks. Now, in our air-conditioned 4x4, it was a two-hour drive uphill, the last half-hour of which was on unpaved road.

In the sixties a road was built to the summit so that scientists could conduct tests to decide if the site was good for astronomical observing. At about forty-two hundred metres above sea level, the summit is an ideal location because of its dark skies, low humidity, clean air, good weather, and proximity to the equator. It has since become one of the most important land-based astronomy sites in the world, forming a sacred convergence with a common goal—to connect with the heavens.

Ian and I rode in the backseat, while Tammy, our Hawaiian host, sat up front gazing at the endless landscape of lava rock formed from previous eruptions. When Tammy heard about One-Week Job, she felt inspired to get involved. She wanted to bring me to Hawaii because she believed the project symbolized an important message for Hawaiian youth. As a result, she organized two one-week jobs on the island for me and scheduled several talks where I could share my experience at area high schools.

Tammy was an earnest single mother with tireless patience. Her black hair hung past her shoulders. She had a youthful face and a slender physique, toned from her years as a hula dancer.

A couple of days earlier, on our way to dinner, she had confessed, "I feel good," with a candid sincerity. "Even though my life seems a mess. I can't explain it. But . . . I feel joyful." She spoke with the elation that only comes from those who have left charted territory and taken the helm of their own destiny. Recently divorced, Tammy once again set her sights on pursuing her passions—something she'd neglected for a long time. She was being honest with her dreams, taking risks, and challenging herself, and she recognized how that contributed to her happiness.

"Growing up, things always had a way of working out for me," she said. "Then things started to go differently. I stopped listening to my inner voice, which had guided me so well in the past." She looked out the car window, shook her head, then smiled to herself. "Sean, for so long I've settled just short of what I really wanted to do—for so long. How many years I've wasted."

We stopped at the visitor information station, located at twenty-eight hundred metres, and stretched our legs. The summit of Mauna Kea is so high that scientists and other visitors are advised to stay at the visitor centre for thirty minutes to acclimate to atmospheric conditions before completing the ascent. I picked up a book on meteorites (pieces of a meteoroid or asteroid that hit Earth), which rather dryly discussed how to determine their composition. I put it down and picked up another one, with colourful pictures of constellations.

With a break in the clouds, Kenyan decided it was a good time to head to the top. We hopped back into the truck and drove the gravel road to the summit. Only two hours earlier we'd been at sea level. Now at 4205 metres, we felt like we were on top of the world. Measured from the floor of the Pacific Ocean (10,204 metres), this was the tallest mountain in the world. Taller than Mount Everest (the highest mountain above sea level).

At the summit, it was a blanket of white. We were above the clouds, and telescopes the size of houses were sparsely placed over the landscape. It felt like we'd landed on another planet. Bundled in my winter jacket, scarf, and gloves, feeling gusts of cold wind on my face, surrounded by snowbanks as tall as me and locals taking runs on their snowboards and sleds, I had to remind myself that I was in Hawaii.

We took refuge from the weather in the Subaru observatory, where Joe, a young and passionate graduate student in astronomy, greeted us. He explained how the photos are taken with the telescope and told us a little bit about the Subaru Telescope. The mirror of the telescope has a diameter of more than 8 metres, is 20 centimetres thick, and weighs 25.1 tonnes. The mirror has to be large in order to collect the most amount of light possible to see objects far away.

"That must take some pretty pictures," I said. "Well, more so than my 3.2-megapixel camera anyway."

"Yeah." Joe laughed. "But scientists are more interested in explaining the hows and whys of these pretty pictures. It's the same when someone appreciates art versus trying to explain why the paint is red or yellow. Astronomers are trying to get details out of the pretty pictures, out of the beauty. Some people would say, 'Oh, you're cheapening it—you're not appreciating the art.' But I like to think I'm explaining it. I'm able to appreciate the art and help understand why that art is there in the first place."

We continued to walk through the observatory.

"Can these telescopes see to the edge of the universe?" I asked.

"Actually, the edge of the visible universe is the beginning of the universe," he said.

"The edge . . . is . . . the beginning? What do you mean?"

"Because the speed of light is finite, the farther away you look, the farther back in time you're looking. So when we're looking at the sun, we're looking at a picture of the sun that's eight minutes old. When we look at distant galaxies, sometimes they're billions of years old.

"When we look at the edge of the universe, the very edge of what we can see, we're looking at the baby picture of the universe—the moment the universe opened up and the light was allowed to shine. That's the edge that we can see from where we're standing, but if you were to travel to that edge, and look back at us, you would see the same baby picture."

I stood with my mouth wide open. Then he added, "Just because we have a horizon, or edge, that we can't see beyond, does not mean there's nothing beyond that horizon. It just means we can never know what's beyond that horizon because of the time it takes light to get to us. So the galaxies that we're looking at no longer exist in that form. Some stars have died, some have been born. We're looking at old pictures—the photo album of the universe."

While Joe searched to discover the answers of the universe, I searched to discover my meaning within it.

As I had seen this week, one astronomer might be seeking to discover the source of our very existence, how it all came to be, the interconnectedness of everything, and the implications of cause and effect, while another might simply have an affection for rocks.

Either way, two things had become clear to me. One, my view of the universe had forever been altered, and two, I was buying a telescope when I got home.

WEEK  JOB: **PARK RANGER**

LOCATION: **HILO, HAWAII**

EMPLOYER: **HAWAII VOLCANOES NATIONAL PARK**

WAGE: **$46,625 YEAR** **[Source: www.rangercareers.com]**

JOB DESCRIPTION: A park ranger's main duties are park maintenance, conservation, incident relief, interacting with visitors and ensuring their safety. I spent my time with the eruption crew. We were positioned down at the coastline, where lava has covered the roadway as a result of various eruptions (until June 2007 lava was flowing directly into the ocean). Visitors can walk down the road until it meets lava rock. There's a NO PARKING sign, half-buried yet still visible after being caught in the lava.

INDUSTRY IQ:

- Park rangers are very well educated; most have a bachelor's degree in environmental studies.
- There are two main types of lava, *pahoehoe* ("pa-hoy-hoy") and *a'a* ("ah-ah"). When it cools, *pahoehoe* lava is smooth and dense, whereas *a'a* lava forms individual rocks (several centimetres to about a metre) and is porous and jagged.

You gotta look within yourself to see what you enjoy, what you believe in, what you want out of life. Some people think it's money that'll make them happy. I believe that people who join the park service believe there's a bigger calling—whether it's for sharing the environment with the public or protecting fragile ecosystems.

—TALMADGE, chief park ranger,
Hawaii Volcanoes National Park

HAWAII VOLCANOES NATIONAL Park was founded in 1916, though native Hawaiians have enjoyed the land for centuries. They regard the park as a sacred place where the deity Pele—the goddess of fire—lives. A recognized World Heritage Site, the park extends from sea level to 4169 metres and encompasses the summits and rift zones of two of the world's most active volcanoes, Kilauea and Mauna Loa.

I spent most of my time this week with Rob, a park ranger since 2001. Rob must have been in his late fifties, but he was in great shape and could no doubt have outhiked me at the height of my varsity sports days. He was never in a rush, constantly joking—he seemed to have an infinite supply of slow-delivered, perfectly timed one-liners.

On Thursday afternoon, Ian and I accompanied Rob on a hike to survey trail conditions. The landscape at the park has a vastness that's difficult to fully take in. The dark lava rock stretches to the edge of the ocean, then drops off in a sharp cliff toward the bright blue water below. Looking back at the gradually tiered mountainside, you get the incredible view of the various lava flows throughout the years and the path they took, revealed by the sparse trees they left behind and differing types of lava.

In some places during our hike with Rob, there were lava rocks as far as we could see. Then, in the middle of what seemed like a barren landscape, we'd encounter a rain forest of lush

vegetation—a remnant of the former landscape before any of the eruptions. We came upon one such patch of forest and ducked under the trees to escape the rain and eat lunch. Rob pulled a tarp from his sack for all of us to sit on, while Ian and I dug out our respective Lunchables kits.

"Lunchables again, eh, guys?" said Rob.

"We're on a budget," joked Ian, assembling his first cheese-and-cracker sandwich. Between bites, he admired the beauty of the landscape and the vitality in the air. "I could see myself as a park ranger," he said, crumbs spilling onto his jacket.

During lunch, I asked Rob about his time in the navy and the years leading up to being a park ranger. Reflecting back, he said there were things that he'd change if he'd known then what he knew now, but he was quick to offer his perception on our tendency to be critical of past decisions. "I see life as if it were one continuous trail," he said. "There's no use thinking about what you should have done or what would have happened if you had chosen another trail. The best you can do is cope with the conditions in front of you. And if you're lucky, you've come well enough prepared."

Many jobs require that you invest in years of training to build expertise and professional standing. While much job satisfaction can come from that, Rob reminded me that a career choice is not necessarily a life sentence. I found comfort in that. If I don't like a certain career, I can always move on, try something else. It's my choice. As I get older, the challenge will be to preserve this choice to choose, even in the face of factors beyond my control—a house foreclosure, or a struggling economy. For my part, I can always ensure that I'm responsible with my finances and that I build the relevant skills so that I never feel trapped in a situation.

I think that as my generation enters the workforce, having a single career for one's entire life will be less and less common. Perhaps the word *career* will take on a new meaning as we do more independently and start to incorporate a healthy balance of work experiences, training, and education as well as family and community involvement, interests, and hobbies. Maybe it will be perceived as a series of mini life experiences, understood collectively as our "career path"—not clearly defined or requiring a predetermined destination.

Rob assured me I can have many "careers" in my life, and can commit to each one fully, see where it leads, have fun, develop my skills, then confidently look forward, excited, to the next trailhead.

Back on Kilauea Volcano, even though I was very wet and cold, I found a sense of calm, sitting sheltered beneath the lush vegetation, watching the rain gather and stream off the vibrant greenery, our chosen trail fixed before us.

I finished my last cheese-and-cracker sandwich, stuffed my garbage into the backpack, and headed out into the dripping jungle.

The day before we left Hawaii, I received a phone call from New York City.

"Hi, Sean, my name is Paul. I'm a production assistant at the *Rachael Ray* show. How's work going?"

"I can't complain. Right now I'm in Hawaii."

"Yeah, I saw that on your website. I'm jealous. February isn't the warmest month to be in New York City."

Turned out they wanted to film a segment with me trying out different jobs at their studio. Then I'd walk out in front of the live studio audience, sit on the couch, and chat with Rachael about my previous forty-six weeks.

From Hawaii, we had a flight to Los Angeles (with the help of Tammy, our Hawaiian host, and her travel points), but I hadn't figured out how we'd get to my next job in Florida. Paul said that the show would pay for my flight to New York City, then, after the interview, the flight to Florida. It was an offer I couldn't refuse.

There was a time when I would have been happy for the Rachael Ray stamp of approval implied by the invitation. But now I saw it as a chance to share my story and send out some positive ripples, an opportunity to experience something cool that not a lot of people get to do, and of course, free transportation to my next job.

At LAX, the ticket agent handed me my boarding pass for my flight to JFK. It had a shiny gold strip at the top that caused me to take a closer look. Elite class, baby!

I walked past the long lineup at security. When I reached the departure gate, I noticed two paths designated to enter into the tunnel, separated by two aluminum poles connected with a single rope. On one side, just carpet. But on the other side, the elite-class side, a red-carpet mat was neatly placed to protect us elite-class passengers from the dingy carpet below.

I boarded the plane and passed the first few big comfy-looking seats where people seemed so relaxed, already with drinks in their hands. In a short couple of minutes, I'd be in my big comfy-looking seat, sipping on my glass of hand-squeezed pulp-extracted organic orange juice with a splash of champagne. I walked down the aisle, glancing at my ticket, then back up at the seat numbers, and tried to guess which one was my big comfy-looking seat. Only a few rows remained. Then I passed the last row, wondering what happened to my elite-class status. Seemed that elite class didn't mean first class. I took my middle seat in economy just in time to hear the young girl sitting in front of me ask her mom, "Mommy, what are those seats up there for?"

"Oh, that's where the important people sit, honey."

Touché.

Shortly after I arrived in Manhattan, my cellphone rang. It was my sister, Natalie. Even though we're close, I found myself not wanting to answer. We hadn't spoken since we'd found out about Mom.

"Hey, Nats."

"How's it goin', little brother?"

"Not too bad." Knowing we had a heavy topic to discuss, I attempted to get in a moment of lightness. "I'd be better if I was sipping on a glass of hand-squeezed pulp-extracted organic orange juice with a splash of champagne."

"What?"

"Never mind. How are things going with Mom?"

"She's been very strong, staying positive. You know Mom—she's not one to look for sympathy."

"And what about Dad?" I asked.

"What *about* Dad?"

"Well, has he been there for her?" I felt a familiar pang of resentment toward my dad, and for some reason I couldn't get rid of it.

"Of course, Sean. You know Dad has always been there for us," she said. "He's being very supportive."

"Oh, yeah? How so?"

"How so?" In her tone, I could hear her questioning why I'd ask such a thing.

"Yeah. Like what's he doing?" I asked.

"Well, he takes her to all the appointments, he's helping out around the house, and he's just being very positive about everything."

"Hmm. Well, that's good," I said, not fully convinced.

Two days later it was time for my interview on *Rachael Ray.*

As I waited backstage, I couldn't help but fidget with everything in front of me. I peeked around the set. A large studio audience anxiously awaited their first glimpse of Rachael and her introduction.

"Relax," said Ian, seated confidently in the other chair. "It's only broadcast to millions of people."

He was always there to boost my confidence.

Rachael stepped onstage. "Sean Aiken can't hold a job for more than one week, and he likes it that way . . ."

The day before when I was backstage, I hadn't felt nervous. I'd felt like a television host. The producers had sent me around with a director, a camera operator, and a sound technician to shoot the job-sampling segment. I'd tried different jobs on set, asked questions of the employees, and reported what goes on behind the scenes. I'd chopped onions in Rachael's prep kitchen, organized tapes in the production department, helped decorate the set. For my most prestigious job, as a production assistant, I chose the "snack of the day"—a nicely decorated package of pecan brittle. A high-end, especially-elite-class version of the more traditional peanut brittle.

I felt a hand on my shoulder. "Sean, it's time."

The crowd clapped as the show returned from commercial break. Rachael introduced me, and I took a seat on the couch across from her. We dove into a conversation about my previous forty-six jobs, my experience sampling different jobs behind the scenes at the show. Then she asked the big question: "Have you decided what you're going to do when this whole process is over?"

"I'm getting closer," I said. "It's funny, when I started the project, a small part of me hoped that I'd find that one perfect career. But I've realized over the course of the experience that what makes me happy at the end of fifty-two weeks is not necessarily going to be the same thing five years down the road."

"That's very wise," she said with a wink to the audience.

"Me going out and searching for my passion has kinda grown, and evolved into motivating others to go out there and take some time to think about 'What do I really want to do with my career? And what's going to make me happy?' "

At the end of the interview, I was glad to see that all the onions I'd cut the day before went to good use. Rachael cheerfully broke the news to the audience: "And, because he was so fabulous at chopping onions, there's"—she paused, then sniffed the air—"French onion soup! And it's for everyone!"

The audience shouted and clapped enthusiastically. I sat up a little taller in my chair and grinned proudly. That is, until, Rachael followed up the soup by gifting every audience member with an all-in-one printer, scanner, and copier.

After the interview, Ian and I went back to our hotel (paid for by the show). I sat down at the table to check my emails. There was one from my mom.

It read, "Call me please."

I dialed the number on the suite phone. As soon as she heard my voice, she cried. I started crying too. She finally told me that the doctors had found something on her pancreas that would need to be biopsied, and that she also had polyps (abnormal tissue growth) in her stomach.

"Now, I don't want you to come home now, you hear?" she said through tears. "I told Dad today that I'll be here to welcome you home after Week Fifty-two."

I cried harder.

When I got off the phone, Ian was at the door with his shoes and coat on. We were meeting Mercedes, the fashion buyer from Week 35, for dinner. And we were late.

"Doesn't sound like good news," he said.

I said nothing and aimlessly moved around the room trying to locate my stuff and get ready to go.

I should be there, I thought. Why am I not there? I'm so selfish.

I looked around the room. "Where's my hair elastic?" I put on my coat and stood still. My back to Ian, I continued to look hard at the exact same spot on the carpet next to the bed as if my hair elastic would magically appear.

Fighting hard to keep it together, I pulled my jacket up over my head.

She doesn't want me there. She'd feel bad. It would only make things worse. Wouldn't it?

Ian stood silently at the door. I wanted him to come over and put a hand on my shoulder, but it probably would've just made things worse.

"Where's my freakin' hair elastic!?"

Suddenly, it became obvious—the resentment I'd felt toward my dad was completely misdirected. It had nothing to do with him or his ability to be there. In reality, he was there. I wasn't.

Death scares me. Gone, finished, no more. Forever. For-ev-er. I wish I could always keep the thought close with me, but not too close. Close enough so that I'm continually reminded of the fragility of life and how I must make the most of it. That my time here is finite. With the knowledge comes a certain sense of urgency. Things are quickly put into perspective, I have more energy, am more willing to say yes. It becomes easier to be the person I want to be.

I thought back to sitting across from Eric, the motivational speaker, in his office. He was right—life isn't always what we make of it. Inevitably I will be challenged by things that are beyond my control. And that's okay. But I can't live my life expecting that things will go wrong. I must be grateful when things do work out and, when they don't, always remember that I can still control how I respond.

I located my hair elastic on top of a pile of clothes and reached for it.

"Okay, let's go," I said resolutely.

We headed out the door and made our way to the subway. The next day we were off to Florida.

WEEK  JOB: **FIREFIGHTER**
LOCATION: **FORT WALTON BEACH, FLORIDA**

EMPLOYER: **FORT WALTON BEACH FIRE DEPARTMENT**
WAGE: **$42,370 YEAR**

INDUSTRY IQ:

- If the tone rings, the firefighters on duty must be ready, on the truck, and leaving the station within one minute. If there's a call at night while they're asleep at the station, they have two minutes.
- There are three shifts at the Fort Walton Beach Fire Department, A, B, and C. Each firefighter works twenty-four hours (7 A.M.–7 A.M.) and then has forty-eight hours off. There can be a lot of downtime, so many of them hold a second job.
- To be a firefighter requires completion of a rigorous training program that includes fire sciences, first aid and emergency medicine, and an annual physical endurance test.

WHAT I LEARNED: Life requires effort.

Exhausted from being on the road, I said to Ian, "Dude, life requires effort."

I realized that my experience wouldn't be possible if I weren't willing to leave my comfort zone, try new things, meet different people, and take risks—it requires effort. A conscious decision to make it happen. Most of the time, it was as simple as being open to the experience—saying "yes," embracing the uncertainty, and seeing where it took me. After the fact, I was always glad I did.

IAN AND I checked out of our hotel, then spent the afternoon at Anne's Bed and Coffee on the Lower East Side. A car was scheduled to take us to the airport in a few hours for our 7 P.M. flight to Florida—probably a good time to figure out where we'd sleep once we arrived.

We laughed at having left it so late—the futile laugh that comes when you're extremely tired and everything, including your not-so-ideal situation, suddenly becomes hilarious.

When the producers at the *Rachael Ray* show made our travel arrangements, I'd mentioned that my next job was in Fort Walton Beach, Florida. Judging by the scale of the Google map I had open at the time, the larger city of Pensacola didn't seem too far away. I'd suggested it may be easier to book the flight there, and that's what they did.

Turned out it's over an hour away. Because we'd arrived so late, there was no way of getting to Fort Walton Beach that night.

We had a couple of options. Ian found a cheap hotel near the airport. We could spend the night there and catch a bus the next morning to Fort Walton Beach. That way we wouldn't have to summon the energy to meet anybody new, could catch up on emails and take some time to relax. Or we could check to see if there were any "couch surfers" in the area, see if we could crash at their place, and take our chance on the possibility of adventure.

CouchSurfing.org is a website created by travellers. Those who sign up know what it's like to arrive in a foreign city with no place to stay while trying to survive by spending as little cash as possible. All "couch surfers" have an individual profile on the website that tells you a bit about them, their previous couch-surfing experience, how to contact them, and their current availability to help other couch surfers by offering a couch, floor, or spare bed while in their city. Members can also vouch for other members, which increases the security of the whole deal.

"So, Ian. What do you want to do?"

Ian hestitated. It'd been a long couple of weeks. Each of us wanted the other to let him off the hook. But it was the easy route. We'd be copping out. And we both knew it.

I adopted the tone of a motivational speaker and declared, "Life requires effort, Ian. Let's go on an adventure."

I searched the couch-surfing website in the Pensacola area and sent out some requests. Fifteen minutes later I got a call from Lacey and Ryan, a couple in their junior year at college. "We already have two couch surfers who are biking across the country staying with us tonight, but you guys are more than welcome to stay too," she said.

Turned out they lived five minutes from the airport and even offered to pick us up. Thank goodness for southern hospitality. Now we just needed to figure out how to get to Fort Walton Beach the next day. But there'd be plenty of time for that later.

In my last contact with Danny, the captain at the FWB Fire Department who offered me the position, he wrote, "Sean, if you can somehow make it to the fire dept on Friday my truck will be there and the keys will be in the console. Also I will have my camper set up for you and Ian at our other station, you can get directions from the guys at the station."

If we *somehow* make it to the station? I thought. I guess he figured that by Week 47 I should be able to navigate through any city. Fair enough. Though an address would have been a good first clue.

The next day, Ryan saved us again and drove us to Fort Walton Beach. When we arrived, we decided to go for dinner and drinks. One drink soon became several. By the time we stumbled out the door, it was well after midnight, and my first shift started at 7 A.M.

Ryan dropped us at the station, and sure enough, there was Danny's camper parked out back for us. Inside was one comfortable-looking double bed already set up and made. Clean folded blankets were set on various cushions and tables that transformed into beds—way too much effort at that time of night.

"I call the double bed," Ian quickly declared.

"No way, man." I hopped onto the bed.

"Yeah, right. I called it. Get up! Make up one of the other beds."

"Dude, I'm not moving," I said, already lying on my side with my eyes closed. "You're welcome to share it with me, but I'm not going anywhere."

"You are such a thief," Ian said as he flopped down on the other side. "Well, you better stay on your side then."

"No—*you* better stay on *your* side."

"Fine."

"Fine then."

You'd think that the benefit of sleeping in the parking lot of where you work is that you can wake up five minutes before you start. It didn't help me.

I woke up parched. My head pounded, and my mouth felt like I'd eaten an entire box of saltines before I went to sleep. Not the best form to start my first day as a firefighter.

Outside, the firefighters were ready for me. They rolled into the garage one by one, each beefier than the last. There was no wasting time.

"So, Sean, you ready for some training?" asked firefighter Larry.

"Well, I had a pretty late night last night, we went out for some drinks and . . ."

They chuckled, and I trailed off. I knew that chuckle could only mean one thing—I was in trouble.

I suited up in all the gear: pants, boots, jacket, gas tank, helmet. Together it weighed about thirty kilograms. After I put on the gas tank, I thought, Hey, this isn't so heavy. Five minutes later, my opinion changed.

First, I hauled out the fire hose. They pressurized it, and I ran with it slung over my shoulder for about thirty metres. By "ran"

I mean exerting myself as if in a full-out sprint, though with the weight of the hose and my gear, my effort translated into a full-out crawl. Next I tried the "Denver Drill," a technique used to lift an unresponsive firefighter out a window to safety. I dragged an eighty-two-kilogram dummy, climbed the twenty-three metre ladder, crawled into the training building with the hose, and sprayed the interior.

I felt like I was going to pass out from exhaustion. Or be sick to my stomach and come up short in a valiant attempt to reach the toilet. Either way, it wasn't going to be pretty.

I wanted to show them that I could hack it. I pushed myself as hard as I could. And they pushed back, trying to break me down. These drills would have been difficult in my final year playing varsity sports, let alone hungover.

I discreetly said to Ian, "Let's do . . . Sean's thoughts. Tell them . . . you want to . . . film." I struggled to breathe, let alone compose a complete sentence. The gas tank felt like it had tripled in weight. The slightest nudge and I'd surely fall flat on my face. Ian got the message.

"Before we start the next drill, I want to get Sean's thoughts on camera about the job so far," he announced to the group. Honest enough. It was something that we did each week.

We walked away from the group of firefighters.

"Okay, Sean, what did you want to say?" Ian pointed the camera at me.

"Dude, just pretend you're filming me. I'm exhausted. I swear I'm going to puke."

Ian smirked and held up the camera. I struggled to catch my breath. "Serious, man, don't make me laugh. I feel like I'm going to die."

Several "takes" later, we made our way back to the group and I tried my best to appear as if I had everything under control. But with my red face, sickly bags under my eyes, and my sudden interest in learning about every aspect of the fire truck before starting the next drill, it was obvious—I was hurting. What made the experience even more humbling was that I knew they were taking it easy on me.

That afternoon, we finally met Danny.

"Thanks so much for having us, Danny," I said. "We really appreciate you setting up the camper. It's perfect."

"No problem. How'd ya sleep?"

"I slept great. That bed is super-comfortable," I said.

"Oh, so you got the good bed." He smiled at Ian as if to say, "Tough luck."

"Actually, we shared the bed," Ian said matter-of-factly.

Danny had a puzzled look on his face. "You guys know that camper sleeps ten people, right?"

We realized that sharing beds is probably not something that firefighters regularly do.

I have a lot of respect for firefighters. Not only do they put their lives at risk for others, but the physical fitness they must maintain is truly impressive. Firefighters are tough. I'd say many of them are intimidating. But those whom I worked with were extremely good people. They have integrity, a great sense of what is right, and I'm sure they know how much what they're doing matters.

Ian and I were quickly accepted into their close-knit group. All the firefighters at the department are like family—their profession demands that they work as a team.

"No matter where you go—you could be stranded in Illinois, California, Washington, New York—if you're a firefighter who needs help, they'll always open the doors. I was in the military, but the camaraderie and the brotherhood of fire service, you don't find that in any other job," said the batallion chief, Dave.

And like all families, they have their differences.

"We could be ready to punch a guy out in the TV room, but when that tone goes, we're on that truck, and it's all left behind," said firefighter Calabro.

My second twenty-four-hour shift got off to a much better start than the first. We walked into the office and met with Dave, the battalion chief. With his tough demeanour, greying hair, and handlebar moustache, Dave was the kind of guy you'd expect to see on a Harley-Davidson. Leaning back in his chair with a stern look on his face, Dave asked, "Sean, what is your objective here?"

I couldn't help but feel nervous and started into a rather long-winded formal-job-interview-type answer about One-Week Job, why I'd started it, where I'd been, and what I hoped to get out of my time at the fire station. His serious face made it difficult to gauge his reaction. When I finished, he paused as if in deep reflection. Then, calmly, he replied, "Well, that's great. My objective at the moment is to get breakfast." We all laughed, then went to a local diner, where he treated us to breakfast.

That afternoon I learned that fighting fires is nothing compared with getting eight men who love eating to agree on what they're going to cook for dinner. Ian and I decided to let them sort it out and went back to the camper.

On our way, I said to Ian, "We should bring some food for the guys to help out with dinner."

Realizing that we hadn't been eating very healthy on the road, Ian made an earnest suggestion: "How about we bring a fruit plate?"

I thought back to our conversation with Danny about the previous night's sleeping arrangements. "How about some buffalo wings instead?"

WEEK 48 JOB: COWBOY
LOCATION: LA BARGE, WYOMING

ONE DAY IN late January, I got an email from Cody in Idaho. It was two lines long: "My brother is a real cowboy, he makes his living going ranch to ranch. His name is Chet, and right now he's on a ranch in Wyoming."

I thought, A cowboy. Named Chet. In Wyoming? I'm in.

Chet didn't have an email address, he didn't have the internet, nor did he have use for a computer. He would wake at dawn, put on his boots and chaps, lodge a piece of chewing tobacco in his bottom lip, saddle up his horse, and head out to the fields to check on the cows. He said things like "Yep," "I reckon," and the classic "Uh-huh." His duties changed depending on the season, and he wasn't tied down to anything but the open range. Yep, Chet was a real cowboy.

From Florida, Ian flew back home to Vancouver and I caught a flight to Salt Lake City. Chet's wife, Billy, picked me up from the airport, and we drove into Wyoming. About fifteen minutes into our drive, Billy said, "Sean, we're throwin' ya right into it—we're headin' to a ropin' today!"

"Awesome!"

I had no idea what she was talking about.

An hour later we arrived at the roping. We met up with Chet and his two teammates, and I was quickly immersed in the cowboy lifestyle. The roping was organized in teams of three. Each team would enter the enclosed dirt area with about ten calves. The judge announced the number of one of the calves, then the team of three cowboys had to successfully rope the front and back legs of the assigned calf in the shortest time possible.

Back at the ranch, Chet told me more about a cowboy's duties. It was calving season, which meant that for the next couple of months new calves would be born every day. Chet's main priority was to make sure everything went smoothly, that there were no complications with the birth, that the calf was feeding properly, and that each one got tagged. It's an around-the-clock job, and Chet had to wake up a couple of times each night to go check on the heifers (female cows that have yet to give birth for the first time, usually around two years old).

It was early March, and there was still snow on the ground, so all the cows remained at the ranch. During the summer months, Chet said, typically the cows graze on government-owned, undeveloped land in their natural environment, and he will then ride out to check on them daily.

My horse's name was Hiccup. He was very gentle, though in his old age he'd become lazy, stubborn, and often reminded me that he was the boss. He walked as fast as he wanted, when he wanted, where he wanted, though he managed to comply just enough so I could never get mad at him. Even though Chet and Billy found my random "yeehaws" funny, unfortunately Chet never said "yeehaw" or "giddy-up"—not even "heyah" when he wanted his horse to go faster. I knew I was a poser, but I still couldn't resist giving ol' Hiccup a solid "heyah" when I was certain no one was in earshot and I wanted him to gallop.

Throughout the week, I helped sort bulls, drove the tractor, fed the cows, checked to see if there were any newborn calves, and if so, tagged their ear. It requires a lot of hard work and long days to be a cowboy, with little pay. Chet didn't care, though. He loved his job, and it provided him with enough money to get by. As with all questions that seem complicated, the answer to Chet is simple: "Money don't matter, unless ya don't got none."

In the past, I had often heard the maxim "Go after what you love, and the money will come."

I was relieved to hear the same thought from someone like Chet, who put his passion before money and would have it no other way. Or, in his words, "If I was doing this for the money, I'd be a stupid son of a bitch."

WEEK 49 JOB: NHL MASCOT (WASHINGTON CAPITALS)

LOCATION: WASHINGTON, D.C.

I LEFT THE ranch as the sun started to rise, sending a pink flood over the flat terrain. A few hours later, I arrived at the Salt Lake City airport with plenty of time to catch my flight to Washington, D.C.

I found a quiet corner, then pulled out my computer to check email. Not long after, I heard an announcement on the intercom: "Sean Aiken, please proceed to gate forty-two."

I looked at the clock on my computer. My plane wasn't scheduled to leave for another two hours.

"Final boarding call. Sean Aiken, please proceed to gate forty-two immediately."

A few months earlier I was bored on Facebook and thought I'd search my name. Seven other Sean Aikens came up (I added all of them). The chance that there was another Sean Aiken at this very airport was unlikely, but as I packed up my things and headed to the gate, I figured that I'd catch my flight that was perhaps rescheduled for an earlier time, or I'd get to meet another Sean Aiken. Both positive outcomes.

As I approached the gate, I looked around. Nobody but the airline worker at the desk.

"Hi, I'm Sean Aiken. I heard my name called?"

"Hi, Sean, you're heading to Washington, D.C., through Chicago, right?"

"Yeah."

"The flight to Chicago is running late, and so you'll miss the connecting flight. But this flight is leaving right now. It's a direct flight to Baltimore, and there are a couple of empty seats."

Balitmore, located forty-five minutes northeast of D.C., was a lot closer than Salt Lake City, so I took it. I walked toward the tunnel. Then, a few steps later, I stopped. I turned to face the airline worker, who aptly chose a "Yes, you forgot something, sir?" face.

"Are my bags going to be able to make the change in time?" I asked.

"Yes. They're changing the bags over now, and the plane is waiting," he assured me.

I paused a moment. "Are you sure? Like, you promise when I arrive in Baltimore my bags will be there?"

He looked me directly in the eye and said, "Yes."

Not even a "Should be" or a "Most likely." Nor did he even opt to put it into favourable percentage terms. The man said, "YES."

I arrived in Baltimore hopeful, but my luggage was nowhere to be found. I made a mental note to one day return to the Salt Lake City airport and have a conversation with that man about the dangers of creating false hope.

When the Washington Capitals marketing director, Joe, arrived to pick me up, I was sure he must have questioned his decision to extend the One-Week Job offer to me. I had scruffy facial hair, no luggage, and carried a distinct odour earned from a week of hard work on a ranch.

Luckily, the political correctness of the nation's capital runs deep, and Joe didn't put me on the next flight out of town. My bags arrived the next day, and I was able to clean up before heading to my first day on the job.

The Washington Capitals are a team in the National Hockey League (NHL). Their mascot is Slapshot, a large bald eagle that sports a furry head, large shoes, and a Washington Capitals jersey with the number 00 over his hockey equipment. During the week, I'd help out with promotions and in-game entertainment (when those overly cheerful people dressed in full tracksuits throw free stuff into the stands). Fortunately the Capitals weren't playing my hometown Vancouver Canucks that week, otherwise there clearly would have been a conflict of interest.

When I first got the email from Joe to come try out life as a mascot, I thought it would entail giving some high-fives, making people laugh, starting the wave, and getting to see some professional hockey games. I quickly learned that being a professional mascot is a full-time job. And when I saw the six-figure salaries of some professional mascots in other sports, such as major league baseball and the NBA, I learned that many make a great living doing it. When it's not a game day, there are many other job functions: appearances at community events and private functions, practising new stunts, taking care of the suit, maintaining physical fitness. Although getting fans excited and making sure they have a good time can appear somewhat trivial, mascots play a very significant role. They become an extension of the home team as they help provide that important competitive edge by energizing the crowd.

I also learned how much goes on behind the scenes at a sporting event. As members of the audience, we grab our seat and wait to be entertained. Everything, from the announcements, to the music, to giveaways, seems seamless, effortless. But the truth is that it's all planned down to the minute—when they will do each promotion, run certain contests, play a particular segment. Most promotional nights are planned weeks, even months in advance.

At the end of the first game, I was given the opportunity to go onto centre ice and use the Pucker Chucker—an air-powered gun that shoots foam pucks up into the crowd.

Turned out I'd be the third consecutive victim of the Pucker Chucker.

I stepped onto the ice and was suddenly surrounded by a stadium filled with seventeen thousand noisy fans all wanting their fair shot at a foam puck. I instantly became everyone's best friend—I had free stuff. Everyone loves free stuff. It doesn't matter what the item may be—the fans want it, they *need* it, and they're more than willing to scream, "Over here!" with their arms flailing, then dive in front of the person next to them to get it.

After they announced the three stars of the game, I started firing. The first two shot out with a loud *pop*. I was surprised how far they flew.

This is so cool, I thought.

You want your pucks, come and get 'em. What? You want them over there? I can't hear you. How about over there? You want them over there? All right, you asked for it. Here they come!

I unleashed the fury of the Pucker Chucker upon the crowd, and on my next shot, the compartment that held the extra pucks exploded. The remaining seven pucks scattered all over the ice.

I scrambled after the pucks and threw them into the stands one by one. Now that I was out of pucks, all of a sudden the 16,990 fans who didn't get one weren't so thrilled about me anymore. I modestly made my way off the ice, my malfunctioned Pucker Chucker in tow.

The next afternoon I suited up and attended the Kids Open Skate at the Washington Capitals practice rink. Slapshot's costume was large, cumbersome, and pungent. Each time I put Slapshot's head on, the fuzz from the inside of the beak rubbed on my mouth, offering a unique flavour that could only be attributed to layer upon layer of Febreze fragrance spray and rubbing alcohol pooled with years of old sweat. After ten minutes in the suit, it became so ridiculously hot that a couple litres of my own sweat joined the aroma.

The hardest part was putting it on the following day only to discover that it was still wet. It reminded me of my high school days when I'd play in a basketball or volleyball tournament and having forgotten to bring an extra pair of socks, I was forced to put back on the same wet ones from the earlier game. Maybe *this* is why mascots get the big bucks.

As I stepped out to greet the kids, I heard a parent say, "Wow, Slapshot grew a few inches." Those parents can be difficult to fool sometimes.

Even though the suit was not ideal, it was fun to put smiles on people's faces and to see the different reactions—some kids were scared, others latched on to my leg and refused to let go, and then there were the ones who found it hilarious to ram into my tail.

Like most mascots, Slapshot didn't speak, so I had to wildly exaggerate all of my moves. The real Slapshot told me that if I held a certain expression on my face, it would come across in my mannerisms. Kind of like smiling when answering the telephone. So even though the kids couldn't see my face, I still carried big expressions—super-happy, huge smile, my arms out to the side dancing with a little shake of the tail.

Afterward we went downtown to create some excitement about the team and the upcoming play-off run. I had a great time interacting with the crowd, playing practical jokes, goofing around, and making people smile, though I did have a few close encounters with some scary-looking dogs who didn't understand why there was a six-foot-two guy wearing an Eagle costume dancing around in front of the U.S. Capitol. Dogs can be difficult to fool sometimes too.

WEEK 50 JOB: **ASSOCIATION EXECUTIVE**

LOCATION: **AUSTIN, TEXAS**

"SEAN, WHEN ARE you available? We want you in Austin, Texas! There are twenty-four thousand professional associations in the United States. We have sixteen hundred associations in Texas. This will be the best week of the year for you!"

When I got an email from Beth, president of the Texas Society of Association Executives (TSAE), I was excited at the chance to go to Texas. Then I asked myself, "Do I really want to work for an association?"

I imagined a week of long board meetings, luncheons littered with those HELLO MY NAME IS . . . stickers, and networking events where the highlight is seeing who can amass the most business cards. I had enough One-Week Job offers that I could keep going for another three years, but I only had a few weeks open and wasn't sure what to choose. Beth continued to sell me on the idea in a follow-up email.

> It will really be an eye opener for you—from CEO of an association, to lobbyist, to professional-membership director, we can have you experience everything about the association profession.
>
> You will also get to see beautiful Austin, stay with wonderful people, eat real Mexican food and BBQ . . . and you might get to see one of my son's baseball games! Please say "yes"—let me know when we can talk about confirming your trip to Austin.

Even when we spoke on the phone, I had a difficult time wrapping my head around the job and what exactly an association does. "So, you're an association?" I asked.

"Well, yes, though we are the association *of* associations," Beth replied.

While I was intrigued simply by the fact these actually existed, I wasn't intrigued enough to work for one and didn't give it much more thought.

Without a doubt, Beth was the most persistent person I'd encountered over the year. She never failed to deliver more convincing, fun-filled facts with each email. A few weeks later, she wrote again.

> Our offer is still good for coming to Austin. You would learn so much about the wonderful world of associations—did you know there are over 1 million people working for associations? For every job you have had, there is an association representing and educating that profession or trade. Learning about what an impact associations make in this world would be a great way to end your year long adventure.
>
> We'd have a great place for you to stay, wonderful food, great people and Texas sized hospitality. I am keeping my fingers crossed!

I wrote back and said that her persistence put a smile on my face. It felt good to be wanted. She sounded so keen to have me.

> Hi, Sean, OK . . . you've left the door open a crack, so now I'll push it a bit more . . . Let me know what you have in mind and we will make it happen. . . . What you will learn about associations will be very interesting and fun. Don't forget, Austin is the home of Lance Armstrong and Michael Dell (Dell computers) and everyone who comes here loves it (but maybe not in August and September 'cause it's hot).
>
> Not only are my fingers crossed but my toes too!

Admittedly I didn't have a great association *with* associations. But in truth, I didn't have any reason to associate associations with the negative associations I'd previously held. Besides, maybe an association *of* associations would be different.

It didn't matter anyway; Beth's persistence paid off. I already had visions of Texas barbecue, night cycling with Lance Armstrong, and discussing produce with Michael Dell in the supermarket. The decision was made. I was going to Texas.

On the plane from Washington, D.C., I sat next to a woman in her late twenties named Heather. She was coming back from visiting her boyfriend, currently in boot-camp training with the army. They rarely got to speak on the phone, let alone see each other. And so we connected in sharing stories of the hardships that accompany long-distance relationships.

"How long have you and your girlfriend been together?" she asked.

"Well, let me think. We met in Week Eleven. So . . . I guess about thirty-eight weeks."

She laughed.

"Yeah, that does sound funny." I smiled. "This year my entire life has been organized in weeks."

"Have you been able to see much of each other over this past year, with you travelling all the time?" she asked.

"Not too bad, I suppose. We've managed to make it work somehow."

"When was the last time you saw her?"

I had to take a moment to think about it. Then was surprised when I figured it out: "Wow, I haven't seen Danna in over two months."

I hadn't really thought about it before—Danna had been my girlfriend for the better part of a year, but most of it we'd spent apart.

I gazed out the window and thought back on the limited time we'd spent together. It was as if we were living in a fantasy world, forever trapped in the honeymoon stage, only seeing each other for short stints in extraordinary circumstances. A week in New York City. A weekend in Vegas to attend a Hollywood premiere. Her picture was on the desktop of my computer. But did I really know this girl? I questioned if it was the longing that comes with distance that had kept us together. Perhaps I was simply in love with the idea of being in love.

I continued to stare out the window, watching the moonlight reflect softly off the tops of clouds, every few seconds rhythmically joined by the light fastened to the plane's wing. Heather decided to change the subject. "So for the entire year your life has been organized in weeks?"

"Yeah, I guess that's true," I said, turning to face her again. "If I thought of any day this year, I could pause and think where I was and what I was up to."

"That's really cool," she said, hanging on the thought. "It seems like as we get older we tend to organize our life in years. Months somehow don't mean as much—it's more about the change of seasons. It's like when I was younger, there was no way I could think past the next holiday. But yeah, now many of us can make five-year plans and think nothing of it. Our perspective gets longer, I guess."

"And do you think that's a bad thing?" I asked.

"Well, no, not necessarily, but it can be—like if we start to focus so much on the long term that it causes us to neglect the present."

Perhaps Heather's right, I thought. We fixate on the future to provide meaning to the present. Doesn't much matter what that future is, as long as we believe that it's better than our current reality. Things will be better when exams are over. When this semester is finished. When I get my degree. When I find a job. When the kids move out. When I retire. Days blend into weeks, weeks into months, and before we know it it's time to make a new five-year plan. We wish our lives away with the hope that better days lie ahead. Until one day we might come to the cold realization that the better days we'd longed for are now in the past, and that amid the noise we somehow missed them.

As John Lennon sang, "Life is what happens to you while you're busy making other plans."

It's important that I always maintain a vision of my long-term goals and ideals to guide me, though I need to focus on enjoying my present situation—doing whatever it is that I'm doing in that moment, the best I possibly can. In the end, that's what will allow me to achieve those long-term goals; that's what will allow me to lead a more fulfilling life.

I arrived in Austin, uncertain but excited to be there nonetheless.

I spent my first morning at the TSAE office trying to grasp the intricacies of association life and the vast number of acronyms that pepper every conversation.

But abundant acronyms and overusage of the word *association* aside, I must admit, once I drew an organizational chart and got my committees, boards, chairs, co-chairs, and subcommittees sorted out, the semantics started to make sense.

TSAE provides educational training for the professionals who work for all the associations in Texas. Basically, they help the people who manage associations manage them better.

Associations are generally formed when a group of people within the same profession or trade come together to further their cause. Many associations will form for legislative reasons, since a larger body can have a more significant impact on legislation than one indiviual. For example, a main priority of the Texas Medical Association (TMA) is to monitor legislation to protect the best interests of doctors. This allows individual doctors to focus their time and energy on providing quality care instead of on fighting to defeat bad laws.

Another important function of associations is to provide networking through social events so members can meet like-minded individuals and learn more about their industry. Beth told me that they also offer continuing education for their members to help them stay current in their industry.

I never realized how common associations are and was surprised to learn that nine out of ten people have a membership in some association. Driving downtown, Beth pointed out all the buildings where various associations were located. Previously, I would have paid no attention to such landmarks. Now, with a tuned eye, I suddenly saw them everywhere. As Beth often said, "There are associations for everything." And she was right. She was not only the president, she was a member too—of a national association called Alliance, an association for presidents of associations of associations. Seriously.

In the end, Beth came through on her promises. Austin is a beautiful city, everyone was very kind, I tasted some great Mexican food and Texas barbecue, and spent some quality time with a wonderful family, as Beth, her husband, David, and their son, Matthew, showed me some tremendous southern hospitality.

The TSAE annual summit in Texas was scheduled for the following September, and Beth urged me to attend. "I'd love to," I said. "But these days I have difficulty committing to anything two weeks in advance, let alone six months."

When I'd met Danna nine months earlier, I needed to decide in those first few weeks if I was up for the struggles of a long-distance relationship. I hadn't questioned that decision once, until now. It had been over two months since I last saw her.

I decided that I'd go and see her in Banff for the weekend en route to my next job, and called her to tell her the news.

"Hello?"

"Hey, Danna, how's it going?"

"Good. Haven't heard from you in a while," she said coolly.

"Yeah, sorry. I've been really busy with everything," I said.

"Not checking your emails anymore either?"

I remembered that she'd sent me a heartfelt email weeks earlier when I was in New York City. I'd made a note to respond when I had the time to write her a decent response, but I'd never gotten around to it. It had now been over a month.

"Ouch. Sorry I didn't get back to you. I don't know, I just had lots on my mind I guess."

"I understand."

"So guess what?" I said, deflecting the subject.

"What?"

"I'm going to come and visit this weekend," I said, anticipating her excitement.

"Oh," she said. "Uh, okay, sure. But I'm kind of busy right now with work."

"What, you don't want to see me?"

"No, of course I do," she said. "But this weekend they have some events at the restaurant. And, I don't know, I don't want to get in the way of the project. You're so close to the end now."

"But I'm willing to come all that way," I said, slightly agitated.

"What? Why are *you* angry?"

"Sorry, I just want to see you."

When we were leaving Trois-Pistoles, I'd said I'd go anywhere in the world for Danna once I was done with the project. Maybe that hadn't been realistic. Maybe it wasn't a good idea that I come then.

"Sean, I don't mean it that way," she said, now irritated. "It's not always about you, you know."

"Fine, whatever. Go."

There was silence on the other end. I waited for Danna to say something.

Finally, I broke the hum of the receiver, "Hello?"

There was nothing. She'd hung up.

I packed up my suitcase and shipped out. To join the air force.

WEEK 51 JOB: AIR FORCE RECRUIT
LOCATION: TRENTON, ONTARIO

IMMEDIATELY AFTER I arrived at Canadian Forces Base Trenton, I got fitted in combat gear: combat shirt, pants, boots, jacket, and hat. Then I met with the big boss on base, eight-wing commander Colonel Hood.

For many coming out of university, joining the military is not typically seen as a preferred career option. For Colonel Hood, it's the only job he's had since finishing school. "As a student I took a summer job with the reserves. I enjoyed the challenge—it was mentally and physically challenging—and from that summer job I came back and applied to get into the regular force. And a year later I was in basic officer training."

After twenty-two years, Colonel Hood still maintained, "There hasn't been a day that I haven't been happy to come to work."

Many who join the military have had a parent, relative, or family friend in the forces and so grew up accustomed to the military lifestyle. I'd heard that the military would put you through university in return for a commitment to serve for a number of years, but I'd never thought of it as being a sustainable career. Colonel Hood understood that many young people have a false impression of what the military is all about, and correcting that impression was one of his motivations for allowing me to be a guest on the base. I had no prior exposure to the military life, and he was curious to hear my perception of the military before my week began and how it had changed by the end of the week.

The first thing that struck me was the military lingo. Packed with acronyms and short form, it's like a dialect. When Colonel Hood and Captain Meszaros discussed some ideas for my time on the base, it seemed as if they wanted to communicate something discreetly using top-secret military code. Then Colonel Hood turned to me and asked, "Does all that sound good to you, Sean?"

I smiled, having tuned out the conversation several minutes earlier. "Yeah, sounds great," I said. "I'm up for anything."

I thought that I was accustomed to the use of acronyms and short form after the previous week with TSAE in Austin, but the military took it to another level. I'd love to see an all-out "talk-off" between Association of Associations president Beth and wing commander Colonel Hood.

Captain Meszaros handed me a detailed schedule for the week (broken down by the hour) and briefed me on base etiquette. "All buttons and zippers on the uniform must be done up at all times, and a headdress must be worn when outside—unless you are on the flight line. Also, commissioned officers must always salute those officers who by virtue of rank are superior to them."

I surveyed my combat gear, did up my buttons and zippers, and made sure that everything was in order. Then the captain added, "I should also mention that although a memo has been sent out regarding your visit that explicitly states to overlook the dreadlocks, expect some comments."

I laughed. I was curious about how my hair would be received in the military. It's not every day, rather, any day, that you see a guy with long blond dreadlocks fully suited in military combat gear.

Twenty minutes later I was sitting in the front seat of a CH-146 Griffon helicopter. The engine started up and the entire frame of the helicopter rumbled. The propellers sliced through the air, creating a deafening, yet somehow muted sound, which made it impossible to communicate without the radio in our helmets. I plugged in the cord attached to my helmet, strapped in the various seat belts, then looked at the pilot to my right. He smiled. "You ready to go flying, Sean?"

"Roger that!" I said, then flashed a *Maverick*-style thumbs-up.

The helicopter lifted off the ground. The pilot applied pressure to the stick, we tilted forward, and the tarmac quickly sped away.

Ten minutes later, we hovered two metres off the ground in an open field. "Okay, Sean, take the stick. Try and keep us steady in this exact spot."

I took the controls. Within moments the helicopter started to sway side to side, up and down, as I overcompensated one way and then the next a metre at a time. The pilot took over and stabilized the helicopter. I didn't realize how difficult it would be to keep the helicopter in one stable position. It's an important skill to master, as many times the pilot will have to remain hovering as search and rescue (SAR) technicians rappel to the victim below. What makes it more difficult is that the terrain and weather conditions don't always cooperate in a rescue-type situation.

Next it was time to execute a training rescue. I hopped into the back next to a couple of SAR techs suited up in orange jacket and pants with various gear in hand. We hovered fifteen metres above the ground while the techs rappelled out, followed by a stretcher. The helicopter then lowered and I was able to get onto the ground to get an amazing view from underneath. I knew that helicopters generate a lot of wind, but I was still surprised when I had to drop to my knees in order not to be blown over.

We headed back to the base and I took the stick once again. It wasn't until I began the descent to the tarmac that I realized how fast we were going. As the ground got closer and closer I felt as though I was coming in too fast and wouldn't be able to control the helicopter. Luckily they don't allow people to land a helicopter when it's their first time in one. The pilot took over and brought us in safely.

When we arrived back at the base, I was escorted directly across the tarmac to the C-130 Hercules, a four-engine turboprop military-transport aircraft that's close to thirty metres long and twelve metres high. As I walked up the extended rear ramp into the cargo-storage area, I was handed a different helmet and harness. With several SAR techs on board, we buckled up, the back ramp closed, and minutes later we accelerated down the runway. Once we hit our cruising altitude, I got harnessed in and helped open the side doors as well as the back ramp in preparation for the training exercise. We were making three drops to deliver supplies to troops on the ground. The drop would need to be timed perfectly, taking into consideration the speed of the aircraft and the wind, in order to hit the designated zone.

That morning we'd tried to find the largest helmet possible to fit over my hair. It's important that the helmet fit snug, first, to prevent it from popping off, and second, because when attached to the radio, it serves as the means of communication over the noise of the engines. After removing some of the interior padding, we finally found one that would work, but my hair had to be spread flat and set in a particular position. With all the confusion and noise on the ground switching from the helicopter into the transport aircraft, I hadn't been able to replicate that same position. The helmet sat too far forward, placing the earphones on the top of my jawline. I could barely hear the communication from the other guys on board—a crucial detail if I was to throw the items at the exact right moment to hit our mark below—but I didn't make a fuss over it. There was no way I wanted to blow my chance at chucking stuff out the back of an aircraft cruising at over six hundred metres.

I made my way to the edge of the open ramp and kneeled down as the plane circled around to approach the dedicated drop zone. Only my harness attached to a cord in the cargo area prevented me from plummeting toward the houses, paved streets, and cars that appeared as mere specks below. Through the muffled communication, and yelling over the noise from the wind and engines, I pieced together my orders from the SAR tech next to me. With his two fingers, he pointed to his eyes and then at the SAR tech who peered out the side window. It was his responsibility to time the drop and wind so that the item would land in the correct location. After a countdown, he'd say "Now," and drop his arm. The SAR tech next to me demonstrated the motion with both arms above his head, then followed through. "HARD!" he yelled over the wind. "STRAIGHT. DOWN."

I nodded accordingly. Then he added, "DON'T. HIT. THIS." He pointed to the ramp we were kneeling on.

I caught a faint, "Ten!" through the radio. The countdown had begun. The SAR tech next to me tapped my shoulder and once again pointed toward his two eyes, then at the SAR tech whose focus was out the side window to gauge the drop. I turned to face him and raised the object above my head with both arms. I could only make out a couple of numbers and so concentrated on his arm, while the other crew members fixed their attention on me. The object hoisted above my head became heavy as I anxiously waited to let it fly. His arm lifted up. He paused a moment, then quickly dropped his arm. "NOW!"

I threw it as hard as I could straight down, barely missing the edge of the ramp in front of me. The safety cord pulled snugly on my harness as my forward momentum urged me to continue with the object out the back of the aircraft. It was now in the distance, and I saw its small parachute catch the wind. It was safely on its way. I turned to face the crew behind me. All smiles and a few thumbs-up. Whether it was a job well done or a mere courtesy, I wasn't sure, but either way I was pumped.

Back on the ground, I gazed out across the tarmac with a big smile, the Griffon helicopter I'd flown earlier to my left, and to my right the Hercules whose ramp I'd dangled my feet over as it cruised at over six hundred metres. Could this day get any better?

"Sean, ready to dispose of expired C-4s at EOD?" asked the captain.

"Pardon?"

He laughed, then translated, "You wanna blow some stuff up?"

"Yes, Captain. Yes I do."

Before long it was time to report back to the wing commander about my experience on base. We sat down in his office, surrounded by replica aircrafts and military pictures. The window offered a view overlooking the base.

"So, how was your week, Sean? Was it what you expected?" Colonel Hood asked.

"It really opened my eyes," I said. "When I thought of the military, I always thought of fighter pilots, weapons, infantry, that sort of stuff. But after working in the different squadrons, I realize there are so many jobs on the base."

Whatever someone may be interested in, whether it's policing, photography, engineering, teaching, there seemed to be a suitable position in one of the squadrons. In my conversations throughout the base, I spoke with many who had been with the military for over ten years and in that time had held almost that many careers. I doubt there are many other organizations in the world in which this would be possible.

Colonel Hood is a prime example. "I've been in the miltary for twenty-two years. I'm an air navigator by trade, but I've had fourteen different jobs over that time. There's never been a dull moment at what I've done here. I've been able to travel around the world. If you're looking to get the most out of life, really bite off a challenge, the military offers a great opportunity for that."

I'd become accustomed to uncertainty over the past year, but I always knew that I could go home if things didn't work out, if I got into a situation I couldn't deal with, or if I simply wanted to call it quits. In the military, things will inevitably become difficult. It will challenge character, build a strong sense of self and independence. Trying times and uncertainty are in the job description. On any given day, you could show up to work and be told that you're being shipped off to another base in a foreign country for an indeterminate amount of time. I couldn't imagine having to go home and tell my family and friends goodbye, uncertain when I'd see them next. It had been hard enough over the past year, popping in and out of lives and trying to maintain meaningful relationships. When military leave their families, their spouses and children will inevitably adapt to life without them being around and will get comfortable in a new routine. It must be difficult to come home after a long stint away and try to reintegrate into "normal" life knowing you could easily be shipped off again in the near future.

When I asked Colonel Hood about this, he said, "We're all aware of what we're getting ourselves into when we sign up."

Later that Friday afternoon, I handed in my combat gear and returned to Private Lavallee's house, where I'd stayed during the week. I sat at the kitchen table and opened up my laptop. Once it loaded, there was Danna sitting on my desktop wallpaper staring back at me (my favourite picture from Trois-Pistoles).

She'd been so patient this whole year; I'd just been unfair. I was the one on the road. It was my choice not to be with her, yet I expected her to clear her schedule and be waiting with open arms whenever it was convenient for me. As I stared at her picture, all I wanted to do was hear her voice. To tell her about the incredible week I just had. To tell her how much I missed her.

I needed to see her. I called Danna, convinced her to let me visit, and, the next day, left to spend the weekend in Banff.

When I arrived at Danna's apartment, we were excited to see each other, yet our greeting carried an awkward undertone.

"How was the flight?" she asked rather politely.

"Good, good. Can't complain."

Pause.

"So, can I get you a drink?" she asked.

"Uh, yeah, sure . . . Thanks!"

It was as if we'd just met but shared an inexplicable sense of familiarity.

After some casual conversation, I asked, "Can we go for a walk?"

"Yeah, good idea. Let's do that."

We followed a forested trail next to the river that runs through town. It wasn't long before we were holding hands, cracking jokes, and once again comfortable in each other's company. It was as if we both needed to make sure that in fact the other was the same person we'd remembered during all this time apart.

As we strolled along the trail, I finally had a moment to tell Danna what had been on my mind for the past few days.

"I want to apologize," I said. "I've been really selfish this year, coming in and out of people's lives, expecting past relationships to stay the same. Almost like everything would be put on pause until I returned."

"This whole thing hasn't been easy for me," she said. "But it's not like I'm pining away, awaiting the day you finally return to rescue me." She laughed. "I understand that you couldn't always be around. I've tried my best to keep up. And I'll be at the finish line too." She smiled. "What's another week, right?"

I had been nervous about seeing Danna. But every time we were together, I was reminded how strong my feelings were. I didn't know everything about her, and it'd likely take some time to get used to being in the same city for more than a week. But I knew enough. She made me happy. I loved her. And for now, that was all that mattered.

We said goodbye the next evening, and I continued home for Week 52.

WEEK 52 JOB: MAYOR
LOCATION: PORT MOODY, BRITISH COLUMBIA

FOR THE FIRST time there was no pressure to have a job lined up, make travel plans, or worry if I'd have a roof over my head the following week. This was it. Week 52.

In a full suit and tie, I marched toward Port Moody City Hall, a contemporary building with steel arches and a glass galleria inspired by a traditional European train station. The roundabout leading up to the front entrance was lined with cherry blossoms in full bloom offering a picturesque setting for this significant day.

I opened the front door, followed by Ian with the camera. It was a familiar environment. I glanced to my right, acknowledged the attached library, and took a deliberate moment of reflection. It was in there at the desk in the dimly lit back corner that it all began. It was where I'd spent most of my time leading up to Week 1, busily preparing content for the website even though I wasn't sure that I'd go through with it.

I'd come a long way.

I turned and walked toward the offices of city staff. They were expecting me. The mayor of Port Moody, Joe Trasolini, greeted me with a big smile.

"Welcome home, Sean," he said.

Joe had lived in Port Moody for fourteen years and had held the position of mayor for the previous nine. His family emigrated from Italy when he was young. He still carried a slight accent, and he walked with a smooth swagger. He was a politician, but as I found out throughout the week, he was sincere.

We shook hands, and Joe led me into his office. It was spacious, with a large window that offered a view of the city's recreation complex, and a table and chairs neatly arranged in one corner for visits from members of the community. Various plaques and pictures of people in business suits hung on the wall, alongside a glass cabinet that housed the Chain of Office, a long necklace made up of a series of attached gold medallions, from which one larger medallion hung. Joe reached to the cabinet, opened its doors, and carefully pulled it out.

"Have a seat, Sean," he said, motioning toward his big, comfy-looking leather chair.

He stepped behind me, then placed the Chain of Office over my head. "Congratulations, Sean," he said. "You're now the mayor of Port Moody."

It was only fitting that my journey ended here; I'd lived my whole life in Port Moody. A town of about thirty thousand, Port Moody surrounds an inlet and has a mountainous landscape with large old-growth forests and nearby lakes.

It was a busy week in the mayor's office. A few committee meetings, an art unveiling, a visit with the Port Moody Scouts, a presentation for newly appointed police constables, an exhibition/reception for delegates from China, and the opening ceremony for the Port Moody Festival of the Arts.

Our first engagement was at the police department, where the presentation for the newly appointed officers was held in the upstairs boardroom. The room was filled with people milling around a large conference table. The two officers being sworn in were noticeably excited. They'd worked hard for this moment. Other police officers were dressed in special-occasion uniforms. Everyone mingled, picking away at the snacks on the table, and waited for the formal ceremony to begin.

In many of these situations, the mayor is faced with a tough crowd. He is there to recognize the significant role the police force plays in the community, and to show the city's support; however, he also must contend with people's skepticism, the belief that he's merely making an appearance to win some votes.

I shook some hands, spoke with some residents, had some snacks, then it was off to the next engagement at the local scouts chapter.

All the kids were seated in a semicircle around me and Joe. I'd just finished explaining One-Week Job and the importance of doing something you love. Immediately a kid's arm shot up. "Did you get to blow anything up?"

Then another one. "Did you meet any girls?"

I was relieved that I could at least answer yes to both questions.

I learned how the mayor and city council members control the overall direction of the city—they're the decision makers behind it all. The goal is to make these decisions based on the wants, needs, and best interests of the citizens. It's a big role, and after seeing it from an inside perspective, I wished more citizens would get involved and voice an opinion. There's so much that goes on in a city that the majority have no idea about. We see buildings go up, people move in, and landscapes change, and we wonder how it all happened.

"You can't please everyone, and you have to make tough decisions," said Joe. "Many times a lot of people resent what you're doing and they don't care that democracy is based on the majority carrying the day."

I take a lot of pride in Port Moody. It's a beautiful place and I've seen it grow tremendously since I was a kid. I enjoyed participating in various committee meetings and discussions that would impact its future growth. After spending my whole life here, I finally felt like I was "in the know."

But it wasn't all smiles and handshakes. It seemed that in every conversation I had this week, I was asked for something. Most often it was a request that more of the budget be allocated to an interest group. We'd discuss my past year, my week as mayor, then whoever I was talking to would try to persuade me of the importance of a program they were involved with, and that when I had the opportunity I should speak with Joe about it.

"Many people think the mayor has the final decision in all that goes on in the city," said Joe. "But I only have one vote, just like the other members of City Council. Yet if things go wrong, the mayor typically gets the blame in the newspapers."

When we place ourselves in a highly visible position, we open ourselves up to criticism. At times I'd experienced this during the past year. I commented on it in a blog post and subsequently received some advice from Eric in an email: "In anything that you do, there will always be critics—a third of people are going to love what you do, a third will hate it, and another third won't care."

In an elected position, I guess you can only hope that a third will be enough for you to receive the majority vote.

A sense of adventure was instilled in Joe from a young age, and he was passionate about preparing youth to take over in the future.

"When I was sixteen I emigrated from Rome with my family, and that experience taught me that change can be good," he said. "You don't have to be born, raised, and die in the same town. You don't have to choose one job and that's the end of it. You can explore, take chances. I want young people to give themselves the freedom and the courage to say, 'I'm embarking on a career—and if I find that it doesn't agree with me, then I give myself the opportunity to try something different.'

"How many people do we meet on a daily basis who hate their jobs?" he continued. "Do they really have to put themselves through that? There may be opportunities to make a change. We always fear change. We put up with all sorts of things in our career because we're scared of losing that security. But there really is no security. In the old days, you found a career, you raised your family, and then you were pensioned out at the end—with basically one career. Not anymore. We have a lot of freedoms, a lot of opportunities, but many folks don't take advantage of those opportunities."

One day it will be my turn to pass the lessons I've learned throughout my life on to the next generation. When that time comes and I reflect back on my life, I don't want my lessons to be rooted in regret. Lessons from failed dreams that I never found the courage to pursue. Lessons from years of settling just short of what I really wanted. Or lessons from not taking the time to learn about myself and what it is that I needed to be happy.

Right now I have the opportunity to take the advice that so many shared with me and put it into practice. I want to be able to say, "Look, kid, I had the chance to learn from my parents' generation who had done this whole 'life' thing before. They gave me some pretty great advice when I was young, and even though I thought I knew everything, I took that advice, trusted in their experiences, and that has allowed me to live a more fulfilling life. Now I want to share with you those lessons and a few others I picked up along the way. Then, how you move forward is your choice."

On Thursday night, Ian and I walked home from City Hall, stopping long enough to pick up a six-pack of beer. The sun had disappeared behind the mountains, but the blue glow of the evening would hover for a while longer.

When we reached the playground of Mountain Meadows, our old elementary school, Ian cracked a can and passed it over.

"Your Worship," he said. It was the official title of the mayor, a perk I admittedly enjoyed. And I was still dressed in my suit from the day's work.

I sipped the beer, the cold liquid welcome. Ian cracked his own, and we sat on the steps leading up to our old gym. It was here that we'd played basketball as kids, losing every game to the older teams in the league. It was quiet for a time, punctuated only by the noise of an occasional car, its headlights appearing in the distance, then faded quickly to darkness.

"So tomorrow's the last day," Ian finally stated.

"Yep," I replied, feeling a bit like Chet the cowboy.

"It's been a long time. I can barely remember last year when you came over and we made the website."

"I know."

I felt I should say something to Ian. I wanted to tell him the difference it made to have him on the road as I started a new job each week, meeting new people, making new friends. Every time I doubted whether I'd be able to do it one more time, I'd look over, see my best friend watching intently from behind the camera lens, and shrug off my fears.

But I didn't know how to convey the true meaning of the message. It was too big to cram into an awkward few sentences. Besides, he knew I appreciated him.

It was Ian who spoke first. "Hey, man, I wanted to say thanks."

"Really?" I asked.

"Yeah. You know, last year when I quit my job. Part of that was because of this One-Week Job thing taking off. It gave me a reason to leave. I mean, I would have quit eventually, but I couldn't let you do this by yourself. It'd seemed too fun." Ian laughed and took another sip of beer. "Thanks for taking me along for the ride."

"You're welcome."

I couldn't think of anything else to say. Nothing else needed to be said.

I held up my beer and we tapped the cans together. It was another hour before we finished the rest of the six-pack and headed back to my house.

Back at City Hall on Friday evening, it was time for my last function as mayor—the opening ceremony for the Port Moody Festival of the Arts. Many people I'd met during the week at various functions or committee meetings were in attendance—delegates, council members, residents, business-interest execs. Some congratulated me, knowing that it was my final day of the year. Others exercised their last chance to ask me for more money.

Ian and I soaked it all in.

Joe stepped onstage and began the ceremony. "Excuse me, can I have everyone's attention," he said, adjusting the microphone. A silencing "shh" spilled to the back of the crowd.

He thanked all those in attendance and then spoke about One-Week Job. "This young man embarked on an interesting journey about this time last year. Sean Aiken has been travelling the world, trying to figure out what he wants to be when he grows up. He has performed fifty-two jobs in fifty-two weeks. His final job has been here, in his hometown."

I remember it had been just over a year earlier that I stood at the edge of the bridge staring down at the river 160 feet below—a countdown urging me to jump. I knew the cord was attached properly, that my harness was securely fastened, and that many before me had taken that same leap. Rationally I knew that everything would be okay. But when it came time to jump, I hesitated. I had to consciously take the next step, to trust myself.

Joe continued. "And now I'd like to invite your mayor for the week up onstage." He motioned toward me. "Come on up here, Sean."

The audience clapped, I stepped onstage, and Joe presented me with some nifty City of Port Moody gear—a hat, a shirt, and some coasters. With the bright spotlight on me, I gazed out into the shadows of the crowd. They couldn't possibly understand the feeling that I had. What this meant to me.

They weren't there when preschool kids referred to me as Mr. Sean. When I lost $1,000 in the stock market, shopped for multimillion-dollar homes in Beverly Hills, or suited up as the mascot of an NHL team and stepped onto centre ice.

Nor were they there when Danna and I watched our first sunrise in Quebec City. When I'd forgotten why I started this project and wanted to give up. Or when time and again complete strangers on Monday morning became close friends by Friday afternoon.

To them, I was a five-minute interlude. A nice story to kick off the formal proceedings. To them, my project was over. But for me, the journey had just begun.

A few minutes later, Ian and I said our final goodbyes to Joe and the rest of the city staff. I shook Joe's hand. "Thanks, Joe. I really appreciate everything."

"It was a pleasure, Sean," he said. "It's an impressive thing you guys have done."

Ian and Joe shook hands.

Then Joe looked at both me and Ian and added, "You guys are very lucky to have the friendship you have."

"Yeah," I said. "We are."

Five minutes later, we were standing outside my house, where inside both our families eagerly waited to greet us.

I opened the front door. Heads turned our way. Smiles. Claps. Danna was there, along with my sister, brother-in-law, grandma, Ian's parents and siblings, Karen. My dad approached. He's a good man. We communicated in silence as we always have. I gave him an apologetic hug, even though I knew he couldn't possibly understand the meaning behind my prolonged clutch. My mom stood close by. Her cancer treatments had had encouraging results, and she appeared strong. Joyful tears filled her eyes. I stood, appreciating the familiar scent of the house I grew up in. No longer my home. But always a part of me.

I stepped inside, then closed the door behind me.

WEEK 53 **EPILOGUE**

THE STUDENTS FILE into the high school auditorium, one class after the next. Ian adjusts the video camera on the tripod, then unravels the wires of my microphone and attaches it to my shirt.

"So, you ready for this?" he asks.

"Yeah, man, I think so," I say.

"Do you know what you're going to say?"

"Not *entirely.* But, I was a motivational speaker in Week Forty-three."

The auditorium is now packed with a few hundred impatient high school students. In the hallway, out of view, I anxiously pace, thinking about what I want to say and how I'm going to say it. I glance at the clock. Ten minutes until I begin my first presentation about the One-Week Job project.

How had it come this far? How had *I* come this far? I had set out to try a different job each week for one year with one simple commitment—to find my passion.

Evidently my story resonated with people all over the world who were struggling with the same question: "What should I do with my life?"

Thousands of people began following my journey, looking for inspiration in their own lives. They commented on the website, wrote about the journey on their blogs. I received emails from people in Australia, France, Israel, China, Sweden—high school and university students, mothers and fathers, employed and unemployed, young and old. Some wrote looking for guidance, hoping that I could shed light on their situation; others wrote simply to say "Thank you." My project was causing them to question the choices they'd made and encouraging them to take a leap.

Even though I started the One-Week Job project to discover *my* passion, it was incredible to hear how my search inspired others to dig a little deeper themselves, challenged them to discover their own passions in life.

For a long time, I thought that finding my passion—that one thing to devote my life to—was the key to happiness. But as I learned throughout the year, many different things contribute to our happiness at work and, by extension, our happiness in life. The two biggest factors are (1) the people we work with, and (2) the feeling that our work is significant. The truth is, I could be happy doing many things. I'd love to be a teacher. I'd love to work at a non-profit. I'd love to be a professional speaker. I'd love to start a small business of some kind. I'd love to work for a marketing firm, or sell real estate, or be involved in some aspect of television. But I've realized that a career is merely a vehicle to fulfill our passion.

I discovered that my passion is to explore.

By starting the One-Week Job project, I inadvertently created a situation in which I was fulfilling this passion to explore—I just didn't know it at the time. I put myself in a position where I was able to try new things, travel, meet interesting people, learn about myself, and then share these lessons with others. But what made it complete was that I believed the project mattered, and not just to me. Knowing that my wages were going to a good cause each week and receiving emails from complete strangers who were inspired by my journey was an incredible feeling. My project was creative, self-directed, and satisfied my passion to explore. Most of all, it allowed me to have a positive impact on others.

For now, I want to continue on this path. I want to find ways to share my story, through speaking, writing, and developing a program that will give others a similar opportunity to try out different professions in an industry that interests them and help them find their own passions.

When this project no longer drives me, then I will continue down my career path and look to another situation. I know I'll be happy as long as I continue to find opportunities to challenge myself, keep the flexibility to try different things, and hold the belief in my heart that what I'm doing *matters.*

Back in the auditorium, I glance up at the clock—five minutes to go.

Last year I would have been nervous about giving this presentation. I'm still nervous—not because I'm standing up and speaking in front of an entire school but because it's so important to me that I make them understand what I didn't. I want them to understand that they don't need to have all the answers. That planning is good, but life can deal some unexpected surprises, both good and bad, to change even the best-laid plans. That even if they know where they're headed, they'll have to clock a lot of hours to get there. Or that they can aspire to be rock stars, but if circumstance should thwart their goal, that doesn't mean it won't lead to an alternate path that works for them. And that they're defined not just by what they do, but by who they are.

I want them to grasp the weight behind my words and remember them past the end of the school day.

With all the students seated, the principal approaches the podium. She asks for silence. I slip into the back of the auditorium and take a seat among the students. Ian is across the room, standing behind our camera, which is directed toward the stage. He's wearing headphones to ensure that the audio is clear. I whisper into my microphone, which for the moment only he can hear, "So . . . ah, where's the exit at?"

He laughs quietly, then scans the audience to try and locate my whereabouts.

The principal begins. "Today we're lucky to have a very special guest . . ."

I remember being in the students' shoes, sitting there listening to someone preach, "You can do anything you set your mind to," or "Believe in yourself and anything is possible." They were phrases that I'd quickly dismiss because I heard them all the time. After a while, they lost their meaning; they became clichés.

Now I realize that I would never have started this adventure if I hadn't already suspected the truth of these statements. The belief that you can have a meaningful career is the first step to finding one.

Knowing what I do now, how can I make these overused phrases real for the students before me?

The reality is, I can't. To truly understand, to really grasp what they mean and the implications, each one of them must experience it in his own way, on her own personal journey. But maybe I can help them take the first step.

As the principal finishes her introduction, I stand up and walk toward the front of the auditorium. The crowd claps and the attention in the room turns to me. I hop onstage, grab the microphone, then look out at the hundreds of faces, their eyes fixed on me.

It's time to share my story.

FACTS FROM THE ROAD

Kilometres travelled: 75,130 kilometres (or twice around the world)

Total wages donated: $20,401.60

Total sponsorship money received for travel expenses: $10,000—NiceJob.ca (also received $400 in donations from individuals during the first five weeks)

Farthest distance between jobs: 6917 kilometres
Hilo, Hawaii (Park Ranger)—Fort Walton Beach, Florida (Firefighter)

Longest daily commute: 2 hours
Week 32—Exterminator

Shortest daily commute: <1 minute
Week 47—Firefighter

 # Beds, couches, and floors slept on: 55

# of plane trips: 24

# of rides hitchhiking: 17

# of bus trips: 9

# of train rides: 2

# of one-week job offers received: 204

Most unusual offers: Male Grooming Products Salesman, Paint Ball Referee, Anesthesiologist, Live Poultry Slaughterer, Carny, Priest, Mobile Dog Groomer, Tattoo Laser Removal Assistant, Zamboni Driver, Professional Race Walker, Celebrity Matchmaker, Porn Actor, Sorority Girl

# of offers of work as a nanny: 16

Ratio between time spent writing and time spent marvelling at how difficult it is to write a book: 1:5-ish

52 JOBS, 52 WEEKS

WEEK 1—JUMP MASTER
Whistler Bungee

WEEK 2—TV TALK SHOW INTERN
Urban Rush

WEEK 3—SNOWSHOE GUIDE
Mount Seymour

WEEK 4—COACH: VOLLEYBALL CAMP
Volleyball BC

WEEK 5—REPORTER
Vancouver 24 Hours

WEEK 6—FLORIST
Best Buds Flower Company

WEEK 7—YOGA INSTRUCTOR
Lotus Soul Gym

WEEK 8—DAIRY FARMER
The Slomp Family

WEEK 9—SKI-RESORT STAFF
Lake Louise Ski Area

WEEK 10—COMPUTER-SOFTWARE SALES
SustaiNet Software Solutions

WEEK 11—ELDER CARE WORKER
Villa des Basques

WEEK 12—FRAMER
Portes et Fenêtres Bernier

WEEK 13—RESEARCHER ASSISTANT
Le Centre d'accueil, de développement et de formation en langues (CADFEL)

WEEK 14—JOB RECRUITER/HEADHUNTER
Venatus Conseil Ltd.

WEEK 15—INNKEEPER
McGee's Inn

WEEK 16—RACE DIRECTOR
Freely Altered States Triathlon (FAST) Club

WEEK 17—STOREKEEPER
Agnew's General Store

WEEK 18—CATTAIL PICKER
J-Philippe Desjardins

WEEK 19—BREWMASTER
Steam Whistle Brewing

WEEK 20—TATTOOIST / PIERCER
New Tribe Tattooing and Piercing

WEEK 21—CANCER FUNDRAISER
Princess Margaret Hospital Foundation

WEEK 22—RADIO DJ
Dave FM 107.5

WEEK 23—HOTEL WORKER
Holiday Inn Kitchener/Waterloo

WEEK 24—VETERINARY ASSISTANT
Hespeler Animal Hospital

WEEK 25—FILM-FESTIVAL REPORTER
Roots

WEEK 26—ADVERTISING EXECUTIVE
Cossette Communications

WEEK 27—BARTENDER
Gus' Pub & Grill

WEEK 28—ROCK-CLIMBING INSTRUCTOR (INDOOR)
The Boulders Climbing Gym

WEEK 29—TRADE-SHOW SALESPERSON
Fundamental Designs, FIFO Bottle

WEEK 30—SMALL-BUSINESS OWNER
SnorgTees

WEEK 31—AQUARIUM HOST
Georgia Aquarium

WEEK 32—EXTERMINATOR
Truly Nolen Pest Control

WEEK 33—STOCK TRADER
Horowitz & Co.

WEEK 34—BAKER
One Girl Cookies

WEEK 35—FASHION BUYER
Global Purchasing Group

WEEK 36—PHOTOGRAPHER
Time Traveler Arts

WEEK 37—PIZZA MAKER
Sweet Tomatoes

WEEK 38—WINEMAKER
Two Mountain Winery

WEEK 39—MARTIAL ARTS INSTRUCTOR
Dojang Studios

WEEK 40—CHIROPRACTOR
Dr. Shawna B.

WEEK 41—REAL ESTATE AGENT
Victoria, Coldwell Banker

WEEK 42—HOLLYWOOD PRODUCER
Emmett/Furla Films

WEEK 43—MOTIVATIONAL SPEAKER
Generation Why Inc.

WEEK 44—PRESCHOOL TEACHER
Nature's Childcare

WEEK 45—ASTRONOMER
University of Hawaii Institute for Astronomy

WEEK 46—PARK RANGER
Hawaii Volcanoes National Park

WEEK 47—FIREFIGHTER
Fort Walton Beach Fire Department

WEEK 48—COWBOY
Chet the Cowboy

WEEK 49—NHL MASCOT
Washington Capitals

WEEK 50—ASSOCIATION EXECUTIVE
Texas Society of Association Executives (TSAE)

WEEK 51—AIR FORCE RECRUIT
CFB Trenton

WEEK 52—MAYOR
City of Port Moody

ACKNOWLEDGMENTS

I'm forever indebted to my fifty-two employers for extending me their one-week job offers. Thank you so much for your willingness to get involved, and to share your professions, homes, families, and wisdom with me. This project could never have happened without you, and I wouldn't trade any of our experiences together.

The kindness that I encountered and the limitless enthusiasm of complete strangers to help me on my journey was truly inspiring. Thanks to everyone who picked me up when I stood alongside the highway, provided a couch to sleep on, treated me to a meal, offered a one-week job, emailed or called with messages of support, or left comments on the website. Your ideas, thoughts, and optimism have contributed to what I believe is a paradigm shift in work consciousness, a revolution in how we as a culture view work and our relationship with it. May the One-Week Job project be a means to continue this dialogue and help move us closer to a time when having a fulfilling career becomes the norm rather than a rarity.

Thank you to my literary agent, Amy Moore-Benson, for her navigation of the publishing world; to my initial editor at Random House, Abby Plesser, for believing that I could capture this experience on paper, and for providing immense encouragement and direction to help guide me through the writing process; to Lindsey Schwoeri at Random House, for seamlessly picking up where Abby left off; to associate copy chief Beth Pearson and all the people behind the scenes at Random House who worked hard to bring this book together; to Helen Reeves, senior editor at Penguin Group (Canada), for signing this book even though she had no idea how it would turn out; and to Alex Schultz at Penguin, for his valuable editorial input during Helen's maternity leave.

Thanks to Alan Kearns, Robert Manolson, and Carla Shore, for their advice, support, and encouragement throughout the year; and to Dan Parker and Kirby Dow, for reading the manuscript and providing terrific feedback.

My deepest appreciation to Manuel Francisci, at NiceJob.ca, for believing in the project early on, and whose sponsorship afforded me this experience; and also to those individuals who made personal donations to help with expenses: Jenny Lepage, Alison Ireland, Garry Rathbone, Karolina Bejm, Leslie Evans, Kyle MacDonald, Irene and Darren Bagley-Heath, Neil Jain, George Reid, Kirsty Henderson, Jonathan Kobz, and Erin Malloy.

A very special thank-you to Dad, for encouraging my pursuit of passion, and to Mom, my number one fan and an extraordinary human being. I love you both very much.

Danna, I can't thank you enough for your endless patience when I was on the road, and yet again when I returned home but was completely engrossed in the writing process. You are my yin. Or yang. Your choice.

And finally, to my best friend and role model, Ian MacKenzie. Thank you. Neither this project nor this book would have been possible without you. I'm forever grateful for your friendship.